DATE DUE

JУ 31 '01			
FE 7 02			
NO 4 02			
DE 5 02			
DE 21 02			

WHERE RIVERS
CHANGE DIRECTION

WHERE RIVERS

CHANGE DIRECTION

M A R K S P R A G G

THE UNIVERSITY OF UTAH PRESS   SALT LAKE CITY

© 1999 by Mark Spragg

ing-in-Publication Data

k, 1952–

ction / Mark Spragg.

m.

-8 (alk. paper)

1. Spragg, Mark, 1952–   —Childhood and youth.   2. Ranch life—
Wyoming—Park County.   3. Park County (Wyo.) Biography.
4. Shoshone National Forest (Wyo.) Biography.   5. Park County
(Wyo.)—Social life and customs.   I. Title.
F767.P3S67   1999
978.7′42033′092—dc21

[B]

99-33890
CIP

Several of the essays in *Where Rivers Change Direction* have appeared in
an earlier version in the following magazines and anthologies: *Northern
Lights,* "In Praise of Horses," "Recoil," and "Tommy Two"; *Thunder of
the Mustangs,* a Tehabi/Sierra Club Book, "Wintering"; *Mark of the
Bear,* a Tehabi/Sierra Club Book, "Adopting Bear"; *High Plains Literary
Review,* "Wapiti School"; and *Ring of Fire: Writers of the Yellowstone
Region,* the Rocky Mountain Press, "Greybull."

"In Praise of Horses" also appeared in *Life in the Saddle,*
a Tehabi Book/Harcourt Brace, and *Northern Lights: A Selection
of New Writing from the American West,* a Vintage Original.

With grateful acknowledgment for use of the excerpt from "White Pine"
in *White Pine: Poems and Prose Poems,* copyright © 1994 by Mary Oliver,
reprinted by permission of Harcourt, Inc.

Printed on acid-free paper

For Virginia,
because of Virginia,
and
for my family,
with love

I have read that, in Africa, when the body of an antelope, which all its life ate only leaves and grass and drank nothing but wild water, is first opened, the fragrance is almost too sweet, too delicate, too beautiful to be borne. It is a moment which hunters must pass through carefully, with concentrated and even religious attention, if they are to reach the other side, and go on with their individual lives.

MARY OLIVER, *White Pine*

CONTENTS

ACKNOWLEDGMENTS

I am indebted to my wife, Virginia, for her insightful suggestions and tireless review of the manuscript; Terry Tempest Williams, for her guidance and encouragement; Jennifer Brice, Pam Painter, and Teresa Jordan, for their careful readings, thoughtful comments, and enthusiasm; Deborah Clow, at *Northern Lights* magazine, and Nancy Cash, and the crew at Tehabi Books, for giving my early essays a home; John Giarrizzo, for his friendship and lovely painting; and I am grateful for the rare good luck in finding Dawn Marano, my precise and generous editor.

WHERE RIVERS
CHANGE DIRECTION

IN PRAISE OF HORSES

When I was a boy my father had horses, over a hundred of them, some of them rank, and I sat them well. He believed that horses were to use and that boys were nothing if not used. He believed that by putting me with horses he was tending to some obvious plan of economy. It was his hope that we would redeem one another. More practically, that we would prove compensative, the horses and I, of our demands for feed and housing. I went to work for him when I was eleven. I was paid thirty dollars a month, had my own bed in the bunkhouse, and three large, plain meals each day.

I was raised in a family business. I was raised at Holm Lodge. Some of our guests called it the Crossed Sabers Ranch, because that is its brand. It is the oldest dude ranch in Wyoming; it opened for business in 1898. When my parents owned the lodge in the 1960s more buildings had been added, there were electric lights, propane heaters in the cabins, but the land remained the same—the high Yellowstone Plateau, straddling the Continental Divide, its water falling away to the east and west.

It is easiest for me to remember the land. I close my eyes, and the heat of midsummer swells through me. I see tar-black butterflies at work in the meadows along the Shoshone River, the grasses come thick in seedheads. I smell white-cupped blossoms, bursts of lavender, the weedy scent of the bloodred Indian paintbrush, the overpowering tang of the banks of low-growing sage. I can step my memory onto the backs of the big boulders and hear my boots scuff against the black and rust and corn-yellow lichens that covered them.

When I was a boy I knew the lodge was six miles from the east-gate to Yellowstone Park. I knew it was on the Shoshone National Forest, but I did not know I lived on the largest block of unfenced wilderness in the lower forty-eight states. That is what I know as a man. As a boy I knew only that I was free on the land. If asked where I lived, I replied, "Wyoming." I meant the northwestern corner of the state; parts of Idaho and Montana. I meant the country itself—a wild, unspoiled part of the earth.

The main lodge building—dining room, bar, kitchen, office, great lounge—is built in the shape of a long, blunt ell. It sits on a leveled rise west of Libby Creek; on the alluvial alleyway of detritus the drainage has deposited between its east and west ridges. The toe of the ell and its length are positioned to catch the high summer sun. The building entire is roughly eighty-by-forty feet and constructed of log. The slope in front of the lodge is grown up in sagebrush and mountain grasses. There is a stand of aspen tucked in against the ridge. Their leaves quake silver and apple-green in the slightest breeze, in the mere flux of air temperatures as the sun rises and falls through the sky. Behind the lodge and along the creek is the thick, emerald press of pine and fir. At sunset each single fir throws a perfect triangle of dark shadow to the east. I liked to stand in tree shadows and stare at the skymost branches dipping against a wind, each branch weighted with the knotted clusters of cones. I would stand and wait to watch a cone drop, to see if I could witness its fall to the ground.

There is a bathhouse, girls' dormitory, barn, tackshed, workshop, storage cabins, bunkhouse, and more than twenty guest cabins. They are arranged along both sides of Libby Creek for a quarter of a mile. My family—mother, father, brother, and I—the wranglers, cabin girls, woodcutters, handyman, and cook all ate together at one long table in a room on the eastern side of the lodge. It opened out onto the porch, had a fireplace at its northern end, and a bank of windows that overlooked the creek. We called it the "Savage Room." I liked the name, liked thinking of myself as an untamed and rugged boy. There were usually at least fifteen of us for meals. It took that many savages to tend to the entertainment and comfort of our guests. Through the summer months we were busy with as many as ninety dudes each day.

Our guests were New Jersey gas station owners, New York congressmen, Iowa farmers, judges, actors, plumbers, Europeans who had read of Buffalo Bill and Sitting Bull and came to experience the American West, the retired, the just beginning. They came to us to fish, and hunt, and ride. They arrived with their different accents, mannerisms; their stories. They wove parts of themselves into the story of my boyhood. They delivered the news of the world in half a dozen languages.

No one ever asked why we had no televisions, no daily paper. They came for what my brother and I took for granted. They came to live the anachronism that we considered our normal lives.

When we moved into the place it was powered by a diesel generator housed in a small log cabin behind the main lodge. My father's first order of business was to sell the thing to an oil company and get us connected to the Rural Electric Association. Farther behind the lodge was an icehouse for summer refrigeration. We did not use it, but it stood in good repair. We made and received our phone calls on an eight-party line.

The lodge itself was heated by four fireplaces, each of them three and half feet in height, and four feet across. Almost every summer morning was cold enough to see our breaths. My brother or I arose at four o'clock to start a fire in the dining room. My mother thought our guests should be able to eat their breakfasts without their coats and hats on. She thought if eggs were paid for they should be served above freezing.

We walked or we rode horses. The tools in the workshed had no power. There were drawknives, hand-augers, slicks, adzes, chisels, hammers, axes, saws, planes, and sledges. One of my father's first purchases was a chainsaw. When I was out with him cutting wood he never tired of revving its engine, his face opened in mock wonderment, whispering, "What's that sound?"

It is easiest to remember the items that a boy can actually put his hands on. In the lodge I remember doors latched with elk antler. Chairs and bookcases made of burled wood and poles, their seats of woven leather and cane. The buffalo skulls nailed above doors to the dining room, office, and savage room. A bench fashioned from a ten-foot length of sixteen-inch-diameter pine, sawn in half lengthwise. A stuffed turkey in a glass case. Head-sized chunks of agate and petrified wood mortared into the fireplaces. A stuffed golden eagle, his wings outspread, suspended from a wire and turning in the peak of the ceiling of the lounge. There were the heads of moose, elk, deer, antelope, and mountain sheep. And rugs of bear and mountain lion tacked up on the walls. The whole bodies of owls and trout. Drawer pulls made of the sawed-off butts of deer antler. Pole curtain rods held up by forked antlers. The panes of glass were handblown and as uneven as ice.

There was a pole and plank gazebo on the crest of the west ridge. It was the best place to sit in the evenings, alone, staring into the shifts of shadow and light the mountains cast as the sun set. Ridges would come bright out of the labile folds of shadow-blackened pine. The rockface of Sleeping Giant Mountain would stand sunslapped white as water. And finally there would be the last gray slants of light as weak as mist, and then the fuzz of evening, and the night.

When the lights were turned off at night it was dark. If the moon was new it was dark enough to walk full-stride into the trunk of a pine. There were no traffic sounds. The fall of Libby Creek washing across its bed of stone seemed to swell in the night to provide the only constant sound. And then a wind would come up and catch, and lift, and rattle in the forest of pine needles that surrounded us. It would produce a sound that made the listener fear the approach of bigger water; the gathered flash of a flood. I learned the constellations by sitting out at night. I knew the different voices of the separate families of coyotes that worked our drainage. I knew the phases of the moon more accurately than the days of a month.

I knew the horses as I knew my family. When we did not have them out on a week packtrip, loaded with foodstuffs, duffels, the canvas tents, with our dudes, we worked them at the ranch. There were day rides, half-day rides, rides by the hour. We caught them, used them, turned them back into the kidney-warm manure cake of the corrals, into the ridden-to-dust round corral. They rolled and stood and shook and milled. When I was separated from them I felt wrong in the world. When I was separated from them I took no comfort in the sound of the creek. I felt chilled without the heat of them. In the short lulls between rides I leaned against the corrals, watching them roil like some captured pod of smallish whales, multicolored, snorting at their handicapped buoyancy. When I stepped in among them they would turn to me, roll their eyes until the whites showed, flick their ears. They were used to the sight and sound of me. I was the boy who straddled their hearts.

They would move away from me, parting, snorting, and in my wake re-adhere. We trained them to show us their heads. I have walked in other men's corrals and known the man—by the way his horses lounged—to be a horse's ass.

It was my daily job to remind our horses of the union of man and horse, to gather them, halter them, grain them, doctor them, handle them, ride them, to ride the younger ones again and again until they became convinced that I was part of them and other men a part of me. They were my father's horses. I was my father's son.

When I was twelve one of the older cowboys I worked with gave me a cheek-full of sugary and long-stringed chewing tobacco. Beech-Nut original. He held open the red and white pouch, and I pinched out a ball of the stuff and loaded it into my cheek. I smiled. The man turned and walked toward the tackshed. I felt the hot seep of the juice pool under my tongue. I turned to spit, and when I looked back to thank the man, found that he staggered; that the ground heaved against him as he walked away. I laughed.

The air sparkled. I gagged, stumbled, and remarkably managed to swallow the wad. I fell to my hands and knees. The temperature soared. My clothes soaked through, and I fell to my side and vomited. I opened my mouth to call for help and vomited again. The strings of tobacco stuck in my throat and I pulled them out, one at a time, and snapped them away from me. I wanted to get to the bunkhouse. I wanted a drink of water. I crawled in circles in the corral. I rolled in the manure. I bumped my head against the bottom rails. I could have flattened out and crawled under, but it did not occur to me. I was looking for the gate. I was no longer a boy. I was in trouble, a sick colt, trapped. The man found me, and dragged me to the creek. He held me while I finished puking and washed my face. He asked me what I thought I was doing. I told him I thought I was a horse, and he smiled, and said I sure as hell smelled like one.

In the evenings we turned the horses out of the corrals and hazed them upstream in the tight valley where we lived and left them to fan and separate and feed. All of them except our wrangle horses, the colts, the four- and five-year-olds that still needed the instruction of experienced riders.

The leaders of the separate clans wore fist-sized copper bells on neckstraps tightened up snug against their throats. We ran them up past the cabins. The guests stood on their porches and clutched their smallest children to their hips. We ran them three miles above the cabins. Their shod hooves struck sparks from the boulders worn up out of the earth. The earth smelled newly plowed, musty, spiked acrid from the crushed and broken pine needles. The sound of their passing gathered against the ridgeside and crested and curled back over us. I felt myself stirred into the mix of them—become large as the accumulation of their tons of heated muscle. We left them to divide and graze the rifts and slant of the young mountain range, and rode our hot colts back to the corrals and spilled hay for them to eat in the night.

In the mornings, before six we gathered them—the other cowboys and me—riding in the dark, listening for the bells, forcing the separated knots of them into a common mob. Each bell was pitched differently, clapping, and combined to a primitive melody as we moved them downstream. We brought them thundering together through the downfall, scree, and fast water, impossibly up and down the steep and careless landscape, back to the corrals, where I would spend the day reviving their marriage to me, proving myself useful in the world.

I was a boy, and I believed deeply in the sightedness of horses. I believed that there was nothing that they did not witness. I believed that to have a horse between my legs, to extend my pulse and blood and energy to theirs, enhanced my vision. Made of me a seer. I believed them to be the dappled, sorrel, roan, bay, black pupils in the eyes of God.

I was a small boy. The first horse I was given to ride was a good-natured gelding named Boots. He was a horse that could be trusted to stand still while I struggled the saddle onto his back, yet not so docile that he was unwilling to deliver a day's work. He was middle aged, big boned, and thoroughly usable. He was named for his white front feet, the rest of him the exact shade of worn-brown as my saddle, his mane and tail running to a darker brown. He owned the obvious, raw sturdiness of some giant farmboy. I thought of him as a hapless and mildly retarded cousin. I considered him a horse with training wheels.

But Boots got me out working with the men on trail rides and packtrips. And he was a horse, and that put him above dogs, cats, and most of the people I knew. He was so rough gaited that only a boy could ride him fast and not break apart. He would have sent a full grown man to a chiropractor.

I would loop Boots's bridle reins at the hitching rail and work back and forth adjusting the hairpad and saddle blanket to fall evenly to either side of his withers. I had to approach him with the saddle turned upside down and balanced atop my head. I would lift it straight into the air, the way a weight lifter presses the bar above his head, step forward, my arms fully extended and drop the thing onto his back.

To tighten the latigo I would turn my back to him, the leather strap over my shoulder, and strain up and against its weight, ratcheting the cinch tighter, and tighter still, my thin shoulders curled under his warm and trusting belly. Think of a man handed a rope tied to a block of stone and asked to drag the thing. It was that kind of job.

If the deck at the tackshed or a stump was not handy I would clasp my left knee, pull it toward my shoulder, and guide my foot into the stirrup. The stirrup hung about even with my shoulder. I would use the saddle strings to pull my way, clumsily, up to the top of him.

"You look like a goddamn chimp humping an elephant," my father would say.

I'd even my reins and turn Boots away from the hitching rail. I would usually be a little out of breath, but once mounted, my toes turned out, my spurs lightly in his ribs, I was impervious to criticism. And I didn't think my father could get much work out of a monkey, even one bigger than I was.

He'd rein his horse in beside mine and by way of apology stare into the sky and say, "I guess I'll keep you." He'd look down at me and add, "You can dress yourself now, and you're pretty reliable about not shitting near the kitchen." He'd smile. I'd smile, and we'd go to work. I liked my father best when we were mounted.

For birthdays and Christmases I received new saddle blankets, an occasional bridle or breastcollar, spurs, once a pair of elk-hide chaps. My toys fit my work. My work became my play. The gift of horses liberated me. It was horses that allowed me early on to step away from the love affair I maintained with myself. I was encouraged—out of necessity—to be a man, to do a man's work; to grow into something broader, wiser, and kinder than a boy. I wanted to grow up fast. I wanted hotter, faster horses underneath me. And I got them.

For two winters we pastured our horses in the McCullough Peaks northeast of Cody. The Peaks are a crumbling open country of badlands and prairie grasses, and hills that shoulder and fall in patterns of stark and mostly treeless erosion. There are a few springs. We pulled the shoes off our horses' feet in October and turned them out into the waning sun and wind of the Peaks.

Through the fall and winter, their lives, and their deaths, were their own. In the McCullough Peaks they mingled with bands of wild horses and ran truant, and when necessary fought for their personal dignities. When we gathered them in May they had become as suspicious as deer, and as proud. They did not smell like domesticated horses smell. There was no odor of leather about them. Their sweat did not own the sweet tang of cultivated grain. They smelled wild. Like sage. Like the earth. Like the water that spills from the earth. Their hooves were not stained by their own piss and corral muck. Their coats would be grown out long, the guard hairs catching the sun, fuzzing them in a dull diffusion of light; their manes and tails tangled, twisted into knots of dreadlock.

We drove them the five miles into Cody, down Cody's main street, and out west of town, traveling upriver, toward the lodge, fifty miles in all. They shied, and snorted, and nipped at each other's withers, and kicked and bucked, and finally lined out in the borrow ditch for the long march back to a life of oats and work and new steel shoes.

When I was eleven and twelve I rode drag down the center of the highway, lagging a hundred yards behind the herd of horses. Ahead of me they frayed and grouped and swept back and forth over the macadam. The men kept them moving west. The sound of the hundreds of hooves on asphalt rolled back to me. I could feel the vibration of our passing. If I closed my eyes it was as though I rode in the wake of a hailstorm. I wagged a red kerchief tied to a stick at approaching cars. I reined my horse toward their grills. I shouted to the drivers. I asked them to drive slowly. I told them that in Wyoming horses have the right of way.

I remember a young man in a yellow Volkswagen Bug with Rhode Island plates, a young woman with him in the passenger's seat. He swerved around me honking his horn. My horse skittered on the pavement and nearly fell. The horses ahead of me were on the highway, the mob of them, and he slid into their ranks standing on his brakes. He drove at their heels, honking, his brake lights flashing on and off. I remember a leggy sorrel we owned. He was smooth mouthed, could be ridden or packed. If we put a child on him he sidestepped around the trunks of trees, careful not to rub their knees. His name was Sterling. The Rhode Island man pressed his yellow car hard on Sterling. His horn produced a constant wail. Sterling stopped, and turned. His ears were pricked. He stood for just a moment and then stepped onto the hood of the car. The metal winged up on either side of him to his knees. He was not panicked. He was simply getting out of the car's path. He stretched his head and neck to the river and snorted.

When he came over the Volkswagen's roof every window in the car splintered and fell onto the road. The honking stopped. He walked the back bumper off on his way down, and trotted to the side of the road, looped into the borrow pit, and continued west. The yellow car huffed and stalled. When I rode past I reminded the man that in Wyoming horses have the right of way. His girl-friend held up a hand in a jerky wave and nodded. She was laugh-ing. She was trying not to let it show. Her other hand was held to her breast.

We started our packtrips after the Fourth of July, when the deep snow had melted out of the passes and the high water settled clear. I loved being out in the mountains for a week with only mounted people, only the sounds of footfall, wind, rain, the squeal of leather and hemp, the snap of a fire. I did not mind that the people dropped their reins, lost their hats, complained that their knees and asses were worn. We were out together in the mountains, and we were with horses. I knew that by the end of the week they would, each of these strangers, become more comfortable on a horse. By the end of a single week, regardless of their various backgrounds, they would become more comfortable with them-selves. Actors hauled water. Congressmen chopped wood. Judges helped strike camp. Farmers identified the wildflowers and bird-song.

Most of our campsites were positioned in a hem of pine, facing the open grass of a meadow. There would be a spring or small stream within walking distance. Our dudes fished, and snapped photographs, and lounged in the grass. I watched the horses. I knew their names. Their personalities. Their classes; some were women's horses, some would tolerate a rough and clumsy man, some would keep themselves carefully centered under an inexperienced child. Some we could only pack. Some were touchy about their hindfeet and would kick. A few were headshy. There were horses that had to be hobbled or they would leave us in the night. There were those that even hobbled would travel like some large rocking toy and be found the next day miles away. Some could be counted on to buck. They all stood as individuals, but by degree shifted nervous, curious, lazy, crazy, frightened.

At night I would often leave my tent and sit cross-legged in the grass close by my picket horse. It was a comfort to hear his careful steps, the pull and snap of grass stems, the rhythmic grind of his teeth. If the moon was nearly full I could sometimes make out horseshapes in the meadow. I listened for their bells. I wondered how far I would have to ride in the morning to bring them into camp. If it was a clear night I would drag my ground cover and bedroll out of the tent and sleep in the open, under the spread of stars, closer to a horse. If the horses were jumpy, or I had seen bear sign, I would sleep with a rifle. The tents were filled with my father's dudes. It would not do to have one mauled.

In the hot, late part of the summers we would often be camped in Eagle Creek meadows. Our camp was near the head of the long, tight valley, and the meadows spanned the half mile of the valley's bottom, the length of them stretching along the border of Eagle Creek for almost two miles. The mountains rose up abruptly in rock and timber on each side of the meadow, and down its center the creek wound and flattened, lost from view in the waist-deep grass. My brother and I would ride to the creek. We would strip off our clothes, saddles, boots, bridles, and remount cleanly, our naked heels against naked ribs, our buttocks clenched on the warm, haired spines of our horses, and ride stiffly into the water.

On the short, straight stretches the animals walked warily, as though on the skulls of mice we thought, belly-deep in the water, their hooves sucking at the graveled bottom. And in the bends, the water sluiced and deepened into a thick emerald green against green banks overhung with green grass, we would have to swim. We would grip the tufts of hair at the napes of their manes and rise toward the sun, slowly towed as the animals momentarily fell away from us, cooling in the water, lightly connected by our heat only. We would come out into the sun dripping, goose bumped, smiling wildly. We laughed. We hardly ever spoke. We lunged the horses into the water again.

By the time I was fifteen and my brother fourteen we were trusted to take four- and five-day packtrips by ourselves. We rode and packed twenty horses if we had ten dudes. I remember their faces. The worry there, the doubtful expressions, wondering why they were being sent into the mountains with only boys. They did not know that we would die for them.

By the second day they would begin to relax. They would have seen us move the packstring, raise the canvas, side-walled tents on ridgepoles supported between A-framed poles we had cut and lashed. We would have spread out their bedrolls, hauled water and wood, set up a kitchen. They would have eaten steaks, fresh vegetables, an angel food cake my brother had made from scratch and baked in a collapsible steel woodstove. They would have finished their morning coffee and watched us magically produce horses turned out into the night, strike camp, repack the panniers, saddle the stock, and have them mounted and on the move, well fed, warmed by the sun, unharmed.

They did not know who we were. They did not know that we were horseboys. That we looked for hazard through the large, dark eyes of horses. That we scented the earth and the wind that moved across the earth, with wide, open nostrils. That we felt the gravity in river water against our legs and stomachs, that our feet became hooves that skated for balance on the round and moss-covered rocks of streambeds. They did not know that we nibbled at the world with blunt, soft lips.

When we brought them back safely they stepped up to us and pumped our hands. They smiled and squeezed us next to them and asked new friends to take our pictures by their sides. The possibilities of their own children looked new to them, and they joked with their kids, and tousled their hair on the way to hot showers, and my brother and I would unsaddle and unpack and turn the horses into the corrals.

On days out of the mountains I would often have a spare hour after lunch. I'd slump in the shade the barn threw by the side of the corrals, close to the noise and smell of horses. I would worry over my love for them. I would look out into the corrals and watch them stand with their heads hanging low in the still, sunstruck air. I would imagine the corrals emptied. I would wonder what my life might be like without horses, and then I would close my eyes and reconstruct a fantasy that made me happy. In this midday dream I was on a horse, on the back of a mixed blood, gently broken to saddle, unshod. I pictured him feral and unfettered—windblown. I pictured him fast. I felt the slap of the world against us as we moved. I was a boy who rode wildly in his dreams. I was a boy who stood startled from his daydreams, ashamed that his body was so little haired, held upright by only two thin legs.

In the afternoons I handled the colts; I gentled them by routine. I haltered them. I ran my hands along their necks, under their bellies. I pinched their flanks. I lifted their tails. Checked their teeth. Spoke to them. I swatted their rumps, and withers, and backs, and legs with an empty gunnysack. They shied, and snorted, and turned and came to realize that they were not harmed. I bridled them. Led them. Saddled them. I reminded them that we were put together to serve.

There were times when I swung into the saddle and a young horse would rise into the air and to earth again, and again, twisting, grunting, screaming his frustrations, bent on divorce from me. If I did not come loose he would finally spend himself, stand quivering, sweating his hot, sweet scent. I would shift my weight, step him out, work him in circles. I would slap his neck with a short, flat quirt to reinforce the pressure of the reins. First one way, and then the other. I would stop him. Start him. I would feel smaller for his loss of recklessness.

❦ EVERY FALL in mid-October we packed out our hunting camp on Mountain Creek. It was a thirty-mile ride over Eagle Pass, over the lesser Dike Creek Divide. I would leave school for a week to help. There were usually six or seven of us and at least thirty-five packhorses. The packhorses ran loose. They wore muzzles of wire mesh to keep them from grazing. A single man led, and the others spaced themselves back through the packstring to keep the horses in line and moving at the same speed, to watch for a slipped pack; to be ready for accident. We ran half a dozen four-year-olds un-packed for extra mounts in case a young horse played out.

The fall I was fourteen I rode a blue roan colt on the trip out of Mountain Creek. His name was Sky. I knew he was sick when I got on him. His nose ran, and he had the shits. He felt hot and stumbled in the creek when I gathered the horses out of the meadow by camp. I meant to say something to my father about the horse, but the weather was threatening, and I was trying to be more help than problem. I knew I should have roped out one of the other young horses to ride, but we'd gotten a late start. The tents were frozen and had to be beaten with lengths of stovewood to fold them into squares small enough to toppack. It had begun to snow. I thought that Sky was normally a clumsy horse. I convinced myself that that was all it was.

I rode at the end of the packstring and kept his head up. My father was six horses ahead of me, and then Gordon and John and Phil spaced farther up the line, with Claude in the lead. The horses knew they were going home. They shouldered one another in the timber, and fanned off the trail in the meadows trying to get around the men ahead of them.

Sky lagged back on the Dike Creek Divide. I spurred him harder. In the big meadows on the Mountain Creek trail he wheezed and coughed. When he farted he sprayed his hindquarters with shit. I whipped him with my bridle reins to keep up with the others. The clouds lifted, and Pinnacle Mountain and Eagle Peak to the north, both more than eleven thousand feet, came clear and bristling with new snowcover.

On the backside of Eagle Pass, Sky tried to lie down twice. He ducked his head back toward his left shoulder and buckled at the knees. Both times I spurred him into a staggering walk. I felt him grow unsteady between my legs, strain in his solid work.

At the top of the pass I stepped off and tied him to the limb of a stunted pine. His eyes were glazed and out of focus. He did not turn to look as the packstring moved away from us. I walked to the downwind side of the pine, as though I had to piss, and stood with my back to him. My father looked back. I waved, and watched them descend. Sky labored to catch his breath. I walked to him and he nickered softly, and I stroked his nose and knew I might be killing a horse to hide my bad judgment.

I hung two switchbacks behind the others. I walked slowly and led Sky. He skidded and pulled back against the reins. When I was nearly to the bottom of the pass I heard the men shouting, horses screaming and neighing, the pounding of hooves. Two packhorses came up the trail toward me. They were running and kicking into the air. I waved my arms and turned them straight down the slope, dropping from the middle of one switchback to the trail below it. They squatted on their haunches and slid and furrowed the ground and disappeared into the trees below me. I looped Sky's reins around the limb of a deadfall and slid on my ass until my heels bit into the hardpacked level of the trail, and then released and skidded down to a lower switchback. I met my father coming back up the trail. His horse bobbed its head and double-stepped, and worked against the bit, fighting to run.

"Where's Sky?" he asked.

"Up the trail."

"Keep him there." He stepped off his horse, a lean, gaited bay we called Secret, and handed me his reins.

"What happened?"

"We rode into a hornet's nest." He turned and started back down the trail at a jog. The wings of his chaps flared and slapped at his calves. I tied Secret's reins to the limb of a pine and fell in behind my father.

We stopped on the last switchback over the creek that ran against the bottom of the pass. Three horses were staggering on its

apron of stone. One trailed his packcover and lashrope and a broken box pannier. A fourth horse was turned on his back in the
water, the weight of his pack holding him down. John and Gordon
had their knives out. They ducked between the flail of his hooves
and cut him out of his cinches and breastcollar and breeching.
They kept his leadrope taut, his head above the water. They rolled
him onto his side, and pulled on the leadrope, and slapped his ass
and got him out of the creek. We watched as John led him into the
timber and tied him. We watched him stand, and stomp, and
shake, and cough.

We skidded down the cutbank and into the creek. Gordon stayed
in front of the horse trailing his pack. He waved and cussed and
kept the horse pinned against the creek. My father waded out of
the water and caught up his lead. The horse's right rear pastern
was rope burned, and his knee was skinned to its cap, and he bled
from the back of his hock. Gordon lifted off the unbroken pannier,
and my father knelt down at the damaged leg. The horse was a dull
blond palomino we called Poco. The blood came away bright from
his yellow-haired leg.

I dragged the panniers, and the packcover, and pack saddle out
of the creek, one at a time, each water soaked and heavy.

"How's his leg?" Gordon asked.

"Nothing's broken." My father was binding the shag of torn
flesh back up over the horse's kneecap with his kerchief. "You got
any duct tape?" he asked.

"By God I do." Gordon ran to his horse and dug the tape out of
his saddlebags. He knelt down by my father and they taped the
kerchief in place. "That might get him home," he said.

"It will if we get out of here before he knows how bad he's
hurt."

John led the other two packhorses out of the trees and tied them
by his saddle horse.

"How are they?" my father asked.

"Just shook up." John stepped up onto the bay he was riding.
"I'm going to see if I can catch something," he said, and turned the

bay into the trees. We could hear the horse snapping through the downfall.

"Where's the rest of them?" I asked.

"They got by us," Gordon said. "Phil and Claude stayed with 'em."

"Where's the hornet's nest?"

"There," my father said and pointed into the limbs of a Douglas fir at the elbow of the switchback above us. He dumped the wet tack out of the unbroken pannier and sorted through it. He held up a cinch and a tobacco tin of nails and a shoeing hammer. "Good to know our medicine bag's not completely filled with shit," he said, but his voice didn't sound like he thought we were lucky.

Gordon went to work on the broken pannier with the nails and duct tape. I shook out the wet packcover and spread it over the rocks. I replaced the pack saddle's front cinch with the spare one, and opened my jackknife and started to splice the cut breastcollar and back rigging.

We looked up at the clatter of stones. John had one of the loose colts roped and dallied and was dragging him right to us. He stepped off his horse and walked the rope back to the colt and made a halter out of the slack in his lariat and tied the colt to a tree.

"Is that all we have left?" My father asked. He tried to make it sound like a joke.

"Claude got ahead of most of them. He's holding them against the bog at the far end of the meadows. Nothing's hurt, but some of the packs have worked loose."

"How many got past the bog?" my father asked.

"Seven," Gordon said. "Phil's gone after 'em. He thinks their packs held."

"You better get down there and help Claude." My father looked to where Poco was tied. The yellow horse bowed his head back against the leadrope and stepped his torn hindleg toward his head and snorted. "When you get everything squared away start for home. The boy and I'll pack this colt and come along behind with him and Poco. We'll come about as fast as that palomino can walk."

John nodded and Gordon did too, and they turned the two undamaged packhorses down the trail and stepped on their saddle horses and were gone.

The colt just stood with his legs splayed, braced against us as we got him packed. He whistled and rolled his eyes but that was all.

"That's a miracle," my father said. I told him I thought so too. "Lead him away," he said. I walked the colt to where the trail came out of the creek and tied him. He walked stiffly, hunched, turning his head to stare at the pack, but he didn't buck.

I followed my father straight up the mountain, the way the packhorses had slid down. When we cut the switchback above the hornet's nest we followed the trail to where Secret was tied and led him further up the pass to Sky. Sky was down. He had fallen uphill. His feet were notched into the trail. He didn't lift his head as we walked up to him.

"This surprise you?" my father asked.

"He's sick," I said.

"How long's he been sick?"

"Since this morning."

My father looked away at the horizon. The sun was already low in the sky. When he looked back at me his face was red. He looked at me longer than I expected. He lit a cigarette, and exhaled, and held the cigarette between his lips. "Let's see if he'll get up," he said.

I pulled on the reins, and my father took his lariat off his saddle and got behind Sky and slapped his ass hard, and then again, and shouted. The roan groaned and struggled to his front feet and stood, but kept folding his head back, trying to lie back down. My father untied my slicker and denim jacket from behind my saddle and shook out the jacket and hung it over Sky's head. He handed me the slicker. "Put this on," he said, and went to his own horse and untied his jacket and slicker. He put on his slicker and turned up the collar, and eased his denim jacket over Secret's head. The horse balked and snorted and stood quiet.

"You ready?" he asked. He seated his hat tighter on his head.

"I guess I am."

We ran down the trail leading the horses, and across the creek. The hornets were busy above us and to the sides, but they did not land or sting. We stopped in the dark timber where I had tied the colt. He whinnied and pulled back against the lariat. We pulled our jackets away from our horses' heads and Sky folded his legs and laid down. My father looked at me and then knelt by Sky's head. "You're going to have to stay with him," he said.

"I'm not afraid to," I told him.

He undid my saddle's latigo and breastcollar and pulled it away from the downed horse. He stood the saddle under a tree and laid the hairpad and blanket over its upturned skirt.

"Get that bridle off him," he said, and looked down the creek to where Poco stood. He went to his saddlebags and came back with a flashlight and hatchet and the lunch that he hadn't eaten. He handed me his slicker. "Do you have matches?" he asked. I nodded.

"How far is it to the lodge?" I asked.

"Twelve miles."

I nodded again.

"If you can get him up in the morning try to walk him out. I'll start back for you. I'll bring a spare horse in case we need one." He lit another cigarette and looked straight up from where we stood. "It doesn't look like the weather's going to change."

"It doesn't feel like it," I said.

My father led Poco up the creek, took off his wire muzzle, and half-hitched the halterrope to the horn of his saddle. He slipped John's lariat over the colt's head and put the muzzle on the colt. He stood for a moment recoiling the lariat and then stepped onto his horse and measured his reins and held Secret on the trail. The packed colt stood in front of him.

"You nervous about this?" he asked.

"No, sir."

"You should be," he said. He stuck his chin out toward Sky. "That's a good little horse you rode down. I'll see you tomorrow."

He started into the trees leading Poco, pushing the colt ahead of them. Poco walked badly, slowly, his light hair gathering the light and holding it against the black and green of the pines. The shadows stood thick and dark as a second growth of trees. When I could not see them any longer, when the echo of their hoofstrikes was gone, I sat on the ground in my wet clothes and cried. I tried to cry because of what I had done to Sky, but I was crying for myself, and because I was afraid that careless boys grow into careless men.

In the last light of the day I broke away armloads of dead branches and stacked them and gathered dry cones and dug up the sap-loaded roots from the rotted stump of an old fir. I used the hatchet to scrape away the pine duff and chopped a firepit into the earth and built a small, hot fire. I stood my saddle on its fork by the fire and used the hairpad for a ground cover and sat and leaned back into the fleece that lined the saddle and stared into the fire. I had spread my saddle blanket over Sky's neck and front shoulder. He watched me, but did not lift his head. I thought he had come to the bedrock of himself. I felt him fall out from under me; I felt myself fall with him.

I put on my jacket and pulled my father's and my slicker up to my chin and my head nodded and I fell asleep. When I woke the night was black and cold and the slice of sky I could see directly above me, busy with stars. The fire had died into a circle of embers, and I stacked on the fir roots. They sizzled and flared and burned hot as coal. I sat cross-legged on the hairpad with my saddle cupped around my back and ate my father's lunch. There were two elk steak sandwiches and an apple and a Snickers bar. When I was done I wadded the paper sack and put it on the fire and walked to the creek and laid the flashlight on the rocks and stretched out and held my chest off the ground on my palms and drank until I was full. My ass was still wet and stung in the night air, but my legs were dry. I stomped my feet to warm them and took up the light and walked to Sky. He nickered when I played the light across his head.

I knelt by his ears and lifted his head and scooted my knees under it and laid the broad thick bone of his skull against my thighs. He did not struggle. I closed my eyes and prayed for the strength to lift him and carry him to safety, and felt no stronger, and began to cry again. I bent my mouth to the soft, furred cup of his ear and whispered that I was sorry. I knew it did not matter to him. I knew that it mattered only to me. I said that I was sorry again.

I stood away from him and straightened the blanket on his neck and shoulder and walked back to the fire and squatted with my back to the flames until my ass warmed. The black night pressed down like water. My chest felt heavy. I had to stand to get a breath.

I sat back against the saddle and pulled the slickers over me and slept. There was only the sound of the fire, and in my sleep I dreamed that I lived on the back of a horse. In the dream I was fully grown. I was a naked, gaunt, and happy man, and I never stood down upon the earth. When I was tired I lay along the horse's back to sleep. When I was thirsty the rains came and I opened my mouth and drank. I was filled with rainwater and ozone. I draped forward on the horse's neck to rest. My arms hung to the sides of his neck. My hands clenched and relaxed. I breathed into his coarse, dark mane. My lungs filled with the salted, sweet-meat taste of the horse on which I lived.

In my dream I stood on the horse's rump and pissed a yellow arc into the air and my head fell back and I screamed into the vault of the black night sky, and turned and walked to his withers and sat.

He was a pinto horse, dark eyed, dark nostriled, dark stockinged with one white hoof, front left, slightly softer than the darker three. Each foot stuck out a single note as he stepped to graze. He made music as he ran. The lighter hoof slapping the earth in a tone shallower than the other three.

I sat upright on that horse and held my arms high like the ar-matures of long, slim wings and leaned slightly forward, and he broke into a run. I could feel the cool air tighten my flesh. I could feel the horse grow hot and lathered, and I knew that when a horse is running flat-out toward the curve of the earth that all four feet, regardless of color, leave the ground at once. I closed my eyes. I heard us skip into the air and touch the earth again, and I knew that it was in those suspended moments, relaxed from effort, that the rider and the ridden are afforded, in that instant, and in the next, and the next after that, the sight of God. I saw God looking at me in the dream and knew it was a horse I had to thank.

I woke in the early light. A gray jay stepped through the gray ash of the fire, and when I kicked off the slickers he rose into a pine and chattered. The slickers were stiff with frost. I took off my hat and beat the frost from its crown and stomped and shook. I expected to be alone. I felt alone. I expected to find a dead horse, to shoulder my saddle and start down the trail. I didn't look up until I was close to Sky. I almost jumped back when he lifted his head. He focused hard on me and tucked his legs and rolled onto them and stood. He swayed and caught himself.

I bridled him and led him to the creek, and he sucked at the water for a long time. I took a step upstream and knelt and cupped water on my face and drank. The ground and trees were dirty white with frost. It looked as though we stood inside the skeleton of a cloud. I felt better than the boy who had gone to sleep. I felt older than the boy who'd nearly killed his horse.

I saddled Sky and rolled the slickers behind the cantle and put the hatchet and flashlight in a saddlebag. I led him and he came along. I did not try to ride. I walked as fast as his strength allowed. When he grew tired we stopped.

I hoped to meet my father more than halfway between the bottom of the pass and home. I knew I deserved what punishment he thought ought to come my way. I knew I would not tell him of my dream.

MY SISTER'S BOOTS

After breakfast it is just dawn. My father and I stand on the lodge porch looking south. He holds a mug of coffee, and it steams in the cool air. He sets the coffee on the porchboards and lights a cigarette and takes the mug up again and sips and leans against the rail. The thick stand of lodgepole and fir along the creek casts a block of pointed shadow to the west. We stand in the fringe of that shadow. In front of us and to the downlight side of each sage is fallen a furred plum of lesser shadow. The nightchill has dropped and holds fast against the valley floor. The songbirds have risen to the heat. They preen and skitter in the topmost limbs of the pines. The mountain across the valley is thrust up brightly in the morning light. We shift our weight from hip to hip and watch the canted light ratchet its angle upward, the shadows shrinking. I've been out of bed since four this morning, riding the drainage behind the lodge with the older cowboys, gathering horses. We all breakfast in the slice of time between night and day because there is too much work to do in the light to have our mouths full. It is the last of spring, and I am out of school. I am twelve. My father is of medium height. If he were to turn to me, hold out his arms to me, and I were to walk into him my head would not brush his collarbones. I am only as tall as the top of his heart. I feel larger when I am working.

I lift my right foot, turn it, and buff the instep and toe of my boot against my left calf. I stand square and rock back, admiring the polished leather.

My father turns. He keeps one hand on the porch rail holding his cigarette. In the other hand he holds his coffee cup. The cigarette smoke fans and spreads to the west. He looks down at my boots. "You buy those new?"

"Yesterday. I went to town with John and Gordon."

"What'd you give for them?"

"Almost thirty dollars."

He nods and sips his coffee. "With new boots you won't get the kind of tips you're used to."

I shine the other boot against its opposite calf and look down at them stepped together. "I guess I won't." The new waxed laces and stitching stand out white as tendon. My last pair had worn apart. Once a week I cut out cardboard insoles and bound the rag of leather sole that remained to the boot's body by circling the thing tight with athletic tape, from toe to instep. And still by midweek they'd worn apart and flapped like feeding-cartoon alligators. The tourists we take for rides and fishing trips felt sorry for me. They tipped extra toward a new pair of boots. It embarrassed them that their guide was nearly barefoot. If I limped they tipped even more.

"You working with John this morning?" He finishes his coffee and straightens.

"I haven't heard about anything else I'm supposed to do."

"Soak 'em through," he says and nods toward the boots. "I don't want you blistered up and thinking about your feet."

"I will."

He hands me his empty mug. "You run this back to the kitchen for me?"

"Yes, sir."

"Take a jaunt up Fishhawk this afternoon. It flooded supreme last week. I'd like to know how much of the trail is left."

"Yes, sir." The hot weather has come early this year and all at once, day and night, and there have been warm rains. The rains stopped three days ago, and last night it cooled to just above freezing. The creeks and river have cleared.

My father stands down from the porch and flicks his cigarette butt into the drive. "Goddamn shame your mother and I didn't have more kids. This place could keep a dozen of you busy."

I step into the help's dining room. The cabin girls sit grouped at one end of the twelve-foot length of breakfast table with the old man my father's hired this summer to cut firewood. His name is Ted. He puts his gloves on when he gets out of bed. He eats breakfast with them on. He buttons his workshirt to his throat, bathes regularly, is expansive in his memory of himself. He's shrunken away from his hands, head, and feet; they appear to belong to a larger man, but he can dropstart a chainsaw on the first try, and his facecuts take a perfect pie out of a tree's trunk. He'll tell you to within a foot where the tree's going to drop before he starts his backcut. There are four big fireplaces that heat the lodge and four cabins with smaller fireplaces. The bunkhouse and shop have wood-burning stoves. We burn half a cord of dead-standing pine a day—lodgepole. Ted hunts out the trees and fells them. It is a six-day-a-week job, only Monday through Friday in August when the nights warm into the fifties.

My younger brother sits to Ted's side. He creases and recreases the bill of his cap. He's ready to go to work. He'll spend the day limbing the felled trees and stacking the rounds cut to length into the bed of the pickup. We both split wood in the evenings.

Ted tells the cabin girls what a randy son of a bitch he used to be. He tells them that if he were still young it would take two good boys just to carry his water. The girls lean forward over their coffee and then fall back against their straight-backed chairs to giggle. I wink at my brother. He smiles, and then politely lowers his grin to the table. Neither one of us wants to risk getting caught mocking a man who's handy with a chainsaw.

In the kitchen the cook asks me if I'm glad to be out of school. I tell him I am. He's a shriveled old man, in his seventies: white shoes, socks, pants, shirt, and white apron. His hair is white. He's already drunk. We've never hired a sober cook. He says, without any sort of pretension, that work is what a man needs to keep his head down. He tells me he's kept his head down his entire working life. He tells me he's watched where he was going. He adds that hard work is where a man finds some peace. I listen because I have been taught to listen to old men. His breath stinks of beer. He's the only one on the place who is up before I am, and his baked goods are soberingly fine. I excuse myself and am out through the pantry and into the shadows still held against the creekbank.

I am thinking of which horse I will ride this afternoon to check the trail up Fishhawk Creek. I kick my bootheels into the loose bank and walk into Libby Creek and stand. Today it's a clear stretch of water; fast; strong enough to tumble gravels of basalt and quartz, some as large as my teeth. Last week it swelled with runoff and rain and moved boulders the size of colts. The big rocks ground like the constant rumble of thunder. We stood along its bank and stared into the brown storm of water and hoped it would not twist out of its bed. It has shrunken in the three days of cooler weather. It will rise again and stay high for another month, but without heavy rain the danger is gone.

I walk into the creek with my new boots on, right into the water. I find a place to stand where the water climbs to within inches of their tops. I pull up the legs of my pants to stare at my feet. They look larger underwater. I become dizzy with the water's movement over my larger-than-life boots and look up into the timber. I feel the water work in through the seams. I flex my feet, and the water drips in through the stitching along the soles. I think that I can hear the waxed thread sing. My socks become cold, and then soaked, and I step out onto the worn-round rocks that line the banks, my feet thoroughly wet and numb. I flex my feet again, and feel the water work the length of my soles, and wonder if I will be as good with a chainsaw as Ted when I am an old man. I wonder if I will be able to make young girls laugh. I cannot make them laugh now. I wonder how my sister would have laughed. I had a sister.

She would be a year older, but she lived for only a few months.

An early birth. My mother has told me about her. Her small hands. Blue eyes. Red hair. Her name was Cindy. My mother has had trouble having kids. She had four miscarriages even after my brother and I were on the ground, and we were born too early, too small. My mother has given up trying to have more children; she satisfies herself with us—the ones who stayed alive. My sister was my mother's only real chance for companionship. Another female in the family. Our dogs and cats are male. Our horses are all gelded studs. I think about my sister when my mind is quiet; almost always when I am watching water. I see a sister as an encyclopedia of feminine advice. I see my sister as a doorway to the second half of the world. I wish I could call her name and have her turn her face to me and smile.

The sun has topped the east ridge, and morning light falls and stands through the timber like a scatter of quarried granite. Wyoming light. Mountain light. I press down with my toes and arch my feet against the boots' insteps. It is the first week in June. I have read in Black Elk's book that the Oglala Sioux called this time of year the Moon of Making Fat. I grip the taut flesh at my belly. I am full of sausage, eggs, bread, potatoes. I feel weighty, fueled for the morning. I look again at my boots. I press my weight down into them.

It will not be a comfortable day, but I do not care. I will walk these boots dry. I will wear them until they shrink back perfectly to the peculiarities of my feet. If they are not dry tonight I will sleep in them. I will trick them to exactly mimic my feet. Only this one day of discomfort for boots that will fit me as closely as if my blood has worked into them and brought them alive. Squirrels chatter from the fanned limbs of a Douglas fir stretched above me. One of them drops a cone. And then another. A raven walks the creekbank toward me, tilting his head, watching. I look down at the boots. Water oozes from their seams.

These are riding boots, with riding heels, and tops of a lighter leather stitched as intricately as stiff sculptures of quilt. They looked good in the store, and they look good on my feet. This is the day I begin to own them; to train them, to break them. This morning they pulled on harshly as rules. They pulled on like what they are, boots made of the thick, hairless hides of cows. I thought of that when I bought these boots, and I think of it now. I think of the boots reduced to their parts. I think that I am wearing boots made from the hide of an animal raised and fatted and killed for my food and clothing. I look up into the squirrel-chatter. I flex my soaked feet. There is little give in the boot leather. It seems as inflexible as the hopelessness of cattle. I look closely at their grain, study it as though it is the hideprint of a slaughtered animal's resentment. For a single moment the boots seem nearly alive; they do not present themselves as just clothing. The thought sends a jolt of fright through me. I think of sitting and pulling the boots off my feet.

The raven has hopped atop a boulder almost within my reach. His eyes glint black in the light. I am still a little spooked thinking of the animal that died for my footwear. I wonder if these new boots hold a memory of betrayal. I wonder if that betrayal will wick its way into me, feet first. I take a step. My toes drift free in the water-filled boot tips. There is a sucking sound. And then again. It tickles. The raven spreads his wings and backs down away from me. John will be at the corrals waiting. Until the water finds its way back through the seams each step makes me smile. I am a boy. Thoughts of my sister, or death, or the misery of cattle, come and go in flashes between the constant delight I feel in my young body. I live each day largely satisfied with who I am. It has not yet occurred to me to be concerned about improvement. It is a trick of boyhood, this contentment I find in each moment. But I am raised mostly by men. I know it will not last.

Last fall my mother hurt her back. My father and brother and I, and every man on the place, were packing in hunting camp, and she was left alone with a sick horse. A thickly muscled gray we call Steel. Each morning she tied the horse up short to a gatehinge and swung the gate back against his side, squeezing him between the gate and corral. She tied the gate's end solidly to a post behind his ass. She'd reach between the gatepoles and inject the horse with a syringe of antibiotic. He dreaded it as much as she did. They both shook from the time she haltered him, the gray horse and my mother.

On the morning before we came out of the mountains Steel felt well enough to fall back and snap his halterrope and kick the gate into my mother as she turned out of his way. She was in bed the evening we returned. She does not drink, but my father prescribed her a glass of whiskey for the pain. I sat in a chair pulled to her bed while she sipped from the glass. Her eyes misted while she talked, but she was smiling. She had been lonely she said. She asked me to bow my head toward her, and when I did she rubbed the palm of her hand against the bristle of my hair. She told me she loved me. She told me she loved both her boys. When she was done with the glass of whiskey she said that my soul was smiling at God— smiling twice. I asked her how she knew. She asked me to bend forward again, and she traced circles on my skull, right, front and rear. "Cowlicks," she'd said. "It's where your soul unravels into happiness. You have two. You have a happy soul." She let her hand drop and laced her fingers together across her stomach and stared at the ceiling. Tears stood in her eyes. I've never seen my mother fully cry. "Your sister had two like yours," she'd said. She looked at me and smiled again. "Cowlicks," she added.

I take off my hat and smooth my palm against my skull. I feel for the swirls of tighter hair. I like it that my mother thinks I smile at God. I like it when she rubs my head. I do not know that I will in a few years come to a self-conscious wildness in myself, be embarrassed by my mother's sweet attention; someday wonder if God notices that any of us smile into His blue and empty air.

John has four horses haltered and tied at a rail outside the corrals. These are the last four barefoot horses off winter pasture. We shoe in the spring. Again in late summer. We pull the shoes before we turn them out in October and their hooves grow long and split and fray. I will work ahead of him; trimming, getting a start at leveling their feet. This is my second year with John. When I am a man I will shoe a horse the way John shoes a horse. With these same tools.

"You got your feet wet."

"Yes, sir."

"Watch you don't slip and get under one of these horses. You won't be worth a shit if you get kicked."

I'm buckling my chaps. I take off my hat and hang it on a peg beside John's. He's curled under the front foot of a big buckskin eyeing a shoe for fit. A half dozen shoeing nails are stuck in the corner of his mouth. He drops the buckskin's foot and walks to the anvil. Our horses are cold-shod. There's not a lot of room for mistakes. He stands the heels of the shoe against the corner of the anvil and brings the hand-sledge down on the shoe's toe. Once. Twice. The metal sings against metal. He holds the thing at eye level and sights that the heel has spread evenly and returns to the buckskin. He refits the shoe and takes up a small claw hammer from the shoeing box.

He drives a nail through the toe of the shoe and hoof. He grips the exposed nailend in the hammer's claw and works the claw back and forth until the nail snaps off nearly plumb with the glossy outside of the hoof. He must do this with every nail and quickly. If the buckskin shies and jerks his leg free he will drag the nailend back through John's hand, or the inside of a thigh. John seats and drives another nail at the shoe's heel and snaps its end. He turns and looks to me. "Anything here you haven't seen before?"

"I guess there isn't."

John's forehead is beaded with sweat. Sweat drips from the tip of his nose. "You waiting for your feet to dry?"

"I was thinking about cows."

He works off another nailend and squares his weight more evenly over his hips. "What about cows?" he asks.

"About leather." His chaps are worn pale and roughed in places. Their insides dark as shadow. "I was thinking that it used to be alive."

John slaps the buckskin in the ribs with the side of the shoeing hammer and tells him to stand up. The horse snaps his head up past his withers and splays his hindquarters, shifting his weight off John's back. John grips the pastern more tightly between his knees and finishes the nailing. He takes a file from the shoeing box and grooves the hoof under each broken nailend and takes a cigarette pack–sized block of iron out of the box and holds it against the broken ends and pounds their heads home harder, turning the nailends down, clinching them into the groove. He drops the foot between his legs and stands against the buckskin's side, an arm draped along the horse's back. He drags his free arm across his face and blows for a minute. He looks at me as though he expects more from our conversation, but I can think of nothing to say. I've become lost in the rhythm of his work.

He shakes his head and steps away from the horse and taps the side of his boot against the buckskin's pastern, and when the horse lifts the foot John crouches and sets it onto his knee. He taps the nailends flat, smoothes them with a file and runs a rasp along the edge of the hoof to knock off any slight overlap. He lets the leg drop and straightens, arches his back, and moves the shoeing box to the horse's left hindfoot. He presses his thumb through each eyebrow to squeeze out the sweat and shakes a kerchief from his back pocket and mops his face. "You're a smart boy," he says. He's catching his breath. "I'll bet if you tried, you could think about cows and work at the same time."

"About leather."

"It'd be worth a try." He smiles and turns and grasps the buckskin's fetlock and coaxes his hindfoot up and shuffles back with the hoof turned up in his lap.

I use just a shoeing knife, a pair of long-handled nippers, and a rasp. I take up the hooves, one at a time, clean them down to the frog, pare what I can, nip back the overgrowth of hoof and rasp it roughly level, shaping the hoof in an oversized version of what I've learned John will expect. The nippers are not sharp, and the hooves are tough. I grip each handle of the nippers and squeeze them together and rock the tool until it bites through. One bite at a time until I've worked my way around the perimeter of each hoof, and the horses lean heavily on me because I am small and inexperienced.

By midmorning our shirts are soaked through, and I can feel beads of sweat run down the insides of my thighs. The flies are out; horseflies, deerflies, noseflies. They orbit singly and in swarms. I've finished the last horse, a bay, and step away and gather my tools. I wonder if it will warm enough to bring the creeks up. John moves the shoeing box to the bay, talking to the horse. The other three are left tied, freshly shod, stamping on their new iron shoes, their winter-long tails working their hindquarters, their skins flexing in shivers against the flies. I take up the buckskin's tail, hook half a dozen long straight, black hairs under my index finger and pull. I drop the hair to my side. I'll work around the tail several times, pulling the longer hairs free; barbering the tail shorter. John prefers a horse's tail to fall just shy of their hocks. I stuff the hair from each horse into gunny sacks. We'll sell most of it and keep a little back to braid into hatbands.

"I'm going to need a pair of oughts for these hindfeet." John is bent under the bay's hindquarters leveling a foot. I bring him the horseshoes from the tackshed and squat by the shoeing box, and he slides a shoe against the upturned hoof, turning it.

"Pigeon-footed little son of a bitch, isn't he?"

"Yes, he is."

"I can take most of that out of him." John stands and walks to the anvil and hammers the shoe, sighting it at arm's length in the light and hammering again. He walks back to the bay, and we stand for a moment and watch my dog sprawled in the shade gnawing on a hoof paring and thumping his tail. His name is Rock. He's gathered most of the parings into a pile by his head. Rock's an all-black dog and stays to the shadows on a hot day. His saliva is thickened into foam at the corners of his mouth, and his eyes are glazed in concentration.

"You ever done that?"

I look up at John. "What?"

"Eat a horse hoof."

"I haven't." His question has caught me off guard.

"Not even a nibble?"

"Not even that."

"Your dog sure likes 'em."

"He eats horseshit too." My point seems sound; conclusive in the differences of what dogs and humans will eat.

"They don't make Jell-O out of horseshit." John is bent back to work. I watch his spine flex and lengthen against his wet shirt-cloth.

"They make Jell-O out of horse hooves?" I ask. I want to see how the statement sounds when I say it. I know it to be ridiculous. I expect John to laugh, but he doesn't.

"Among other things. Hand me over a couple more nails."

"Lime Jell-O?"

"The lime's just flavoring."

I look at the dog and back to John. "I don't believe you," I tell him.

"Ask your mother."

"Why would she know?"

"I imagine everybody knows but you. Your feet still wet?"

"Yes, they are."

"Those boots'll feel good when you pull them on tomorrow."

"I know that." I don't mind being a boy, but I hate being treated like one.

John stands and smiles. He tosses the hammer into the shoeing box and drags a shirtsleeve across his face. "I just thought you might be feeling bad you didn't know what was in Jell-O. I was trying to cheer you up. I thought someday when you were done thinking about leather that you might want to branch out." His eyes widen and he smiles again. "A boy like you could give a lot of thought to hooves and horns."

There are eleven people at lunch, and every one of them knows what's in Jell-O. Even the cabin girls, and they're only a few years older than I am. I'm thankful my brother is still out cutting wood with Ted. If no one gets to him before I do there's a chance he won't have learned the ingredients in gelatin. It's a slim chance but the only one I have not to appear the single dunce.

After lunch I saddle the buckskin and cross the Shoshone River on the Kitty Creek bridge. It's a low-railed wooden bridge, and I listen for the strikes the buckskin's new shoes pound out against the boards. The echoes of our passing fall down and against the river, spread to its banks, and rise back to us. A fisherman waves from the riverbank.

The buckskin steps out into the mile of dirt road along the river that ends at the Boy Scout Camp. We ride through stands of shadow, broad, flat stretches of light, standing puddles, and pine scent so sharp it quickens the horse into a trot. I stand in the stirrups and rest the heel of my right hand against the saddle horn. We move past the camp buildings, and the road narrows to a single trail. I turn the buckskin north up Fishhawk Creek. My boots have drained and feel easy in the stirrups. Their tops have dried and the bottoms are stained impressively with horseshit and soil. I watch them as I ride. I think I will get off easy this year. If I flex my feet I can still make the boots squeal a bit, but almost inaudibly; they are losing their individuality. I am breaking them to walk or ride.

Beside the trail there is a reef of berry bushes come dark green in new leaves. I wonder what it would be like to be a Boy Scout. The few I've seen appeared to have lost something. They stared at me shyly, as though they needed a guidebook to identify me. If I were mounted they would sidle away and group around the fat man who always seemed to accompany them.

When I ride through the Boy Scout Camp the main dining hall and outbuildings are still boarded up. It's too early in the summer for the Scouts to be out. My horse slows to a walk, and I tell him that I'd rather take a beating than have patches sewn on any of my shirts.

We flush a ruffed grouse, and the buckskin snorts and boogers sideways into a scatter of rocks and berry bushes. I spur him back onto the trail, and he gooses like we've just seen a bear cub. I can hear the grouse drumming behind us until the sound of Fishhawk rises out of its drainage and mutes the birdsound.

The sky is clear. The day has just warmed, not gotten hot. It's a good day for a ride and for drying leather. My feet feel fine.

At the first crossing on Fishhawk the creek has cut into the bank and it has fallen away, leaving a ten-foot drop of crumbling earth. Several lodgepole have had their roots exposed and list out over the water. The opposite bank looks just as bad. I work the buckskin up through the downed timber, and almost high-center him on a log he refuses to jump. He scrapes his back shins struggling over. I can feel his mood shift. I step off to see that he hasn't run a stub into his flank or stifle and find just peeled skin. I lead him in a weave through the timber above the creek looking for a place to cross and find one a half mile above the ruined crossing. I remount on the apron of rounded stone along the creek and let him drink. We walk the creek boulders upstream for a hundred yards because the east bank is undercut, and then find a chute made by the elk to get to the water. I turn the buckskin up the chute, and he farts and digs in and we're out of the water and I've managed not to get my boots wet again.

We strike the main trail a hundred yards upslope, and the buckskin swings into a faster walk, shaking his head, mouthing the bit, generally pissed off that he's out alone with a boy banging through the downtimber and up a gutted creek.

The next two crossings don't look like I remember them but they're passable. The trail drops off in a series of eroded ledges that will smooth by the end of the summer. So far it's just a day's work to cut a new trail around the first crossing. I plan to ride the drainage for another three or four miles and then turn for home. I put the buckskin up the northern slope of a ridge that falls into loose rimrock. After we top the palisades the trail humps out to the west and then slides back on itself into a steep-sided dry crease, turns west again, and descends evenly back to the creek.

It is in the crease where the horse humps me up into the air and steps out from under me. It is a trick he manages when he can, and he is the kind of animal that looks for an inconvenient day; just mischievous, not mean-spirited. He'll nicker and nuzzle my chest when I grain him tomorrow morning. Today he waits until we drop down through the steep, dry cut. He catches me preoccupied—catches me, in fact, staring at my right boot, my weight shifted up on his right shoulder—and drops off the trail, kicks over his head, and fades to his left.

When I stop rolling I have plenty of time to stare at my new boots. I squint hard at them, trying to anchor my sight, make of my sight a vortex. My head feels as though it might spin off, but I don't seem to be hurt anywhere, just shook up. When the swirl of trees has settled I lean back onto my elbows and close my eyes. And then stretch flat on my back. There's only a general ache. My hips and lower back feel tight. I can hear the footfalls of the buckskin echo softly, receding. I imagine his satisfaction. The thought makes me smile. I sit up and bend my knees toward my chest. Everything works. I feel just alone when I get to my feet, not crippled. I unbuckle my chaps and hang them over my shoulder. I've got a five-mile walk. It would seem like ten wearing chaps.

I find the buckskin's tracks on the main trail. This side of the ridge faces north, is still damp, and he's slipped in a spot. I smile again. The son of a bitch. He'll make better time than he did with me on top of him. A hundred yards down the trail I find a broken bridle rein and loop it around my neck. I hope he'll step on just the one. The rein falls to each side of my neck and over my chest like some thin, equine vestment. It broke near the bit. Tonight I will make the repair. John will watch and smile, maybe rib me a little, and I will have one rein slightly shorter than the other.

I keep my eyes on my boots as I walk. They still look new, and that is allowed only once a year; to purchase a new pair of boots. All day (no matter what else I have done, and really, it is what got me bucked off) I have watched the smooth, unworn narrow toes of these boots lift me into each next step. Watching them makes me more aware that I am walking, that I am a boy without a horse under him.

I think that walking is different from riding. I am connected to the earth differently, more aware of the strike of my bones against the land, more aware of the surface. My breath comes sharp and strong. I think that when I am walking it is as though I am speaking each word of myself to the mountain's ear. Aloud. I like the sensation. I also like being on a horse. When I am mounted it feels as though I must draw my breath through half a ton of animal to fill my lungs. My breath comes to me fuller, hotter; the breathing expanded, drowsy, and meditative. When I am older I will think of the difference between walking and riding to be the difference between prayer and the effect of prayer. A pair of ravens keep pace with me, in short swings of flight from tree to tree, cawing. There are always ravens here. I know that I am in the Absaroka Mountains. I have read that in the Crow language, the word *absaroka* means "raven." I turn my face to them and say aloud, "Absaroka." The larger of the two spreads his wings and drops and rises into a spruce ahead of me. I think of my sister. I wonder if she saw the buckskin step out from under me. If it made her laugh. If she's laughing now. I close my eyes and listen but hear only the creek and ravenspeak.

The trail descends the wooded slope, hugging the curve of soil and rock, turning back into its depression at a rate that animals may follow easily, climbing higher into the air with leisure, without their hearts having to pump away at their storages of fat. I turn into the crease that runs from ridgetop to creek, widening, carrying excess water from the slope. The timber thickens, and I am lost in the repetition of my movement. I am only vaguely aware that this cut has no spring at its head, and am sorry because I am thirsty, but when I cross its deepest part—where I, in fact, wish for a creek—and turn, there stands on the trail a cow elk, only four feet ahead of me, and between us, exactly as we have noticed one another, she commits the birth of her calf. It drops to the trail at my feet. Her eyes come alive in panic at the sight of me. She cocks back on her haunches and bolts for cover, and I am left staring at her calf, at my new boots, now splattered by her blood.

The calf is mostly bone and hair and moves awkwardly, without smoothness. I think it looks like some blind, emaciated, and smallish Great Dane. It struggles to stand, to come free from the tangle of afterbirth, blood stained, catching transparent and white and ruby in the tree-muted light. I look once to the cow's track. She's gone straight uphill. The slope is wet. Her dewclaws have printed behind the lobes of her track. I hear her neigh, and then bark, just once, and I turn quickly from the trail and down the mountain away from this new calf. I pray as I walk. I pray that the cow will return. That she will offer up her milk-filled teats. I pray that I have not caused a death. I ask my sister to hear my prayers. I ask her to spread the word.

I stop when I am short of breath and look back up the mountain. I see only trees and the slant of afternoon light merely segregating them. It is so quiet that I think for a moment that I imagined the birth of an elk. I close my eyes. On the backs of their lids is pressed the image of the slick new thing; at once common, yet ineffably private. I know that I've witnessed something most boys have not. I know that it has made the day as different as if there were a death. I know I've walked through a door left temporarily ajar into a deeper part of the world in which I live, and out again. I have the blood-splattered boots for the proof of it. But beyond the excitement, beyond the instance of unexpected tourism, I know that I have not seen enough.

I unsnap my shirt and wad it into a rag and try to rub the spots of elk blood from my new boots. They do not come out, but smear and fade and look to be leather cut from the rumps of Appaloosa horses, or I think, and smile, the freckled cheeks of a red-haired girl. I put my shirt back on, and hug my arms around my ribs, and whisper, "Cynthia." And again. I think of her baked alive in my mother's body. Dead in the world. Alive in my heart, in this forest, just on the other side of some closed door.

It takes me an hour to crawl to a point above and downwind from the calf. I nestle in the duff and watch. The cow has circled round and comes out of the cut one cautious step at a time. She steps and stops, and steps again. Her head is up and her nostrils flare. Her body is bunched for flight behind her nose. The calf sits on its left hip, its shoulders squared atop its straight front legs. It blinks and bleats a little when it finds the breath. The cow sniffs her calf and begins to lick the film of afterbirth away. She stops to stare into the timber, first right, and to her left. She lowers her head and noses the calf to its feet, and I sneak on my belly farther downwind—careful not to make the same error twice—and curve down the mountain home. I'm walking fast.

I run through all three fords to keep my boots as dry as I can, at least not soaked from the inside out, and manage not to fall. It's almost dark when I've reached the Scout Camp. I press an eye to the crack where two sheets of plywood meet over a dining hall window and inside it is just gray and quiet with rows of empty picnic tables.

The dirt road is harder than the trail, and I limp against a blister rising on the heel of my left foot. My hips have begun to ache. The light is soft and green and dropping fast. My stomach whines and my hands are thick, packed tight against the skin from hanging down.

I hear the hoofstrikes before I see the horses and then a flashlight beam plays up my body and across my face. I step forward out of the light. My father sits the bay he likes to ride. The horse side-steps on the road and fights the bit. John rides beside him and my brother behind them both.

"You hurt?" my father asks.

"Just a blister. And I guess my pride."

"Your horse got home an hour ago."

"Did he have one rein?"

"He did," John says.

"Your feet wet?"

"They're fine."

"Step up behind your brother," my father tells me, and they turn their horses in the road. "Your mother won't sleep until we all get back."

My brother kicks his left foot out of his stirrup, and I step in and swing up behind the cantle and fidget until I'm comfortable on top of the saddlebags. The men step their horses out abreast, ahead of us.

"You get bucked off?" my brother asks.

"You couldn't really call it that."

"You have him tied?"

"He just sort of ducked and humped me off. He found a good place to do it. He stepped on a rein on his way home."

My brother nods. "You hungry?" he asks.

"For a couple of hours now."

The men have put their horses into a lengthy gait. My brother holds his sorrel back. He reaches inside his denim jacket and brings out a sandwich wrapped in waxed paper. "I thought you might be," he says. "Dad said you might be hurt or dead, but I knew you'd be just hungry." He hands the sandwich back.

"What kind is it?"

"Bones, horns, hooves, and skin." I feel him duck his head in a smile but he doesn't turn.

"Tastes like ham," I say, with as much confidence as I can muster.

"I guess you'll never know."

"Did Mom tell you?"

"I told her I already knew."

"Did you?"

"I guess I didn't." His horse stumbles in the dark and whinnies. The men's horses' shoes strike sparks thirty yards ahead and low. "I don't plan on eating any more of it either," he says. "No matter who serves it up."

"Neither do I," I tell him. I tell him I don't care what kind of flavoring they've put in it.

"Chew back a little," he says. "I don't want crumbs down my collar."

I lean away from him, and he puts his horse into a trot. "You didn't think I was dead?" I ask.

He pulls his hat down tight. "I wouldn't have made the sandwich if I did," he says.

When we cross the bridge on the Shoshone the hoofstrikes echo and fall away and gather in the night, along the water, fading downstream. I ball up the waxed paper and put it down the collar of my brother's jacket. I poke him in the ribs, and he hoots, and spurs his horse, and the sorrel jumps and kicks. "You're going to get us both farted off," he says, but I have my arms around him, and I can feel him laughing.

❧ FIFTEEN YEARS later in New York, in dry shoes, in a restaurant in the Village a slim, brown man recently emigrated from Hardwar in the north of India takes my hand, stares into the lens apparent in my palm, and then into my eyes and tells me that an auburn-haired sister accompanies me every step I take. He is a waiter, and would have us believe a mystic too. I am twenty-seven. I have come to New York to start a new life, to remake my personal history. I have come to New York because I have made decisions about the man I want to be. The process requires that I forget the boy I was. I have come to render myself less parochial.

I tell the palm reader I do not have a sister. I turn to my new friends at the table and shrug. I laugh openly at the man. I tell him there is only myself and one brother, younger. I tell him my brother lives in Florida. That he has graduated from law school. The man smiles. He says that families are not an easy thing to lose. He says my sister accompanies me because she is a sweet and loyal soul, and because she can. He describes the way my dog, the one I've left in Wyoming, bounces in circles in the sage, by himself, chasing something several feet behind his tail. He says he knows I have seen the dog at play. He says my sister plays with the dog to keep herself busy when I am already happy. He tells me my dog's name, spells the name so that there is no mistake, and the animal's exact breed. He says my sister plays with me that way, but that I have become too stiff to bounce in circles.

He drops my hand and leans back in his chair. His face is relaxed. He looks tired. His eyes are brown and soft and sparkle. He tells me that the job of my happiness is a habit my sister's soul has taken on. "For centuries," he says. He pauses, and leans forward. He tells me her name is Cindy. He says it twice. He says my sister is with me now, beside me, next to this table in a New York restaurant dancing slowly in a speckled pair of cowgirl boots.

I close my eyes against the sudden rise of tears. I am like my mother. I do not cry. I hear a raven caw. I smell sage and pine and loamy soil. I hear the creak of saddle leather moving against its wooden tree. I watch the dawn of an actual day. The light looks bold and clear; late May or early June, I think. "The Moon of Making Fat," I say aloud.

No one asks me why.

BONES

The knife must be sharper than John remembers. Certainly not sharper than he intends, but intimacy breeds, to some extent, tedium, and tedium a familiar carelessness. It is part of his kit, and he cares for his kit. He whets its blade each night. As a father would clean the palm of a son's hand. With that kind of easy attention.

John is in his forties. I'm thirteen. We both work for my father at the Crossed Sabers Ranch, but we are a long way from the ranch. We are a long way from help.

We are in northwestern Wyoming, on the western edge of the Shoshone Wilderness. On Grinnell Creek. We have come to help ourselves. We have come to kill this elk. Its body lies between us.

John stands up and away from our work. He does not seem in a hurry. I think at first he is standing to straighten the tension from his back. I expect him to take a step away, shake a cramp loose. We have been working bent, on a sidehill, our footing careless in the mat of fallen pine needles and decaying downfall. He has been bringing the knife's blade from near the dead elk's anus to its breastbone, and because he is unbalanced he has rested his left hand ahead of the incision, on the animal's abdomen. I am standing above him. I grip the animal's leg at its hock and hang my weight uphill; levering the bull open to its butchering. Exposing it to be emptied. The smell of blood and gut and wildness is in the air. It is late fall. We are working for ourselves. This is our winter's meat. I have not been paying attention.

John holds his left hand high and away from his face, as a far-sighted man does the front page of a newspaper. He stares at the hand as though he does not recognize the thing. As though the text of it is written in some unlearned language. I follow the length of his arm. I think he is pointing to something and look into the deeper forest and then back to him. His right hand has fallen to his side. It still holds the knife's handle, loosely. His sleeves are rolled past his elbows for the job of butchering. He means to keep his clothing free from blood. His forearms shine moon-white in the near darkness. I am confused.

I look again to the raised hand. He turns it. The hand's shortest finger falls away at an unnatural angle. I still hold on to the animal's leg. I hang back against the hillside. John revolves the hand slowly, at arm's length, studying it, and then his forearm darkens bright and slick, his blood dropping down like crimson shadow. Just that fast. Just colored shadow fallen before a sudden light. We watch, both of us, as the blood drips from his elbow. We watch it describe a splattered pattern at his feet.

"That gets your goddamn attention," he says. I hear no panic in his voice. I believe, for a moment, that nothing has happened. That everything has remained the same. That we are safe. And then he flexes the hand, and I watch as the flesh lips back, grinning, the bone at its heel shining through like some beaten fighter's smile. The bone shining white as his right forearm. "You want to let loose of that animal's hindfoot?" he asks. "I'd like to get this covered before I puke."

He holds the knife out to me, and I take it. Its steel feels alive and treacherous. Its blade glows faintly in the waning light.

"It's not going to piss me off if you hurry," he says. His voice remains calm. He's brought the hand closer to his face. He sniffs it and turns to me. His legs are splayed, his feet turned out to grip the hillside. "Everybody's blood just smells like blood," he says. That is all.

I pull my shirt out and slice at its tail. All the way around. Circling my waist. The material falls away as though a separate piece of clothing all along. The knife is that sharp. I press the back of the blade against my thigh and fold it away into its handle. I slide the knife into my jeans pocket. It feels hot, aware. My hands are shaking.

"It's a lot worse than it looks," he says. He holds the damaged hand toward me. He's smiling. He's hoping for laughter, but I am too frightened to give him any. "Don't worry, boy. It's just a man's hand. Try to forget it's mine."

I nod, but my hands still shake.

"This has to be done now," he says. He has spoken each word separately.

I nod again. I bind the slabs of his flesh together. I watch as they close over the bone. The blood runs dark. It hangs from his fingers like the drool of an old, sick bull. I work fast. My hands become slippery and then tacky. My fingers stick together. The air is cooling. I spit when I feel the waves of nausea rise.

"Bear down," he says. "And take a wrap or two on that finger. I'd like to keep the little son of a bitch." His face still holds a smile, but it is beginning to loosen at the edges. "If this isn't going to kill me I might need to pick my nose in my old age." He refuses to approve my fear, refuses to stoke its contagion. I begin to calm. I think of my mother. My mother is a nurse, but she is not here. I look up into the trees grown over our heads. The gray jays, the Clark's nutcrackers, the magpies have gathered. They shoulder from limb to limb, anxious for a hot meal.

I stand back. The shirtcloth is already gone soggy, seeping, but the blood on his arm is drying in patches, starting to crack in the dying light. "How does it feel?"

"You got a good scald on your bandage." He holds the wrapped hand down and grips its wrist with his good hand. I think he means to choke off the flow. The veins stand out in his neck, and like small, magenta-colored garden snakes on his forearms. He grimaces. "Fetch the flashlight out of my saddlebags." His voice comes from a place higher in his chest. There is a crackle when he speaks.

"We can be in camp in half an hour," I tell him. The fear is returning.

He clears his throat. "We could probably be in Chicago in twenty-four." He looks up at me. The flesh seems shrunken at his cheeks, around his eyes, but he's freshened his smile. "In half an hour I'll feel this thing throb clear to my nutsack. The hatchet's in with the light. Cheer up, you're about to learn to butcher an elk." I still haven't moved. "It's all right. I'm not killed. This animal needs to cool tonight, or all we've got is ruined meat. We'll quarter him in the morning."

"You need stitches."

"You go to medical school when I wasn't looking?"

"In town. From a doctor." More birds have arrived. Their chatter like the tapping of dried sticks.

"You don't run and get that light I'll bet my good hand can knot up your head enough we'll both need a doctor." He's not kidding anymore. He doesn't care if I laugh. He's an even man, but I've been raised with men. I know that frustration and pain can turn quickly to anger.

John holds the butt of the flashlight in his teeth and trains its beam between the animal's back legs. The place where he began the work. Where the accident happened. I take the knife out of my pocket. I catch my thumbnail in the notch of its blade and snap it open. The blade is smudged with color and still wet. John takes the light out of his mouth. "You afraid that knife is going to bite you?"

"No, sir. I'm fine."

"Then get to work. I'm not feeling exactly relaxed."

With the flashlight back in his mouth his instructions are garbled, but precise. He pulls with his good arm. His shirt sweats through and clings to his chest and back. "Pull the last of that membrane out of there," he says. "Chop up higher. Reach into his neck and grab out the windpipe." The gutpile steams in the cooling air. It's dark and glossy and grim. John moves below me. He pulls back on one side of the splintered sternum, and I wedge a stob into the chest cavity to keep the ribs spread to the air. The whole job takes longer than it should because I am just a boy. I stand away from the carcass. I'm bloodstained to my shoulders and breathing hard. John's hair is matted to his forehead, and the whites of his eyes are crazed red. His shoulders drop forward from his neck.

"Gather up the liver and heart," he says, and turns toward the horses.

The organs are slick as fish. I kneel to get my hands under them and clasp them against my chest and follow. I feel their warmth through my shirt. I feel the knife riding up and down my thigh. It feels as though it is not satisfied. It feels hungry for blood.

At camp John hands me his bridle reins and enters our tent. "I'll start a fire." He doesn't turn.

Our four packhorses stand in a knot in the pole corral. They watch as I unsaddle and picket my riding horse. I lower a section of poles, and they trot into the meadow, dropping their heads to feed. John's horse rolls in the grass and dusting of snow, stands, shakes, and joins the others. They snort. A big, rangy bay coughs once. They ripple their hides and sweep the air with their tails as though the flies are at them, but there are no flies. I allow just a moment to stand and lose myself in the rhythms of this small bunch. There is a peace to grazing horses.

In the tent John sits cross-legged on his sleeping bag. His face is gray. He holds his hand in his lap and stares at it. His hat rests on its crown on the ground beside his bag. His hair is thin, and his scalp shows in furrows as white as his teeth. As white as the skull that lies under his skin. He looks up at me. He tries to relax his face away from the pain we both know he feels. "I'm going to nap if I can," he says. "Wake me when dinner's ready."

I fill a pail with water at the creek. The moon is up, and the horses cast shadows like fat colts at their sides as they graze farther into the deep grass. I wash the heart and liver, and slice them into a skillet on the collapsible steel stove we pack for short trips. We've made a kitchen beside the stove in the stack of box panniers. The tent has five-foot sidewalls and a ridgepole I can't reach. John has lit the lantern and it hangs, hissing from the ridgepole. I slice potatoes and onions in with the frying meat, ladle in two spoons of bacon grease, and sprinkle a teaspoon of cayenne.

I stand above him with the plates of hot food. He sleeps with his head hung back over the jacket he's rolled for a pillow. His mouth is open. His Adam's apple comes out of his throat as his chin comes out of his face. They are stubbled with two days of whisker. There is a smear of blood on his cheek. He is a slim man. There is no place where his clothes draw across him tightly.

His body does not look like much, but it is a body that I know and trust. We have lived together, in the same bunkhouse, for two summers and falls. I've seen him drunk, and I've seen him naked, felt his rage and his laughter. He's told me elaborately obscene jokes while sitting on the bunkhouse toilet. There is no door to the bathroom. There has been no place to closet ourselves from the other. I know the sound of his steps on a board floor in the night, his cough, the rhythm of his breathing when he works, the tunes of the three songs he knows to whistle. I recognize his scent. He smells like home.

I think of the trail out to the highway. It is only ten miles. I could let him sleep. I could catch up the picket horse and be back in five hours with help. Another man. But I know that if I abandon him it will change the family that this man and I have made. It will show him that I do not trust myself. It will show him that I do not trust his guidance in helping me grow into a man.

"John," I say, and he closes his mouth, but does not wake. "John," I repeat, and he opens his eyes. He looks at me and smiles, and sits up in one smooth motion. I set his plate in his lap. He bends into his dinner, eating fast. The bad hand rests at his side. It looks like the rolled and shrouded corpse of some small animal.

"You have water heating on the stove?" He speaks with his mouth full.

"Yes, sir."

He nods. Not looking up from his plate.

When he is done with dinner I help him unwrap the hand. We're careful. I've placed an enameled bowl of soapy water on the ground in front of us. And the spray can of purple horse medicine he's had me fetch: a strong disinfectant that burns and stains the flesh for days.

He lays the hand in the water palm up. He breathes through his mouth, evenly, concentrating on his breath. It's the kind of pain a man can stand, but the kind of pain that drains. I was once careless enough to get behind a colt and get kicked in the chest. I think that it is that kind of pain. A throb that hooks into the mind as talons hook into living flesh. It doesn't release. There is no use in putting up a struggle. Fighting the pain causes it simply to tighten its grip.

The water covers his wrist. He shuts his eyes and turns his head and reaches in with his good hand, tenderly, as though there is something in the bottom of the bowl that will nip at his fingers. He works at the ruined hand with the pads of his fingers. The water muddies with blood. He doesn't watch what he's doing.

"Don't suppose you packed an aspirin?"

"I didn't do the packing," I tell him.

"Or whiskey?"

"No, sir." I watch the water like an apprentice wizard might watch a crystal. There is only the reflected glare of lantern light. There is no hint to our futures.

When he brings the hand up out of the bowl he turns the thing to examine it. The heel is steamed open, swollen, the meat drawn back from the bone. The finger falls toward the heel and is held by just a strip of puffed skin and a band of whitish cartilage. The bone is there too, a shard of it, but angled badly from the squareness of his palm. The hand seems to have left all its blood in the bowl. The thing is unnaturally white, tumescent, and steams in the air.

"You got that undershirt cut up the way you like it?"

"Yes, I do."

"And you can do this all at once?"

"I think so."

"I'm not prepared for a lot of starts and stops."

"I can do it," I tell him.

"Take hold of the wrist so you can turn it if you need." He looks into his lap and holds the hand higher between us. "Get a good grip. I might jerk back."

"What about the bone?"

"All of it," he says.

My fingers aren't long enough to encircle his wrist. I get up on my knees so if he pulls away I can stay with the job. I hold the can of disinfectant in my other hand. It's as thick as his wrist. "I'm not going to hold this against you," he says. He looks up quickly and grins and then back into his lap.

When I start to spray I feel a shudder drop through him, rise, and arc into my own arm. It is like a bared wire has fallen on us both. When I have finished I release the can and take his wrist with both my hands, still kneeling in front of him. The vibrations continue, and the hissing of the spray. I look to where the can has rolled and then realize that it is John who is making the sound.

He does not look up until I have redressed it with the strips of clean cloth. The fingers that stick out of the bandaging are stained indigo and twitch. He withdraws the hand and rests it in his lap. I sit back on my heels.

"Jesus H. Christ," he says. There is a look of astonishment on his face. His eyes have watered, and a tear has run through the smear of blood on his cheek. "That's not something a man would stand in line to have done every day. Help me up."

He pushes down on my shoulder with his good hand and gets to his feet. He staggers a little, and stands breathing hard, letting his balance spread. I can't get the sight of his bones out of my mind. His back is to me. His clothes seem to hang from nothing but his bones. The presence of bone seems more real than the flush of his skin. He takes a roll of toilet paper out of a pannier and pushes back a tent flap and steps halfway out. I hear him suck in the moon-blanched air once, and then again. "I believe I've got the shits," is all he says and steps into the night.

When he returns I help him out of his boots and into a clean shirt. He slides dressed into his bag with the bad hand out, held up by his head. "Don't forget the light," he says.

"I won't."

"You did good, boy. But I wish we'd packed whiskey." And that is all. His breathing falls into the pattern of his sleep.

I throw out the bowl of bloody water and rinse it. I poke the bloodied bandage into the fire with a length of kindling and add more wood. I pull off my boots and sit on my bag. I can smell the horse pads we've used for ground cloths, feel the slight spring in them. I watch John's sleeping face. He seems older than he was just this morning. Older than when he raised his rifle and killed the elk. I lose my belief that anything changes gradually. I realize that there is only the flash of accident and the level times afterwards where we are allowed to gather our strength for the next.

I get up and refill the bowl with the last of the hot water. I set it on the ground in front of me with an unused strip of white undershirt and John's whetstone. I open the knife and lay it in the water. I reach into the water and rub it free of blood and hair. I am careful of the blade. I take it out and dry it with the cloth. It catches the light. It is just a knife. I set the stone against my ankles, where I've crossed them, and go to work. I know what to do.

Every night I've watched John sit on the edge of his bunk, leaning forward, his face, chest, legs drawn into a curve of shadow. The knife held under a one-bulbed lamp set on the seat of a green, wooden chair pulled to the side of his bed. I've watched him oil the stone and bring the blade slowly across its surface, from base to tip. Again and again. I have no oil so I spit on the stone. I close my eyes to bring the bunkhouse into fresh focus and then start again. The knife makes its song against the stone.

It is the sound John makes with the knife. It is the sound of flesh slippery against flesh. The sound of a man's arms working against his sides in the sun. A shirtless man bent into his work. Loading hay. An old sound. The sound that animals make at the end of a day. A sigh. Again and again. Metronomic. I pause. There is always a pause. I bring the blade away from the stone, examine it, reverse the stone and spit again.

I turn the blade as John would turn the blade. I bend closer to its edge. I think of how his eyes and the oil of his hair draw to the edge of shadow, gather the soft, dulled peripheries of cabinlight. I remember that he tests the blade against the slight hairs of his wrist. That he blows them away from the balded skin. That he is never quite satisfied. I barber my wrist. I feel his dissatisfaction. The blade tells me that it is not ready. I bring the knife back, scything against the stone. Its blade shines in the lantern light, red, gold, Spanish orange, mulberry. I think of his hands before the accident; brown, callused, cracked, the nails holding crescents of mountain soil, scraped leather, the dander of horses. I think that my hands will someday look like his. All I must do is live my life with the same kind of attention; the same disregard for accident.

I have seen this knife at work under the noonday sun. I have seen it sever saddle strings, hemp, pine boughs as though they were as insubstantial as wishes. I have seen it at work in the world. Witnessed its ease. I bring it closer to my face. I test it again. It does not scrape at my wrist; it whispers its contentment.

I hold it to the light. I think of it in the sun: the small, curved white reflection that it casts; a thing become so polished that it mirrors the heat of the sun, and if held steadily to the dry, bent underfluff of the grasses could ignite a fire simply by throwing the curve of that reflected heat. It feels hot and right in my hand.

I wipe it clean. I worry an edge of the rag into the groove in its handle and clean the place, and then fold the blade home. I heft it in my palm and rub the pad of my thumb against the smoothness of the bone-sided handle. I lay it by the head of John's bed, on a corner of pad, where he will find it in the morning. I stand and pull off my jeans. I roll them and stuff them to the bottom of my sleeping bag where they will be warm in the morning, and stand on an overturned pannier and put out the light.

In the darkness I feel my bones, my spine, reach through the goose-down bag, through the horse pads and meet the bones of the earth. John's breathing is even and deep. He does not turn in his sleep.

I think of being buried in the earth. Last fall, later in the season, John and I rode out of Mountain Creek and got caught in a blizzard. We had been hunting. We were bringing home meat. The temperature fell faster than we could come off Eagle Creek Pass. The snow moved in and swarmed in the wind. The horses stepped tightly, hunched, heads down, their muzzles spindled with frosted whisker, their nostrils and eyes rimmed with ice. Each step was felt to the bone. Each step crazed the thin sheet of ice that covered our backs and our thighs.

At the bottom of the pass John dismounted and pulled the hatchet from his saddlebags. There were already eight inches of snow on the ground. I held the leadropes tucked under my arm. I could not feel my hands or legs or feet. It was colder. My nostrils froze to the post of my nose. I felt sleepy and fought to stay awake; the snow fell so heavily it curtained off the world; entered me, chilled me, stung in the parts of me already gone numb. I was no longer sure I was mounted. I could not see my horse's head. I looked away from my hand where the reins curved down and seemed to snap off in the biting, white haze.

My horse took a step and then another, and stopped. I thought I heard someone tell me to get off, and I tried. I thought of kicking loose from the stirrup, of swinging my leg over the cantle, of stepping down, but my body did not obey. John's hat appeared at my waist. He gripped my jacket at the shoulder and pulled me off the horse. He dragged me through the snow and leaned me back against the trunk of a tree. I know this now. I did not know it then. I only knew I was out of the wind and snow. He led the horses in behind me, one at a time, and they stood saddled and fanned in a semicircle facing me: two riding horses, four packhorses. I could see them clearly. I could see their breath rise and hang in the air.

John worked his way between two horses and stood in front of me. The horses steamed, and the steam fogged the distance between us. "Dig," he said, but I did not know what he meant. "Dig," he said again and slapped me softly, and I focused on his face. His eyebrows were puffed with frost. "Dig," he said and smiled.

We knelt side by side and dug with our hands. There was no soil, only decades of brown needle. The work warmed me. I looked to my sides as I dug. There was the huge, barked trunk of the tree at my head. The hatchet was stuck into it. I smelled the sap. I recognized it as a spruce. Its limbs grew to the ground and skirted out twenty feet in every direction. John had entered this old cone of tree. He had chopped out a cave and led me and the horses in through a part in the needled branches.

We scooped out a shallow trench and lay side by side and covered ourselves with a mound of duff. Our shoulders and heads rested against the tree. I could feel my hip caught in the notch above John's. I could feel my arm against his ribs, the length of our legs stretched out in the earth. We warmed, and we dozed. The horses heated the place. They lowered their heads and shut their eyes. I heard the storm. I heard a horse chew against his bit. I felt the roots of the tree spread below me; sap loaded, hard in winter as veins of gemstone. I felt the rounded joints of rock into which the tree had grown. I felt the rock rise up and welcome my bones. I wondered if there was some skeleton to this valley, some armature of stone that realized me only by the pattern and pulse of my bones. I wondered if my death could sadden the earth; if my satisfaction brought it peace. And I slept.

John woke me after midnight, and we unburied ourselves and walked out into the night. The moon had risen. The sky was clear and cold, but windless. We led the horses free from the shelter. They snorted and pawed at the foot and a half of snow. We mounted. We were rested—all of us. The horses swung their heads as they walked, the leather and lashropes squealed. We thought of food. We moved across the moonstruck, white landscape as though skating on the surface of a powdered bulb. It was that effortless. We were thankful for our hunger.

I hear the horses in the meadow outside the tent. I feel their footfalls shake the ground. John is breathing regularly. It is too dark to see him. The coals shift and sputter in the stove. I am where I want to be. I am with a man who cares for my safety. I am with horses, and I am pressed against the earth.

I think again of our shelter in the body of the big tree; green, emerald, brown, black, and a single thin shaft of white where the snow had blown in. I think of the wall of shelved books in the cabin where my mother and father live. Their spines are like the wreck of a rainbow. There are thousands of them. My father reads. My father asks my brother and me to talk to him about what we read.

In the whole gathering of books there is only half a shelf of books with pictures. They are about painters and the places where painters have lived. There are reproductions of their work. My favorite is about a man named Bernini. He was a sculptor, but there are no pictures of his hands. I think he must have had the hands of a laborer. When I look at the pictures of the marble he worked I think of his hands on the stone; coaxing the stone to life.

"The man knew about horses," my father has said. "And pain. Look here. Look at the faces he's made."

I keep the book in my cabin on a shelf above my bed where I live with my brother in the winters. In the winters my imagination becomes lost to the cold and the darkness. In the winters I feel frozen away from the earth. I use the book as a compass. The Bernini book keeps me solidly focused; gives my dreams the solid odor of stone.

My favorite pictures are of a fountain in the Piazza Navona. It is the Fountain of Four Rivers. There are men of stone. Horses of stone. Stone cactuses, stone serpents, a stone lion. They are giants. Their bodies are polished from the bones of the earth. I stare at the men's faces. The expressions hold the pain of their creation. I look at the pictures until they blur. I move the pad of my thumb on the page to bring them clear. There is fear in the faces of the stone men. But I do not think they fear their natures. I do not think they fear their tribes. The stone seems simply fresh with the memory of its creation. I wonder if Adam began as stone. If Eve was the inspiration of a single marble rib. I wonder at the pain of birth. Do all of us spring from the earth? And then there are the horses.

I like to believe that horses were fashioned moments before us, under us. I like to believe that they sprang from the earth snorting, lifting man loose from the imagination of God. I hold my hand against the page. The marble is white as bone. I close my eyes and pray that when I am a man I am granted, for even moments, a beauty that reflects as cleanly as polished stone. And I pray for a clan with the eyes to witness me.

In the morning I dress in my bag and roll out to pull on my boots. They've stiffened in the night, and I stand outside the tent stamping my feet until the leather loosens and warms. John is still asleep, unmoved from the position in which he laid himself down. He mutters quietly.

The meadow grass is frozen and breaks under my feet. I halter my saddle horse and work at the buckle on the single hobble where I've tied off the picket line. The clasp is thick with cold, the metal shrunken dense in the night. I'm glad for a patient horse. The sun hasn't risen, and the light is weak. I coil the picket rope, tie the horse long at a rail, and spill him the last of the hay cubes we've brought.

In the tent I drip lantern gas on a piece of kindling and build a fire. I'm quiet, making less sound than John's muttering. The latch on the stovebox squeaks lightly, but it's an old stove and most of the noise is worn out of it. I've left the coffee pot filled with water on the back of the stove. I pour in the coffee and replace its lid.

I saddle the horse, remove a glove, and hold the bit in my hand, warming it. The frost melts and drips from the palm of my hand. A few stars still struggle in the sky. There are no clouds. The weather won't make our day harder than it has to be.

I find the horses grouped in a small park along the creek a mile upstream from the big meadow where we've camped. They're lazy from a night of grazing, but when I circle to start them back they break into a run, a pair bucking for play and warmth. The sound of them in the down timber and undergrowth echoes in the still air. In another hour they'd have been on the move and hard to find.

When I've got them in the corral they mill like bar-braggarts, finally settling, snuffling and blowing at the frozen ground. And then they all stop at once and stare into the timber. Their ears are pricked. I listen with them, but hear nothing.

John's up in front of the stove. He's managed his boots on and holds his jacket out to the heat. I ask him how he feels. He snorts. "Like catshit smells," he says. His shirtsleeve is tight on his forearm. The swelling in the hand has moved up that far. "Help me on with this," he says and shakes the jacket at me. I turn a box pannier on its top by the stove's side and he sits, and I break the six eggs we have left into a skillet. I pour him a cup of coffee.

"Wish I'd thought to pack an adrenaline gun," he says. "I'd press the barrel to my head and squeeze off six rounds." John tries a smile over the brim of his cup, and winces. "Make sure you don't feel sorry for me today," he says and lowers the cup. "It won't help either one of us."

"No, sir, I won't."

"We'll butcher that elk after breakfast and let the stove cool. It won't take as long as you think to tear down camp."

"I didn't think it would take long."

"Well, it won't."

"Should I look at your hand?"

"I already did. It wasn't hard to find."

Breakfast makes him shit again, and I have his horse saddled when he comes out of the timber. He'd saddled the packhorses while I did the dishes and raked the coals out of the stove. I'd looked out once and seen him buckling the breast collars, using his good hand and his teeth. "You don't have to do all the work," he says. He puts the toilet paper in his saddlebags.

"I don't plan to," I tell him.

"There's too much of it," he says, and steps on his horse more easily than I think he'll manage and fidgets on the saddle's seat and then turns his big gelding into the timber. We follow the down-timbered hint of a game trail, climbing the shoulder of a ridge that rises sharply out of the valley. The horses dig in with their toes. Their haunches strain, the muscles standing striated and hot. Their hides glisten in the dawn. I take a handful of my horse's mane and pull myself forward on his neck; lifting my weight away from his kidneys. We stop to let them blow. The ground is frozen, their footing precarious.

The elk corpse is rigid, and the meat cuts like it's store-bought, brought cool and thick from a big walk-in freezer. John works with his good arm, and we take turns at the hatchet. We struggle the quarters into meat sacks, and then into cloth panniers, the thighs sticking out, ending at the knee joints. The backstrap and neck-meat we put in a sack and toppack between the bucks. We have to lift each pannier together, and then I keep it balanced, pinned against the side of the packhorse, while John drops the leather straps over the crossbucks, adjusting them level.

"You care about that rack?"

"I guess I don't," I tell him. I look down at the elk head. He's a young four point; the antlers smallish and uneven. The grass was not good this summer; the clouds rode high and moistureless, bumping eastward. Nothing grew bigger than it had to. I will leave the head. The gutpile has darkened in the night, been scattered, the intestine opened by the birds. We've left some scrap, parts of the rib cage, and the four legs, from the hooves to where we've chopped them away at the knees. The snow is broken and stained with blood.

John hands me his knife. "Dig out the ivory. They're nice to have. They'll help you remember that this pretty son of a bitch wasn't always just dinner."

I kneel at the head. The elk eye that should be looking at me has been pecked out by the birds. If it warms enough today the socket will fill with ants and flies. The lip is black and curled into a grin. I trim it away. It cuts like cartilage. I use the knife's point to pry out the ivory tooth, and turn the head. This downside eye is whole and glazed like some large, dull sapphire. I've robbed the ivory from an elk's mouth before, but this is the first time I've wondered why there are just two; why the whole set of teeth isn't ivory. "Little tusks," I think. I wonder what elk must have looked like a million years ago. I think I'll try to find the answer in one of my father's books when we're home. Were they saber-toothed grazers? Does time evolve us all away from our habits?

"You did a good job with it last night."

"With what?" I ask him.

"With the knife. The edge is right."

"You tested it?"

"While you were out gathering the horses this morning."

I'm scraping the gum and flesh away from the roots of the teeth. "I wasn't tired," I tell him. "I like the sound it makes against the stone."

"I like it too," he says.

We're back in camp in half an hour. John rests while I pack the kitchen, lantern, ax, bucksaw, and picket rope in the box panniers. We've used the newspaper the tins of food were wrapped in for fire starter. I pad the skillet and loose utensils with our dirty cloths. We unstake the tent and drop the front A-frame, and pull it from the ridgepole. It folds into a square that's hard to get my arms around, but I can stand the weight. John helps me slide it on top of the bucks. We stand on either side of a horse and adjust the packcovers. I keep the slack pulled out of the lashropes, and John ties the diamond hitches with his one good hand. I would have to stand on a stump to get high enough to thread and tie off the ropes at the very top of the packs. I am not tall enough to have done this job alone.

It's late morning when we're done. The day is warming. We sit on a downfall in the sun and eat the sandwiches I've made from the leftover fried organ meat and thick slices of onion. The snow remains only in the shadows, lightening them. If I squint, the landscape has the odd look of a photograph's negative. A squirrel comes down the log in a series of sprints. He is gathered for retreat. I tear off a piece of bread crust, and he sits upright, holding it in his front paws. His tail twitches as he eats, and then he is up a tree and scolding.

John stands, and I help him out of his jacket. "You feel like you want to get out of here?" he asks.

I roll the jacket and tie it behind his cantle. "Yes, sir, I sure do."

"This is the best I've felt all day." He fills himself with air but relaxes smaller than he normally seems. His shoulders and chest shrunken, guttered. His left arm is swollen to his armpit and hangs at his side like some bloodied club.

We head and tail the packhorses, and I lead them. "I don't want to risk a wreck," says John. "And I don't feel like trying to stay ahead of this bunch. It's all downhill." The horses know they're going home and line out without mischief.

He rides ahead of me and keeps his smoke-colored gelding spurred to a good walk. He appears off balance, holding the reins in his right hand. His left arm hangs bent into his lap, and he lifts it straight above his head occasionally without looking back.

The trail crosses the creek several times. The drainage is tight and the ridges steep. The packhorses grumble, stepping down off ledges into the unstable bottom of the streambed, lowering themselves toward the end of their work. I watch that their packs don't shift, that they remain untangled, spaced evenly, paced so that not one of them slips and pulls back. There is the clatter of steel shoes on loose rock. We approach and ride through the chatter of squirrels. Big, totem-sized ravens watch us from dead limbs, the sun playing on the oil of their slick, black feathers, their eyes beads of black. The smell of pine is everywhere. The lighter scent of the aspen, along the creek.

When we cross the river the horses are too home-starved to want to drink. Their front hooves beat out fans of water before them, onto the asses of the horses they follow. They're soaked to their bellies and still dripping when we ride into the corrals. My father is at the tackshed when we come in. He's seen the way John sits his horse before he's seen the hand.

"Did you shoot yourself, or let something bite you?" he asks.

"I put my knife in my hand." John loops his bridle reins at a rail by the tackshed's deck.

"Bad enough to go to town?"

"I believe it is."

"I'll run you in as soon as we get unpacked."

"I can make the trip myself if you'll send the boy."

My father takes a step closer to John. "Why don't you go now?" he asks. "There isn't much work here. You look like an hour might make a difference."

"It might," John allows. The men stare at one another for just a moment. John nods. It's hard for him to give up the chance to finish the work. "I've been wanting a drink." He looks toward the bunkhouse.

"You kill a cow?"

"A bull. The boy didn't want the antlers."

"Take the truck when you're ready."

John is back from the bunkhouse with a bottle of whiskey in the time it's taken me to unsaddle only my riding horse. My father is lining the panniers on the edge of the deck. He's turned two pack-horses into the round corral, and they roll and fart.

"If it's worse than you think, you have the boy call from town."

"I'll be fine."

"If you're not he knows the number." My father lifts a pannier away from a horse and carries it to the deck.

I hold the bottle between my legs and steer leaning across the seat when John shifts through the gears. The day has remained solid, cloudless, and warm, and we crack the windows. The air is sweet. The windshield, blotched with the shattered bodies of insects.

"When we get to town, you want to come in with me and watch?"

"I don't like doctors," I tell him.

"I don't like them either." He shakes his head.

I hand him the bottle and take the wheel. When he drinks the whiskey dribbles from a corner of his mouth and stains his shirt front. He hands the bottle back without looking. I wedge it between my legs and twist its cap on. John starts to whistle. His cheeks and neck are hollowed. His eyes seem to have sunken away from their brow. His nose comes sharp in the bright light. It would be easy to imagine that he hasn't eaten for a week. The cab smells of blood, whiskey, horse, sweat, and antiseptic. I lower my window a bit more and look toward the river. The aspen splash yellow and incandescent against the waning landscape. My eyes water against their glare, and my chest and face and arms feel pricked by fire.

John taps on the steering wheel with his index finger, tapping out the rhythm of the tune he whistles. His left elbow is hooked on the armrest, and the damaged hand is curled on his lap. It's hard to remember the way the hand looked last night, under the lantern, its bone gone milky and slick. Its fingers have dirtied during the day, thickened. He keeps them still. The hand does not appear to belong to him. It reminds me, as it did last night when he napped before dinner, of some separate animal. I imagine we are just bringing some small hurt animal to town, to the vet's.

I feel unsteady and close my eyes, and there is the image of graves. It does not startle me. It is not the first time I have seen them. I have dreamed of graves. Layer upon layer of grave. The earth cut away and the stratum variously colored in its stages of decay, descending, the weight pressing the first dead finally to stone. I fidget on the seat but keep my eyes closed. I think of the millions of bones that have fallen to the earth—bones like sticks of hail, melted into the earth, nourishing it. I wonder if a girl's bones are different than a gambler's. If different bones are compressed to different stones—to gem.

I think that I know nothing of the singularity of bones. I have picked them up from the ground, held them, and did not know whether I held the bones of a large dog, a deer, or a man. In one of my father's books I have read that there are saints whose bodies do not decompose after they die. There are not a lot of them, but there are some. I wonder if their bones stay damp, and blood filled; if they shine like the ivory teeth in my pocket and arch against the press of sky instead of falling. I open my eyes and squint into the sunlight and aspenglare. My shirtsleeve has ridden up my wrist. My skin appears white as marble.

"I'll bet I keep the finger." John doesn't look away from the highway.

"I'll bet you do, too," I tell him. I hand him the bottle and take the wheel, and after he drinks he continues to whistle.

WAPITI SCHOOL

In Shawnee, *wapiti* is a word that means a white, or pale, deer. In white America it is what we call our elk when attempting to be precious or regionally cryptic. In Wyoming it is a valley that rises gradually westward for fifty miles from Cody to the eastgate of Yellowstone Park. I was raised in the Wapiti Valley. When I hear the word, or say "Wapiti" aloud, it is the place that comes to mind, not an animal—a neighborhood of almost three million unfenced acres.

I remember its sage-covered foothills and open meadows paling in the August heat. Its grasslands blanching to the tan and umber shades of elk-color under the weakening and mostly unclouded autumn sun. And then in November I remember the snows that reduced the valley to the simple dichromatic shades of white and evergreen. Spring was brown, and fall, a lighter shade of brown. The valley was only truly green at the end of May, and all of June and July. Summer was short, never lush. Never long enough to bore.

The valley, in the 1960s, supported perhaps two dozen cattle and dude ranches. The summer days were hot. In the afternoons the skies swelled with cumuli risen up from the Absarokas, and we stood in barns or sat in our pickups to wait out the sudden hail- and

rainstorms. The nights were cool. There was rarely enough moisture in the morning air for dew. We worked the longer days the sun
gave us. The cattle ranchers labored to put up their crops of alfalfa,
fatten steers, husband their pregnant cows. Their winters were
spent feeding, making specific repairs, up in the below-zero nights
of January and February in the lantern light of calving sheds min-
istering to the bawling heifers. America was not yet rich enough
for the coastal populations to buy up the hinterland and subdivide
it into a patchwork of second homes. The Wapiti ranchers worked
their land; they did not sell it. It was a life that lined the face,
leaned the body, and satisfied. We knew our neighbors. We cele-
brated and mourned together. We raised our children as though
the valley had brought them to life and would keep them. I was a
boy then, in a place that saw me as its future.

The bottom half of the valley was puzzled together from sections of deeded land and sections of BLM. The upper half of the
valley, the half that butted into Yellowstone, was Shoshone National Forest. My family lived on the national forest. On Libby
Creek. At Holm Lodge, the Crossed Sabers Ranch. We leased our
buildings from the federal government for ninety-nine years at a
time. We made our living from housing the summer tourists. From
packtrips and fishing trips into the Absaroka Wilderness Area.
From the hunters that came in the spring and fall. It was a mar-
ginal living. Even with a pantry of canned goods and a freezer of
wild game, my father went to Cody some winters to work on a sur-
veying crew to get us through. My mother stayed year-round at the
lodge. She reconciled the books, made reservations for the next
summer, varnished the interiors of cabins, repaired furniture,
oiled the tack, sewed curtains, made a home, made sure my
brother and I got to school.

The Wapiti School was painted a dark, flat brown, the brown
of an elk's eye, and it was not a one-room schoolhouse. It was
five miles off the national forest, twenty miles from our lodge, and
had one good-sized, well-lit room with a bank of windows that
looked east toward the Wapiti Post Office—and in the far distance,
Rattlesnake Mountain—a lesser room, boys' and girls' bathrooms,

a coat closet, and a basement. More like the first home a young couple might own. The basement was used for the storage of out-dated books, broken desks, leftover building supplies, and any over-flow of personal possessions our teachers might want out of the weather. Students weren't allowed in the basement, but all of us got in for a look at least once—we had the run of the place. The building was constructed in 1911. There's a picture in its entryway of the five small children that attended school in 1910. They stand in front of a tent.

We had two teachers. Both lean, clean-shaven men in their late twenties. They were resourceful, honest, used to outdoor labor, and inventive in their approaches to schoolwork and discipline. We were all expected to pitch in. The older children helped to educate the younger ones. All of our desks were lined together in the largest room.

When my brother and I attended the school it housed grades one through nine, its entire student body swollen to eighteen. My class had four students. Several grades were unrepresented. Several more had only one student. Grading on a curve was not par-ticularly functional.

I have a copy of the black-and-white photograph of that year when there were eighteen of us: 1964. It was a record enrollment. Our teachers, Mr. Hedrick and Mr. Dansby, stand straight at the very rear of the photograph, their heads and shoulders above the rest of us. They wear jackets and ties. Their hair is cut short. Mr. Dansby looks directly into the camera. Mr. Hedrick down over the heads of his students. There are two rows of us standing, the taller children in the back, and five of the youngest children sitting on a bench at the very front. Every girl wears a simple cotton dress. Linda Schmitt has a barrette in her hair. Kass and Shawn Sidwell wear glasses that peak at the corners. All of the boys wear jeans. Most of the boys wear plaid shirts that fasten with snaps instead of buttons. My brother and Brian Sidwell wear white shirts. Pete Krone has a bola tie snugged up tight at his neck. He's looking at the girl standing to his left. Six of the ten boys have burred hair-cuts. We other four have allowed our hair to grow out another inch or two. My hair is slicked into a part. I was intent on training my cowlicks that year. Before I went to bed each night I wet my hair, parted it, and pulled on a skullcap made from the knotted thigh of one of my mother's discarded stockings. We're all smiling, Jeff and Bruce Keller wildly. The picture must have been taken just before recess.

Our playground had once been a hay field. The machinery of several generations of children's feet had pounded it cropless. It was fenced on all sides and presented itself as a stretch of common dirt, frozen dirt, or mud. There was a swing set and a basketball hoop. Basketball was, for the most part, unpopular because it was unreliable to dribble on a rocky slope. Many of us spent our playground time climbing through the single row of pine and cottonwood that formed a windbreak on the building's west side. There was also the propane tank tucked in against the trees. We spent a lot of recesses sitting on the tank. We lied to one another, flirted, joked, made up stories about the men and women we thought we might become. Everyone straddled the tank as though it were some horribly obese and witherless horse. Most of us knew only three ways of sitting: astraddle, perched on the top rail of a fence, or squatting. There was one boy whose name I can't remember. It was his first year at the school and his family moved away from the valley midsemester. He was a year older than I and put in his fifty minutes of lunch hour in a squat. He'd shuffle to the edge of our games of tag, red rover, catch, or touch football and naturally fold into a squat—a sort of controlled collapse. I think his family moved a lot. For him it was a posture of exact balance for his long and nearly fatless body. His knees fit perfectly into his armpits, his butt acted as the precise counterweight for his shoulders and head. He ate his lunch squatting, and when he had something to say he spoke from a squat. No one made fun of him. He was one of us, and he was larger than any of us. I've often imagined him as a man, as an accountant or actuary, squatting in the corner of his office plowing through a single column of work stacked between his ankles. He was a sweet boy. I imagine him a sweet man.

There was a sage-spotted bulwark to the north of the playground that fell away for several hundred yards to the Northfork of the Shoshone River. Beyond the river the land rose again in a series of humped foothills and stands of monolithic rock formation— one section of deeded land, and its western neighbor, BLM. The foothills ended at the base of Jim Mountain. The southern face of the mountain always reminded me of a crude, rounded, and out-sized mock-up of a photograph I had seen of a Mayan pyramid; something transported from the Yucatán peninsula and allowed to fall into ruin under the northern winds and snow. The mountain rose to more than ten thousand feet in bands of vertical palisades, the terraces between the diminishing tiers of rock, timbered, its summit a naked dome of hundreds of acres of meadowland. To the northwest we could see the barerock thrust of two taller peaks, both more than twelve thousand feet. When the winter storms came in, those summits reached into the sky and snagged the gray paunch of a snowcloud and held it, and emptied it over the high valleys.

Off the school's front porch, to the south, was a small graveled parking lot that extended to the two-lane highway running be-tween Cody and Yellowstone. To the south of the highway the sage and grassland rose so abruptly that the hills obscured our view of Table Mountain. We were a valley school. Our students' families lived along the Northfork. We all knew the names of the feeder creeks as well as we knew the names of our families. If one child asked another where he lived the answer might be, "Whit Creek." Or Breteche, Big, Nameit, Moss, Newton, Eagle, Green, Half Mile, Pagoda, Goff, Libby, Grinnell, Gunbarrel, Fishhawk, Trout, Jim, Rattlesnake.

The school had no cafeteria. We all packed lunches. They were brought in brown paper sacks or black steel lunch pails. I don't re-member much plastic wrap. There was a lot of waxed paper and tin foil, which most of us were required to scrape clean, refold, and return to our mothers. Most of those same mothers had been teenagers during the Depression and weren't about to have their children precipitate another.

I've always believed a packed lunch to be an accurate barometer of a child's family. Sort through a lunch pail and know a family. Are the parents creative or dull? Practical or innovative? Lazy, poor, uncaring? Most of our mothers cared. Most of them considered bologna part of a balanced diet, but most of them viewed bologna a luxury. Standard fare was an apple, a sandwich, perhaps a candy bar. I've seen sweet potato sandwiches. Once, in the early fall a mayonnaise and sliced zucchini sandwich. A lot of elk, deer, mountain sheep, and moose sandwiches. Twice a turnip sandwich. Nothing went uneaten.

It was from those Wapiti lunches that I gained an almost religious confidence in the free-market system. What was one boy's garbage was another's manna. My brother's and my fall and late-spring lunches were packed by a cook who worked our lodge dining room. He was an exhausted and alcoholic old bachelor, and provided two specific seasons of fried-egg sandwiches. The bread was homemade, but the eggs were never drained and their yolks consistently sunny-side up. When we peeled back the waxed paper what we found was a gray-and-yellow fist-sized wad of dough, congealed bacon grease, and yoke. We saw a mess. The Krone boys saw an entrée. Their eyes would widen when we held our lumps of sandwich to the sun. Their nostrils flared. Not every day. But the majority of days. I have no explanation for it. Their father was the district forest ranger, a decent man with decent tastes, and their mother a cheerful woman, and one of the best cooks in the valley. Perhaps they ate too well? Or perhaps Pete and Kip's fondness for fried-egg sandwiches was a simple example of grace? We didn't care. We traded the things for cookies, brownies, and squares of fudge. Everybody went away a fuller, happier boy.

There were three of us who had to get to school from the national forest. My brother and I, and Linda Schmitt. Linda lived a mile downriver on Goff Creek. The Krone boys also lived on the forest, but the ranger station was close enough to deeded land that their parents drove them to the boundary every day. To get picked up by the school van you had to be off the national forest. Kip, Linda, and I were in the same grade. We were twelve. My brother and Pete were a year younger. Trail Shop was where we met the

Krone brothers and the school van. Linda's parents and our own traded weeks driving the three of us, the upper-valley kids, those twenty miles. The five of us then waited together on the highway by the Trail Shop mailbox. We threw rocks and told jokes. If the wind was raw we took turns squeezing into the package compartment built beneath the mailbox. It was a three-foot-by-three-foot-by-three-foot cube with a little door, made of roughsawn pine. Three of us could fold into the thing at one time. It was more exciting in the package compartment if Linda squeezed in with you.

Linda Schmitt was the only girl in the upper valley, and I was in love with her. She had dark hair, liquid eyes the color of her hair, and a smile that hinted at forgiveness. I was only a boy but smart enough to know that I should look for a merciful girlfriend. Actually I loved Linda when it was my turn. Loving her full-time would have been too stressful. Love brought with it the duty of chivalry, a depressive self-consciousness, and constipation. My brother and I took turns loving Linda—a month off and a month on. We didn't get to town much and were used to sharing. I don't think Linda ever noticed.

There were two kinds of drives from the lodge to Trail Shop. They both held their allure. There was the out-of-love drive that I spent pressed against a backseat window, watching the valley. It was like passing through an earlier century. I once counted more than four hundred elk. The bulls would run beside the car, their heads back, their antlers strewn to their rumps. It was not uncommon to see a winter-killed elk close to the road, and we would stop the car and watch the coyotes duck and snap and worry the fresh and stiffening corpse. Ravens and eagles walked the carcass, flaring their wings, stabbing at the meat with bloody beaks. An apron of magpies chattered from a safe distance and satisfied themselves with scraps. The out-of-love drives seemed to take no time at all. Besides the elk we saw otter, bobcat, deer, mountain sheep, and moose. I remember being dropped at Trail Shop with an unshakable sense of satisfaction and freshness, relaxed.

On the in-love drives I sat stiffly in the backseat pressed against Linda. I watched the delicacy of her thin fingers cupping her

knees. The car seemed filled with the scent of her soap and sham-
poo. The heater, always turned too high. For a thin girl Linda
seemed to throw off a lot of heat. I remember her father's, or my
mother's, face, framed in the rearview mirror, watching me fidget.

In truth I don't think I was actually ever *pressed* to Linda. I
think our knees may have touched. But when you're twelve, and
besides your mother the only women you've seen without their top
layer of clothing are the lingerie models in a Montgomery Ward
catalog, a knee-touch gets your complete attention. The valley
women wore jeans and blouses in the summer. Or long dresses.
After sunset they put on a sweater or jacket, or went indoors.
T-shirts were worn by men under their workshirts. It was
Wyoming, and we lived at seven thousand feet. The rest of the year
girls and women layered themselves in thermal underwear, wool
and down coats. The sight of a woman's body lay largely uncon-
firmed in my imagination. On the in-love drives I struggled, trying
to visualize what Linda Schmitt might look like naked. I tried not
to let that struggle show on my face. I didn't have a sister, so I as-
sume my expression must have mirrored the inaccurate murk of
my imagination. When I looked up into the rearview mirror and
met my mother's eyes I'd smile as though I was simply carsick, and
become nearly sick with the realization that I was fooling no one.

I endured my love for Linda when it was my turn. I shouldered
that love every other month, from the time we were both put together in the car until we were released at Trail Shop. She deserved my love. I had known her since her parents moved to the
valley. She lived only a mile away on Goff Creek.

But Candy Dohse was the girl that kept me up at night. Every
night. She seemed more exotic than Linda. She seemed more exotic than the models in the Montgomery Ward catalog. She lived
in the lower valley.

I watched the clock every day waiting for recess. I got out of
class fast so that I could watch her walk into the sunlight. She had
straight red hair, bobbed just below her ears, and when the sun
struck her hair it stopped there and held. I was the only blond. It
was obvious that we were destined for one another; the only two

fallen away from the dark-haired mob. I spent September and October 1964 stepping away from games of tag, or from the boys I had grouped with to gossip, just to watch Candy move in the sunlight. I'd lean against the schoolhouse, or the fence, and act as though I was catching my breath or examining a rock and watch her from the corners of my eyes. If she spoke to me I dissolved into a general state of sappiness, my mind swirled, my mouth fell open, and when I noticed it was open I would try to form it into a smile. I would then watch her walking away, shaking her head of red hair.

It was not hard to be in love with Candy. She was a girl who was at ease in her body. She moved fluidly, purposefully. She was one of those rare children that threw off an air of confidence and energy. She was a formidable tomboy. She could outrun most of us and throw a ball as far as I could. She did not look to the sides of things. If she looked at you, she looked *directly* at you. If she smiled, you felt the force of her happiness. And there were her freckles. Her face was crowded with them. Her arms speckled to the backs of her hands. I imagined them on her shoulders. I imagined every square inch of her freckled. And because I was an obtuse and wildly optimistic boy, I imagined that she would be my girlfriend.

Just before Thanksgiving her father visited mine, and Candy came with him. I had saved three dollars that summer and bought her a fake turquoise stone on a fake silver chain from one of the tourist shops in town. It didn't matter to me that the necklace wasn't precious. Three dollars was all I had. To keep my brother away from it I'd worked the necklace down into the stuffing of an easy chair that sat in our cabin. The fabric on one of its arms was ripped, and it offered a good hiding place. When Candy came to visit with her father I asked her if she wanted to see where I lived. She said she guessed so. It was the opportunity I'd been waiting for. It was time to pronounce my love. The necklace had been hidden since Labor Day.

She seemed to fill up the cabin when we got inside. The place appeared smaller, shabbier than it had been that morning. There were the two twin beds. Each was heaped with a tangle of quilts.

There was a desk and straight-backed chair, two dressers, the worn easy chair. There was a mirror. I stood away from it so that I would not have to suffer my reflection. The water had been drained from the bathroom pipes so they wouldn't freeze solid. The bathroom door was shut. A little box-shaped propane heater hummed in a corner. All it ever seemed to do was heat its vent pipe. The cabin was a framed building, and built up on posts to level it on the hillside—just an exposed and uninsulated box of lumber. My brother and I could pull off our boots at night and stand them directly in front of the heater and in the morning there would still be an unmelted wedge of snow between the heels and soles. Candy hugged her sides and smiled tightly. "You can see your breath," she said.

I nodded. "I have something for you," I told her. I felt mildly nauseated. Flushed. I looked toward the heater. I expected to see it glowing red. My face seemed to pulse.

"Where?"

"There." I pointed to the chair.

She nodded. I suppose she didn't expect a lot from boys.

I worked my hand in through the ripped fabric. I felt around in the stuffing. The necklace was gone. I smiled at Candy. She stamped her feet and bent at the knees to work the chill from her legs. She was still hugging herself. I took off my jean jacket and wormed my hand deeper into the chair, feeling for the necklace, smiling, fighting back the panic. I felt my blush drop down my neck and spread over my shoulders. I knelt beside the chair to work my arm in deeper. And then raised up off my knees to get the whole length of my arm into the thing. I could feel the springs. They were cold. I kept smiling. I kept tunneling my hand through the interior of the chair. I thought that if I didn't find the necklace that there was a good chance I might cry. "It's in here," I said. My voice cracked. I was losing hope.

Candy held her smile. She bit her lip. I think she was trying not to laugh.

And then I had it. Just the end of the chain hooked around a fingertip. I pinched at it, an inch at a time, pulling it into my palm, and closed my fist around it and stood. There were little wads of stuffing dotting the arm of my flannel shirt. I walked toward her. I extended my arm and opened my hand. We both looked down into my palm.

"What is it?"

"It's for you."

"Why was it in the chair?"

"That's where I hid it."

"It worked," she said, and then she smiled and held it up exactly between us. The stone turned at the end of its chain. It seemed dazzling. Larger than I remembered it.

She slipped it over her head and walked to the mirror and looked at herself and the necklace. She touched the stone and then lifted her jacket away from her chest and dropped the necklace inside. "It's beautiful," she said. She stepped toward me, and she let me kiss her. For one single moment I felt as though I'd stepped away and off the edge of the cabin floor and fallen, was in the act of falling, and put out a hand to catch myself. We both laughed. "It cost three dollars," I told her.

We went outside to stand on the creek. It had frozen, and broken free in spots, the water refreezing over the ice, the thing now two feet of solid iceflow. We took turns running down the ice, skating on our boot soles, and falling, and very conscious of where the other one was all the time. I didn't try to show off. I was just glad to have gotten the necklace out of the chair.

When her father called her to go we came off the creek, and she stepped into his pickup and stared down at the floormat. She did not look up when they pulled away. She did not wave or smile.

My father asked me if I'd had a good time. I said it was fine and walked back to my cabin and pulled a chair in front of the heater and held my hands over its grill. The metal ticked, but there wasn't much warmth.

The next morning I woke gripped with fear. I lay under my quilts, feeling their weight, aware of my slight insignificance. I touched my lips. They were cold. When I closed my eyes and thought of Candy she seemed pushed away, her image blurred, as though we were outside in a heavy snowstorm.

When we were on the playground we stayed away from one another. We did not climb on top of the propane tank at the same time. Our eyes did not meet. I regretted the gift of the necklace. I regretted the gift of the kiss. We had become too large in each other's world, and it pushed us separately down to a sudden shyness, and we stayed that way.

By the second week of December I had become critically hapless. I watched for Candy to wear the necklace, but if she did she kept it inside her shirt. I was desperate to break the tension. I took my brother by the arm and led him to the corner of the schoolyard. I told him that he could love Linda all year long. He was younger. I felt he had to obey me. I told him I was in love with Candy. I said it out loud.

"A lot of good that's going to do you," he said. He actually sneered.

I asked him what the hell he thought he meant.

He walked away from me, and I followed. He stopped and turned. He looked serious. "She doesn't know you exist. You might as well be living on the moon." He sighed. He let me know that having to repeat the obvious was painful for him, embarrassing. He looked at me squarely. "She doesn't even know you're breathing the same air she is." He looked away in disgust, and then back to me.

"I bought her a necklace," I said.

"How much?"

"Three dollars."

His face fell in pity. He cupped his hands and blew into them. He squinted up into the weak sun and then leveled his head and watched Candy. She was building a snowman in the corner of the playground with Kass and Shawn Sidwell. "You should have spent six," he said, and moved away to help the girls push the ball of snow they were struggling against.

It was obvious. I wasn't necessarily unloved; I was only cheap. I hadn't made enough of an effort. It was a busy world. Smallish gestures were overlooked. I decided to make my intentions known. I decided to let them all know that Candy Dohse was my one true love. During the next recess, with love in my heart, I centered a stone in the middle of an iceball and winged it her way. She was the ace pitcher on her side of the fight and had a row of snowballs lined up on a fence rail. She was delivering them rapid-fire. Our team was breaking ranks under the barrage. She turned to throw her last round, and I caught her above her right eye as she completed her follow-through. It stopped her. In fact, every kid on the playground stopped. Their arms fell to their sides. Kip Krone backed toward the propane tank, no doubt thinking of cover. The four Sidwell kids grouped as a family. Everyone dropped their snowballs. My brother looked to me as though he expected to be an only child. My objective had been achieved.

Candy shook her head, dabbed the heel of her hand at her forehead, and then pressed it to the bloody knot that was rising. She did not cry. She scanned our side of the field for someone that was as shocked as she was. That someone was me. I was shaking, caught between hysteria and laughter. I'd always found accident funny. I was caught in an effort to suppress both ends of an unfortunate emotional arc. It caused a general, that is, noticeable tremor to vibrate through my body.

Her reaction was immediate. She was apparently not a girl who considered abuse an indication of intimacy.

She ran the length of the schoolyard, full tilt toward me. I remember her charge as though in slow motion. I didn't have the sense to retreat. I was in love. Her right arm hung straight and low from her shoulder, her right hand clenched into a fist. She'd taken off her mittens to pack snowballs. She didn't throttle back as she ran past me. She simply brought her right fist up under my jaw as though pumping her arms for the finish of a race. My brother said that she did not stop until she was a good twenty feet past where her uppercut had lifted me into the air. He also said that she stopped and turned before I landed on my back. It was the season of frozen dirt.

I don't remember being led into the schoolhouse. I do remember that when my vision cleared I was sitting in the coatroom with Mr. Hedrick. The door was closed. He sat on a little bench we used to wrestle off our overboots. Our coats hung about his shoulders. I vaguely remember that for a moment I thought he was the Angel of Death.

Mr. Hedrick was a big man. He had played football for Notre Dame. Before he came to the valley he had been scouted to play professional football. The Raiders had made an offer. I don't know what position, but I would guess now that it was either linebacker or tight end.

"You okay?" he asked.

I said, "Yes, sir." But I wasn't sure.

I think Mr. Hedrick must have suffered from a thyroid condition because his eyes were larger in his face than they should have been.

I took a stab at redemption. "Is Candy okay?"

"She's stirred up."

"I figured that out already."

"Looks like you did."

"Is she going to need stitches?"

"She needed a Band-Aid. Head wounds just bleed a lot. I don't know why."

"Why what?"

"Why all the blood. Our brains have practically none. Compared to a thigh for instance."

"Yes, sir." Mr. Hedrick was a thoughtful man, but he'd lost me. I was braced for a beating.

"You proud of what you did?"

"No, sir."

"You like Candy?"

"A lot."

"What do you think Mrs. Hedrick would do if I hit her in the head with a rock?"

"On purpose?"

"I don't throw rocks at people by accident."

"Divorce you?"

"I don't think she'd go that far."

"I don't think she'd punch you. You're bigger than she is. I'm pretty much Candy's size."

"I think we've gotten off the subject."

"Yes, sir."

"You think you should get a paddling?" I hated it when adults tried to involve you in your punishment. They usually already had their minds made up, but I didn't know Mr. Hedrick well enough to predict which way he'd go.

I said, "No, sir."

"Have you done other things that you thought you should get a paddling for?" This was a trick question. The answer would indicate whether I was a good or evil boy.

I said, "Yes, sir." Mr. Hedrick looked down at his hands. He had big hands. He nodded his head. A spike of panic jolted through me. There was the possibility that he would decide to punish me for an accumulation of crimes.

"You sorry?"

"I'm very sorry."

He looked up at me. He stared hard into my face. He still hadn't tipped his hand. "Go tell Candy you're sorry." I stood up. I was still a little woozy. "I'd also appreciate it if you sulked around for the rest of the day. It'd help the general morale. I don't want this happening again."

"I can do that."

"You sure you're okay?"

"I think so."

"Whacked the starch out of you, didn't she?"

"Yes, sir, she did."

"I suppose if she feels like she needs to do it again you ought to let her."

"In the face?"

"I'll say something to her."

"Thank you, Mr. Hedrick."

"Get back to class."

Candy was sitting by herself in the back of the classroom staring into her math book. I walked the length of the aisle aware that all the other children's eyes were on me. I tried to affect a limp. Candy didn't look up from her book. I stood beside her desk for just a moment. I shuffled. Mr. Hedrick was watching us. I tried to keep my attention focused on Candy. I hoped I hadn't broken the pattern of freckles on her forehead.

"I'm sorry," I said.

She looked up at me. Her eyes were on fire. "You don't look like you are."

"I am."

"Mr. Hedrick put you up to this?"

"I'd have said I was sorry anyway." It was a desperate situation. "I love you," I whispered. Kip Krone was leaning back in his desk.

"You should quit." That was all she said. She said that I should quit loving her and then looked back into the math book. I took a step away. I admired her for not playing up the pain. Most girls would have fingered the bandage, maybe winced a little. I told her I loved her again, and she closed her book and swiveled in her chair. I could see a flash of silver inside the collar of her flannel shirt. She was wearing the necklace.

"I hope you die," she said.

I smiled. We were kids raised around horse accidents, grizzly bear, high water, and blizzards. She hadn't said *how* she wished me to die. I felt partially redeemed. I looked to Mr. Hedrick. He shrugged.

On the drive upriver my brother sat away from me. Linda sat in the front seat with her father. I thought about Candy. I was sure she still loved me. This was only a setback. I put my hand to my jaw. It was tender.

I stared out the car's window. The clouds were low and the same dull white as the fallen snow. It gave the landscape a bleak, muted quality. I thought about the rest of the afternoon after Candy had hoped me dead and I had gone to my desk and sat and stared at my hands. It was obvious that some of the boys admired the way I had taken Candy's punch and gotten right back up, but they weren't about to say so. Kip Krone at least raised his eyebrows and shook his head and smiled at me. The younger kids whispered and glanced at me as though I was something wild and possibly dangerous. Every girl looked at me with loathing, stared at me for what I was:

the sorry evidence of puberty gone wrong. The light began to fall. I couldn't tell where the snow stopped and the gray air began.

When my brother and I were dropped off on the highway below the lodge Linda Schmitt just stared at me blankly, as though I was an irksome little dog being let out to go to the bathroom. There weren't going to be anymore in-love rides in the backseat with Linda. She smiled at my brother with real pity.

The snowfall and flat light swallowed the Schmitts' car. My brother and I stood at the roadside. We could hear the tires bite into the snowpack on the two-lane, but could not see the car. We turned and started up separate tire ruts toward the lodge.

"I don't think a six-dollar necklace is going to help now," he said.

I nodded, and we walked the rest of the way in silence.

As far as I could see, I had only three true shots to regain my rightful place as an upperclassman in the scatter of grades. I vowed to live with abandon. Shame might be my destiny, but I would revel in my opportunities for celebration.

Some schools blunt their students with events: assemblies, guest speakers, a stray magician. We did not suffer from glut. Wapiti School had the Christmas Pageant, the spring auction, and the rural school track meet held just before summer vacation. I planned to win Candy over by summer. I planned to showcase myself through the three events.

Between Thanksgiving and our release for the Christmas holiday we practiced for the pageant. In past years there had been caroling, poetry reading, a play that begged to have something to do with Christendom, and yards of gauzy material going into the manufacture of a dozen angels' wings. I now think of the Christmas Pageant as a sort of baptism: if it could be survived, so could the numbing cold and darkness of the next three months. The whole valley attended. Everyone's parents, relatives, school alumni, childless couples, old bachelor cowboys with trucks that might not make the round-trip to Cody. Television reception was rare. We were a people starved for even the most meager of entertainments.

The Christmas I was in the seventh grade our pageant had a twist. It had Bill Waller. Bill had briefly owned Nameit Creek Lodge and had an interest in Native American ritual. He had also been a coach. He coached us in the intricacies of the Snake Dance. It did not bother us that he wove several Indian traditions into one spectacle; at the time none of us knew the difference. We were all just white kids who were bored spitless at the prospect of singing "Silent Night" and playing elves, or wise men, or a troop of sweaty messengers of God.

Bill Waller established himself as nearly supernatural immediately by grouping all ten boys together and walking back and forth in front of us on his hands while he introduced himself. He was an old man. He was in his fifties. We were impressed. It was like joining a circus without having to run away from home. We would have followed Bill Waller anywhere.

When I told my mother about the Christmas Snake Dance she said that it sounded like just the kind of thing for a boy who would hit a girl in the head with a stone. But she grudgingly made my brother and me corduroy breechcloths and moccasins.

On the big night, under the eyes of our families and friends, we line-danced onto the homemade stage and hopped and twisted and gyred in a rough circle, stripped naked except for denim or corduroy breechcloths that flapped over our jockey shorts, waving rubber snakes above our heads and hooting. I felt the need for a sustained howl.

Our legs, torsos, and faces were painted with lightning bolts, handprints, geometric designs, stick-horses, and the outlines of pickup trucks. Bill Waller had supplied the snakes and a set of watercolors. I don't know if he was the one who had supplied our black braided wigs, but we had them, and they flew off and we danced on them. Bethlehem it was not. Wapiti it was. I was so enthusiastic that I nearly tipped Pete Krone back into the crèche. We got a standing ovation. Candy Dohse appeared angelic, and unimpressed. I wasn't able to catch her looking at me. Not once.

January and February were bleak. The Krone boys and Jeff and

Bruce Keller would be seen with me for short periods of time. My brother had no choice. All of the girls kept a respectful distance.

The fund-raising auction was held at the schoolhouse in March, hosted by the Wapiti Women's Club to feed their scholarship fund for Wapiti School alumni. The valley's residents were by this time ground down by the winter and anxious for an event. Each family brought at least one hot dish and a dozen cookies, and the evidence of their winter's hermitage to donate to the auction. Canned pickles, beets, meat, preserves. Jars of honey. Loaves of bread. Macramé. All manner of baked goods. Plants. Birds shaped from lengths of driftwood. Horseshoes welded together for bookends. Amateur landscapes. Braided tack. And the big item: the quilt made by the Wapiti Women's Club. Each square fashioned by a different woman, quilted by their majority, so highly prized that its raffle tickets were snapped up in a few weeks. Almost every woman in the valley belonged to the club—the newly married, the widowed, the never married. The quilt was their communal gift.

People bid wildly for show, to court, to swell the scholarship fund, because they could. Neighbors spent what little money they had for each other's crafts so that every year, one of the valley's children could enjoy an expanded education. There were scholarships given to four-year colleges; scholarships given for technical schools. The ice was breaking up on the river. It was a party no one missed. I remember Glenn Fales as the auctioneer. He owned Rimrock Ranch. There was a level of threat in his voice that made the bidders sit up straight. I had saved ten dollars. I bought a cake and an elaborate wall hanging braided and macraméd from the unravelings of a length of thick hemp rope. It had blue wooden beads. Candy Dohse told me she wouldn't hang it in a barn.

The elk and deer and mountain sheep that had made it through the winter, waiting for green grass, fed on browse, and died in the heavy spring snowstorms of April. I watched their deaths without pity, my sap risen and withered.

At the end of the school year we were bused into Cody High's football field and gymnasium for the rural schools track meet—all told perhaps fifty otherwise capable country kids become shuffling and clumsy in the glare of sophistication cast by the urban setting. Cody was a town of almost four thousand. It had a macadam track. There were bleachers. We felt like gypsies brought into the kitchen of a manor house for some rare supper.

Through the winter my parents took my brother and me to town once a month. We shopped for groceries and hardware. We ate dinner at the Irma Hotel, and then my mother, brother, and I would go to a movie and my father would wait for us in the Irma Bar across the street, catching up with his friends.

But the spring track meet was more than a trip to town; it was a frivolous thing. There were no errands to run. The Dairy Queen was open, and there was the opportunity for heroism. We trained hard. For two entire weeks prior to the meet the Wapiti School's student body spent our recesses running the quarter mile from the Wapiti School to the Wapiti Post Office. All of us. We lined up in the school's gravel parking lot and sprinted down the gravel apron of the two-lane. Kip Krone and I ran in the borrow ditch. When we reached the post office we milled around until we caught our breaths, and then ran back to school. No one suggested to us that we should compete for our alma mater. There was a total lack of esprit de corps. We went for individual glory. We went for ice cream. We went because it was a trip to town and it was spring.

My uniform consisted of one of my father's white T-shirts—the sleeves hung past my elbows, the tail past my knees—a pair of everyday jeans, and black, high-top sneakers. Some kids ran in their cowboy boots. There was the high jump, a quarter-mile run, several dashes, and a basketball throw. Our parents stood on the wooden bleachers and yelled until they were hoarse. My brother won a ribbon for the quarter-mile run. I finished last in the fifty- and one hundred—yard dashes, but won a ribbon from the free-throw line. I sank eight out of ten tries. I was short, but rendered utterly Zen by my lack of hope. I threw without any sort of expec-tation. I threw to get the thing over with and sit in the shade and have an ice cream cone dipped in chocolate that hardened into a glaze. I didn't offer my ribbon to Candy. I pinned it on the shoulder of my borrowed T-shirt where any sort of breeze would lift it against my face. Shame had run its course. My mother didn't cringe when I hugged her. Linda Schmitt had smiled at me on the bus ride to town, shyly, but she didn't care who saw her. It was the last of school. The trees had leafed out. In a week we would trail our horses from winter pasture, and our first guests would arrive at the lodge.

The next fall I attended the eighth grade in Cody. I lived in Lillian Hackett's basement. She was a widow with two girls almost out of high school. To help pay for my rent and dinners I shoveled walks, advertised for odd jobs, pulled shoes off horses. I hitchhiked home every other weekend. At Christmas my brother told me he was in love with Linda Schmitt. Full-time.

☞ I CALLED Linda Schmitt's mother last week and learned that Linda manages Norwest Bank in Billings, Montana. Her mother told me that she's married and has an eighteen-year-old son. I told my brother the news. He said he wished he needed a loan. We both plan to stop to see her when we're next in Billings.

Kip Krone manages a ranch outside Pavillion and fights forest fires in the summers. His brother, Pete, turned his pickup over on the apron of rocks that borders the Greybull River and died there in 1979. I've lost track of the Sidwell kids, and Jeff and Bruce Keller. My wife searched the Internet in Wyoming and Montana to find Bill Dansby's phone number and did not get a match. Gene Hedrick died of a heart attack in 1982. He was only forty-six. I sometimes see his widow in a life-drawing class at a nearby college. She told me that one of her daughters went into the forest behind the lodge where they used to live to spread Gene's ashes. She said that a black bear chased the daughter up a tree, and that she had to spend the afternoon in the tree. She told me that a bear was Gene's talisman. We smiled. We were remembering what a kind and solid man he was.

I also called Candy Dohse last week. She's a deputy marshal for San Diego County. She has two children, a granddaughter. She asked me if I remembered the dances in the loft of the barn at the

Lazy KC. She asked me if I remembered that she played Mary in the Christmas Pageant. She asked me if I remembered the necklace I'd given her. Did I remember where I'd hidden it? She said she's kept it. She said she's kept it in a little wooden box Kass Sidwell gave her. On the top of the box is carved the word *WAPITI.*

I think of them now, all of them, as family. And when I wake in the night and am afraid for the land, or the decisions I will make about the man I am, I hear their names, like the names of the creeks that feed the river: Keller, Fales, Ballinger, Rumsey, Royal, Gibbs, Morris, Coe, Wilson, Lewis, McClelland, Kinder, Petty, Dahlem, Hall, Schmitt, Garlow, Selby, Sidwell, Legg, Stonehouse, Fell, Sauerwein and Sowerwine, Van Wagoner, King, Dohse, and the ones who came before them. Their names fall down and out of the Absarokas, to the river, to the Shoshone, and whisper the name, Wapiti.

THE CIRCUSMASTER

"You know how old I am?"

"I don't care," I say, but it's a lie. Every cowboy in the bunk-house wonders about the old man's age. He's a champion drunk. A curio of delinquency. Respected for his stubborn deterioration. The middle-aged men, John and Gordon and Phil, regularly twist off into drinking binges that last three or four days, but they allow themselves a month's rest between their bouts. The old man's consistency makes them brave. They agree that if he has survived his bad habits there is hope that they may become old as well. A life lived in comparison to the cook's makes a man feel wholesome, even virtuous.

But I'm young and stuck with the notion that I might succeed at life. I fear the old man as I fear lightning. He has somehow slipped through the cracks. I fear that when his run of luck is done all those around him will be struck dead. Or not. What I fear even more is that he will simply grow older and die; that there is no justice; that I may be handicapped by a life without the instruction of punishment. I am beginning to yearn for crimes that deserve punishment. I have begun to tremble when around girls. My mind lost to fantasy. My thoughts unthinkable. I'm not so callow that I don't recognize a budding addiction to skin. To sin. I fear the old man because I must be stopped and he's still going strong.

"I may be old, but my feelings can still get hurt."

"I'm sorry," I say, but I don't turn. I press a palm against my saddle horn, stand in the stirrups and arch my back. The old man rides behind me, and I don't want him to see my face. I'll sacrifice learning how old he is before I'll give him the pleasure of a conversation.

The actual truths are that I *do* care how old he is, and that I'm not sorry I've insulted him. Two lies. I'm not only a developing pervert, but a liar. I bring my knees up under the swells of the saddle, bend tightly over the horn, and stand again in the stirrups and stretch. I try to keep the lies flexed away from my skeleton. My mother has told me that lies work into the joints of a boy's bones. She's said they resemble petrified peach pits, but much smaller, that they gather like seeds. She's said that lying is the primary cause of arthritis. That liars cripple early and painfully. Before my mother had taken on the task of my personal enlightenment she had been a nurse. I'm stuck in a descending spiral. Every day I think about girls in a way that requires lies.

"I'm so goddamn old I don't buy green bananas," he says. "That's how old I am." He tries to laugh, a choked cackle, and the attempt sets off a coughing fit. He coughs until he hawks up a mouthful of old-man phlegm and spits the wad of it over his left shoulder, wiping his mouth and chin on his jacket's sleeve. "How far have we come?" he asks.

"About a quarter of a mile since our last stop."

"Age'll wear that smart mouth of yours quiet," he says. "Smooth-mouth you."

"Then I better use it while I'm young." The clouds are massing out of Yellowstone, their bellies dark with moisture, and the temperature has dropped. The day could go either way. It's said in Wyoming that if you don't like the weather you can wait five minutes, or travel five miles. A useless aphorism if caught in an early fall blizzard.

"That's not all you better use." He makes no effort to disguise the leer in his statement.

"There's no good place to sit on this slope," I tell him. "We'll stop in the trees." I turn in the saddle and smile. Worse than a conversation would be having to hear the old man prattle about sex. "We've come about seven miles," I add. I'm looking directly at him, trying to maintain an expression as unruffled as water in a pail. He bobs against the rhythm of his horse like some smallish and desiccated chimp.

The thought that this old man has ever touched a woman he didn't have to tie up has the effect of a snake dropped down the collar of my shirt. If I think about his hands on any single woman—his ruminations about women are precise—all women become suspect. My fantasies become as rank as the whiskey he swills. I prefer the girls in my imagination to know nothing of lurching old drunks. I prefer the girls in my imagination to know only me.

In the timber I tie his bridle reins head high to the limb of a lodgepole pine and get on all fours under his left stirrup. He wriggles over the side of his saddle, steps in the middle of my back and onto the ground. He is as fragile and light as some large, featherless bird, really more bird than monkey, I think. I steady him as he shuffles to a downfall. He sits, grimaces, moans as he rubs his thighs. His face has reddened from the exertion. I go to his saddlebags and pull out a bottle of Walkers Deluxe. Getting the old man into hunting camp is a two-bottle affair.

My brother has bet the old man is eighty. I've said I imagine him to be one hundred. Like the middle-aged cowboys I work with, my hope is that he is record-breaking old. The single reason I want him ancient is because I wish him dead. If he is old enough I can imagine him having lived a full life. It eases my guilt. I may be a liar, and depraved, but I am still capable of guilt. My mother has not told me what guilt might do. This spring my father had given me the job of bucketing a clogged septic tank. I was constipated for the week after the work, and my appetite left for a month, but I would gladly spend my life in hip boots bailing shit if the trade-off meant I wouldn't have to baby-sit this old cook into camp. This is my second time in three years. I consider it a badge of incompetence.

He takes a pull from the bottle, sets it on the ground between his legs, and lights a cigarette. "I'm seventy-four," he says. He's still getting his breath.

"That's going to disappoint some people," I say. I try not to let my disappointment show. Seventy-four is not old enough to get me off the guilt-baited hook.

"I hope to get a lot older." His head is tilted back, and he's exhaling cigarette smoke in little circles above his face. The whiskey is working its magic. His Adam's apple bobs like an extra elbow caught in his throat. His skin has returned white as milled flour, but blotched. In places he looks as though he is beginning to rust. His cheeks and chest are sunken. He has no butt, chin, or earlobes. I try to imagine what he must have looked like when he wasn't just bone and skin, but then his head levels and he grins. There are only four teeth left in the front of his mouth. "I wasn't always a cook," he says.

"What were you before?" I wonder what an actual albatross, an old one, might look like.

"I owned a circus."

"Any birds?"

"No birds. One elephant. A couple of big cats. Some horses. One of the trapeze women kept a snake. She was a nymphomaniac." He drops his head and spits beside the bottle, scratching at a cheek, chortling. His cheeks are constantly furred with a white stubble. So is the bridge of his nose and the tops of his ears. His eyes are clouded and rheumy, but he doesn't look like he's lying. For all his ailments he doesn't suffer from arthritis. "Don't you want to know about the trapeze woman?"

"No, sir."

"Do you know what a nymphomaniac is?"

"I'm trying not to think about it."

"How old are you?"

"Fourteen."

"That's probably all you *do* think about. I was fourteen once."

"I don't like snakes," I say. It's a desperate attempt to derail the conversation.

"She ate, slept, and shat with that big bastard draped around her neck. The son of a bitch got more tit than all the rest of us put together."

"I'll stop the horses more often if we can talk about something else."

He lowers the bottle away from his mouth and squints in my direction, and then smiles. He shuts one eye and sights into the bottle's neck as though witnessing some past event. "A snake can't really generate any genuine heat of its own. There's something for you to think about."

"I'm thinking about it now."

"When you own a circus, life is just generally entertaining. Had a dog act for about a month, but one of the larger cats got loose, and that was the end of that."

He takes another sip from the bottle and struggles to his feet. I stow the whiskey and drop by the side of his horse. He sighs, steps onto my back, and claws up the side of his saddle. He rights himself, farts, and smiles. The booze seems to revive him. He'll be good for another quarter of a mile, maybe a half, but it is twenty-seven miles into camp. Two years ago we'd made it in eighty-one stops. It is the worst kind of traveling I can imagine. We leave at four in the morning, and I consider it a miracle if we make it by dark. With the pack string it's a seven-hour trip, barring accidents. This is already the twenty-fourth time the old man has had to stop, and we aren't seven miles up Eagle Creek. Traveling with him is simply one protracted accident.

When I'm back on my horse I'm seized with the sudden fear that two bottles might not be enough this year. I've seen the old man before he gets his first drink in the morning, and the difference between the old man drunk and the old man getting drunk is the difference between a house cat and a wolverine. The horses are already edgy, but at least the sky is clearing.

There is whiskey stashed everywhere in the kitchen and pantry at the lodge. In the flour bins, behind canned goods; bottles rattle in the backs of silverware drawers. He keeps a bottle wrapped in sackcloth and buried in the ground meat in the walk-in cooler. My mother has found one in an empty milk carton in the fridge. Every week I drag two gunny sacks of empty beer cans out of his cabin. He claims that beer is nutritious. Like taking vitamins. "Gives me gas," he's told me, "but it's a small price to pay for your health."

My father packs in four cases of bourbon to get the old man through the thirty days in hunting camp. I try to imagine how he gets by in the winters. In the summers and falls we feed him, house him, but he never takes anything away. He trades his wages for booze.

"They still have a trail built around that bog?"

"Yes, sir." We're working down off a sidehill into the main drainage. Our horses kick shards of shale loose, and the fragments slide into the trees below us. It sounds as though we've spooked a herd of elk away from their daylight beds.

"You're sure?"

"It was there a month ago."

"It could have washed out."

"Could have."

"A bog's not a hell of a lot of fun."

"I was there too," I remind him.

"You weren't in it."

"I got muddy getting you out."

"Just so we don't have to ride into that goddamn bog."

The first year I'd escorted the old man into camp was the worst. The trail then passed through a stretch of stagnant mire at the mouth of Eagle Creek meadows. His horse had slipped and lunged, and the old man had simply pitched off into the mess. Before I could get a rope on him he'd flopped around in the slime and muck, so panicked that he'd finally quit cussing and simply settled into a constant whimper. It was unnerving. My father wasn't paying me to deliver a dead cook to camp. I scraped the old man off the best I could, filled my hat with spring water so he could wash his hands and face, but he remained so slippery he could hardly sit his horse, stunk terribly, and complained nonstop for the rest of the ride. And yet two bottles were enough that year, and the Forest Service has cut a trail out around the bog. Surely, I think, two bottles will be enough this year.

"I'm a hell of cook," he says.

"I know that." We've come another three miles in only nine stops. The horses are tied in a fringe of timber. The old man sits on the curved dome of a boulder, and I squat beside him. The ground falls away to the creek in a scatter of head-sized stones.

"It's important to be good at something."

"Yes, sir."

"If you aren't good at something and you're a drunk, you're just a bum."

"You make the best strudel I've ever eaten."

"I guess you could call pastry a specialty of mine."

"I like your pies and your tarts, too."

"Dry skin. That's my secret. I was born to handle shortening. An oily-skinned man will never get his crusts to flake. It's a fact. There's just some of us that are born to bake. Women hardly ever figure into the equation. Too high a fat content. Oozes right out of their pores, God bless them."

He takes another sip from his bottle and opens a second pack of cigarettes.

"I'm surprised you're still getting handed the shitty end of the stick." I look up at him, and he exhales smoke directly into my face.

"I wasn't always a drunk," he says. "I used to be a fair observer of situations. I still have the faculty if I choose to employ it. Seems to me that it was your little brother who rode me in here last year."

"I was busy bringing dudes in. Hunters."

"Those fat bastards from Florida?"

"They were doctors."

"They should have prescribed one another jars of diet pills is what they should have done. Your dad hear a complaint from 'em?"

"He didn't have to."

"That how come you got bumped back down to me?"

"I guess."

"Hell, you didn't kill anybody."

"I almost did."

"I just saw the part where they were holding you down in the cook tent and stitching up your head. If you don't turn bald you won't ever have to admit to the scar."

"My hair parts a little crooked."

"I've never noticed." The old man smiles, and he doesn't look so much like a scarecrow. His hands tremble as he smokes, and I wonder if it's difficult for him to hold his bridle reins.

I get him on his horse, and over the next several miles I tell him how hard it was raining when I'd left the lodge with the hunters. I tell him that a mile into the trip I'd loaned the littlest doctor my chaps and dug a pair of rubberized rain pants out of my saddlebags. They were a man's pair, and their waist came up past my nipples. I'd dallied their suspenders around my neck to keep them in place, but they bunched up under my butt and knees.

"They keep you dry?"

"My feet got wet."

"You can't say enough about being dry. What were you riding?"

I tell the old man that I was riding a snaky four-year-old who skittered as much sideways as he walked forward. He was a brown-and-white paint with a black tail, and on a dry day with chaps that fit he was a trick to get on and off. He'd tried to bite me twice. Struck at me once with a front hoof. The doctors thought it was a show. Every time we stopped they'd gather together and laugh at me trying to get on and off my horse.

"Did they stop as much as me?"

"Not that much. But close. They were a lot younger."

"Was that the horse your dad sold to the rodeo company in town?"

"Yes it was."

"I'll bet it makes you proud you survived him."

"Makes me glad I don't have to ride him anymore."

I tell the old man that by the time we got over the pass it was snowing. Three hours later we were a mile from camp, but there was a foot of snow on the ground. The doctors were lined out walking, leading their horses. Their asses stung so badly that they were on and off every other mile. The littlest doctor stopped to remount. My horse was dancing back and forth in front of him. It was snowing hard enough that I could barely see him.

I tell the old man that I guess the doctor's legs were shot because he couldn't swing all the way over the cantle, got a foot tangled in the strap that held his scabbard, and kicked the thing loose. The butt of the gun gouged into his horse's flank.

"Good thing you were transporting doctors and not lawyers," says the old man. He's halfway into the second bottle of bourbon. The old man has a window when he drinks. When the window is open his body feels fine and he grins while he talks. I know it will close before we reach camp.

I tell him that the doctor didn't even look alarmed as his horse stampeded past me. Both reins flapped to the sides of the horse's mouth. The animal's eyes were rolled back, showing mostly white. The scabbard was attached at the front D-ring, and with every lunge it bounced up into the horse's flank. The doctor clutched the saddle horn with both hands, and amazingly rode kneeling on the saddle's seat. He appeared to be some daredevil jockey. I spurred in behind, trying to keep them visible in the snow. And then the doctor started to list. To the right. For several seconds he clung to the side of his horse as a fat squirrel might, and then lost his grip, straightened out, and torpedoed into the snow. I pulled up, but he was lost. And then he was found. He exploded to the surface, having skidded under the skin of snow for more than twenty feet. One of his colleagues actually measured the distance. The slide had badly bruised his right shoulder, and I had a mutiny on my hands. The men sat in the snow and refused to move. They looked as though they wanted to weep.

"I think if I wasn't a cook I might have liked to be a gynecologist."

"Pardon me?"

"Maybe all those doctors were gynecologists." I look back at the old man. His head has fallen forward, and I can hardly hear him. The top of his skull is as speckled as the backs of his hands. He looks up at me and smiles. "Maybe if they were gynecologists they were all more ready to die than your average man. Maybe they'd seen it all and just wanted to die peaceful in the mountains."

"They didn't come to Wyoming to die," I tell him. "They came here to hunt elk." I feel panicked. There's obviously a very real chance that the old man and I share similar ambitions.

"I'm sorry," he allows.

"I thought you were listening." I try to sound insulted.

"I was. Sometimes I drift. It won't happen again."

I tell the old man how I caught the runaway horse and led him back to the doctors. I tell him that I told the doctors that we'd likely die if we stayed out in the storm. I tell him that the doctors said they preferred to die on their feet. That they'd paid to come hunting. Not ride broncs. And then I tell him that when I stepped off the paint the suspenders snapped and the snow pants dropped and tangled at my knees. I explain how I staggered and pitched forward and how my horse spooked and jumped on top of me.

"That's how you bunged up your head?"

"He stepped on it."

The old man was there when I'd arrived at camp. I was walking, leading all five horses, carrying the doctors' four rifles. They were lined out behind me. Wet, unhappy men.

"Your dad said it was dark enough that you'd have been hard to spot if you weren't covered in blood. It caught what little light was left."

"That wasn't all he said."

"He'll give you another chance."

"I guess he will, or I'll get big enough to leave home."

We stop at the top of Eagle Creek pass. It's late afternoon and windless. The sky is free of clouds and a watery blue. I fish my backup sandwich out of my saddlebags, and the old man and I find shelflike seats in a broken escarpment. We look north twenty miles into the head of Mormon Creek.

"Aren't you hungry?" I ask.

"I was for a while, but I'm over it."

"I have a Snickers bar."

"A matter of economics." He smiles. The window is still open. "No sense letting twenty-five cents worth of junk food screw up a thirty-dollar drunk."

"You don't seem drunk."

"I am."

"I guess you'd be a better judge than me."

"I'm taking in more air than I normally do. I can't even get a cigarette lit while I'm riding. That might have something to do with it."

The old man shifts on his rock ledge, takes another sip from the bottle, and holds it out to me.

"I better not."

"Afraid your old man will smell it on you?"

"Yes, I am."

"Got any gum?"

"Some Juicy Fruit."

"That'll do it."

It will mean another lie if I'm asked, but I take the bottle from him, unsnap my shirt at a wrist, so the sleeve hangs down from my elbow like a rag, and wipe off the mouth of the bottle.

"I don't have anything you could catch," he says.

"You can't know that for sure."

"Look at me for Christ's sake. A cold would probably kill me. If you don't have the nerve just hand it back."

I take a timid sip and try to hold the whiskey in my mouth, but my gums start to burn, so I swallow fast and hand him the bottle back to free my hands. I think I might have to stand and hop around. When nothing happens I'm a little disappointed.

"How was it?"

"Not as bad as I thought."

"You feel any different?"

"Maybe warmer."

"Can't do anything but good for you as long as you eat while you're drinking. The French are walking proof of that. You don't have anything to worry about. I've had an eye on you. You're a good eater."

A marmot waddles out onto a ledge of rock to our left. He bounces up and down on his front legs. His head swivels. He looks nervous. As though he's exposed himself on a dare. The rich browns of his fur catch in the sun. I think of a dark-haired girl in my history class.

"You think that deal with the doctors was my fault?"

"If I'd have been French," says the old man, "I'd probably feel better than I do. Lost my appetite about twenty years ago. The booze really went to work on me then."

The marmot chirps and whistles and sits and snaps his tail. His bucked front teeth flash yellow in his dark face.

"If I hadn't worn the rain pants I'd have gotten wet, but I might not have gotten stepped on."

"You didn't do a goddamn thing wrong," he says. He turns to me. His eyes are sunken and bloodshot. "If you were my kid I'd have given you a medal for not losing the whole bunch in that storm."

"Thanks for saying so."

"I'm not sure they make medals for something like that, but maybe a citation could have been typed up."

"You ever have kids?"

"Sure I have. A boy and a girl."

The old man bends forward and works his billfold out of a back pocket. It takes him a while, but he finds a picture and hands it to me. "That's the girl," he says.

The picture is faded, frayed at the edge where it's worn against the fold of his wallet. The girl is about twenty. She wears a blue bikini and leans back against a palm tree, smiling broadly. She doesn't look like anybody's daughter.

"Good-looking, isn't she?"

"Yes, sir."

"Got a boy too, but I've lost his picture. A goddamn genius is what he is." He flicks his cigarette at the marmot, and the animal hurries back into the shadow of an overhang. I look back and forth from the picture to the old man to see if the girl has his eyes, or chin, or forehead. "Couldn't keep up with the boy intellectually. Had to send him off to school. He graduated from college when he was sixteen. How old did you say you were?"

"Fourteen." On the back of his daughter's picture there's a palm tree. Its trunk is made out to look like the body of a naked woman. Underneath the tree it reads: GIRLS OF THE SOUTH PACIFIC. "What's your boy do?" I don't really care what his son does, but I'm not ready to hand over the picture.

"He runs the circus."

"Does the snake lady work for him?"

"She's dead. What grade are you in?"

"Ninth."

"I didn't mean anything when I bragged on my son getting out of college at sixteen."

"It's okay."

He holds the bottle out to me. "You want another sip?"

"I think one was enough."

He takes a sip and checks to see if the marmot's come back out into the sun. "Anyway, genius is something a man's born with."

"I guess I wasn't."

"Most of us aren't."

I hand him back the picture of his daughter, and he squints at it for a moment and slips it into his wallet. He stares at the sky while he works his lips into a pucker to suck on his teeth. "It'll be dark in a couple of hours," he says. "With no moon it'll be blacker than the inside of a bear."

"Your wife must have been a pretty woman."

"Gorgeous is what she was. Prettier than that girl by a long shot."

"Do you have a picture of her I might see sometime?"

"Just the girl. I'd let you hang on to the picture for a while, but it's the only one I've got."

"I understand."

"You ever tire of this life in the mountains maybe you could sign on a steamer. Have a look around the world yourself. There's women out there that don't require a genius. You might find a dozen or so who even think you're cute."

"That'd be a lot."

"There's more women in the world than men. Make a count locally if you don't believe me."

"I believe you." The old man leans forward to spit and folds right onto the ground. I see it only out of the corner of an eye, but the whole procedure looks like a cricket might look if trying to somersault. "Are you okay?"

He sits up. "I'm surprised. Did I spill any whiskey?"

"You have the cap on."

"Good for me. You better give me a hand up. We didn't pack enough bourbon for me to be out all night."

I kneel down and get a shoulder into one of his armpits and lever him to his feet. He clings to the saddle strings while I get down on my hands and knees so he can step up into a stirrup. When he drags his leg over the cantle he coughs and farts at the same time. "Excuse me," he says.

I swing up onto my horse. I check the sun to see how much of the day is left.

"We better get a move on," he says. "I can feel my good mood starting to fade."

A BOY'S WORK

"Your horse is wire-cut." My father has pulled up to the corrals with a four-horse trailer. This is his second and last load. The rest of the horses have been left on winter pasture. The snow still lies in dirty, humped drifts around the buildings and in the timber. The grass has just started to work up through the smear of gray, gauzelike mold that has spread under the winter's snowcover. Our Forest Service grazing lease won't begin for several weeks. Any horses we have on the place will have to be fed hay. Hay is expensive.

"My horse?"

"You have so many you can't remember which one?"

"They all belong to you."

He steps to the back of the trailer. He turns with one hand on the trailer's gate. He looks tired, hungry. "The horse you rode last summer and fall," he says.

"Socks?"

"I think riding a single animal every day of your life allows you some privileges."

He swings the trailer's gate open and backs out a big sorrel gelding and hands me its halterrope, stepping into the trailer again and turning out a black we call Bird.

"Don't let Bird get by you," he shouts from inside the trailer.

"Wire-cut a little, or a lot?" Bird trails his leadrope, holding his head to the side, careful not to step on the thing. I catch up the leadrope.

My father steps the third horse out of the trailer. We have spring bear hunters coming in on the weekend and need just enough transportation to get us all back and forth to the bait-ground.

"I mean he tried to cut a hoof off." I'm following the horse he leads, bringing the other two with me.

"With what?" I know it doesn't really matter.

"With a wire gate. Some asshole left it open on the ground and Socks got in it. I found him when I was gathering these. He worked himself loose of the gate but the damage had been done."

"He's at the vet's?"

"His leg's gangrenous." He pauses just inside the corrals. He turns his horse into the corrals and looks back over a shoulder at me. He's looping the leadrope over the halter's headstall. "I hope you've just gotten hard of hearing. You were a good deal brighter when I left this morning."

"You killed him?"

He takes the two other horses from me. His hat is pulled down. I don't get a good look at his eyes. He speaks softly. "He's in the trailer," he says.

When I step in the trailer I can smell him. It is the smell of something that has died in the sun. A hopeless odor that brings memories of road-killed deer and elk—flies, gums drawn back over yellowing teeth. He nickers softly and I move to his head. He's gaunt. His winter coat is shedding in large, uneven gouts. I run a hand along his side, my fingers tracing the cage of his ribs. There are sprigs of dried weed tangled in his tail and mane. I untie his leadrope and lead him from the trailer. Every time he steps with his right front foot his shoulder sinks as though he's stepping into a hole. Outside the trailer my father lights a ciga-rette.

"Put him in with the others and spill some grain for them."

"Why?"

"Because I told you to."

"He's not going to get any better."

The cigarette smoke rises and holds against the brim of my father's hat. "No," he says, "he's not going to get any better."

There is more light out of the trailer. I can see that Socks's leg is swollen badly. From his hoof to his shoulder the skin has split in several weeping slices. His pastern is as thick as his forearm should be and blackened, crusted with dried blood. When he takes a step the heel of his foot flops loose and snaps back up against the pastern. It makes a sucking sound, and then a click.

My father speaks with the cigarette in the corner of his mouth. He's latching the trailer. "I'd give a lot to get my hands on the son of a bitch who was in such a hurry he couldn't close a gate."

"I don't feel very well."

"You're going to feel worse."

He drops his cigarette at the toe of his boot and methodically grinds it out. He doesn't look up when he speaks. "I've got to be in town tomorrow or I wouldn't ask you."

"I've got school."

"If you think you need to go to school your mother can run you down the valley after lunch."

My father is looking up at me now. He's pulling on a pair of yellow cloth gloves.

"You could have killed him in town," I tell him. "If you didn't have a gun you could have borrowed one." A knot of panic rises in my chest like some small, waking animal clawing its way out of hibernation.

"I want him baited."

"Bear-baited?"

"We don't exactly have the kind of money to kill a usable horse. Everything else'll make it until this fall. Kind of looks like Socks volunteered, don't you think?"

I do not, but I'm part of the family and this is part of our work. I'm fifteen. Old enough to be asked. We bait horses for bear, allowing their corpses to ripen, hoping they will attract an otherwise elusive grizzly. Our hunters fire from a blind at the bear that feeds on the dead horse.

I stand staring at my father's boots. They are worn down to the same color as the soil. Socks lips the collar of my denim jacket. His breath feels warm and moist against my neck. This is the first time I've been prompted to draw any conclusions about sport. The horses we have baited in the past were derelict, their teeth gone, ready to die. I have never before connected sorrow with our family's business.

"Where?" I don't look up.

"That little meadow up Kitty Creek. Where we killed the big boar two springs ago. It's close; there's no creeks to cross. If he's alive in the morning you might get him up there."

I nod. I'm not sure there is enough light left for my father to see the movement of my head.

"I'm sorry about this," he says. "You have your supper?"

"Elk roast."

"Your mother make a dessert?"

"Just canned pears."

"Ask your brother for a hand if you think you need it."

"I'll be fine."

"This won't be the hardest thing you'll ever do. You believe me?"

"Not yet."

"I'll see you tomorrow."

I listen to his footfalls grow fainter as he walks away from me. It is dark enough now that I can't distinguish his outline. But I feel the heat of him leave. The night seems to drop ten degrees. I get Socks in the round corral, away from the other horses, heap a coffee can with oats and pour them in his trough, make sure he has clean water. For a while I stand in the dark and listen to him chew—a blunted, rhythmic rasp; the sound of pack rats at work in a hay loft. And a single owl hooting periodically, well rested, watching us with its wide night eyes.

When I pass my parents' cabin I can see my father at the supper table. He still wears his neckerchief. His hair is so short it hasn't needed to be combed, his sleeves are rolled above his elbows, the brown hair on his white forearms catching in the light. My mother sits across from him at the table. She sips coffee from a mug my brother has made her as a school project and nods as my father speaks. She grimaces. I step back from the light the window throws to watch them. Their conversation is locked away from me, inside with the light. I do not hear their words. I can hear the creek, and the pine needles under my boots when I shift my weight. The air is warming away from winter. It tastes of pine and sage. I can smell the sap risen in the aspen. I wait until my father is done with his meal and walk in the night to the cabin where I live with my brother.

"What's the capital of Romania?" he asks.

"I don't know."

My brother sits at a desk by the gas heater in our cabin. There is just the one room with a closet-sized bathroom that we keep closed off in the winters. The plumbing isn't buried, and the pipes would freeze if not drained. My parents live in a slightly larger cabin just down the creek. It has a well pit dug under the kitchen floor, and their bathroom is capable of running water year-round. We use their tub and toilet. It makes for regular bowel movements. When we have to piss we piss over the railing of our own cabin, writing patterns in the drifted snow.

"Bucharest?" My brother still has not found the answer.

"I said I didn't know."

"It makes a difference."

He's thirteen, a year and a half younger, and smarter than me. He's bent over a report that is due the next day. We don't have television and only get a country-western station—KOMA, in Oklahoma City—if we stay up past midnight, flag the antenna with tin foil, and one of us stands by the radio holding the antenna's tip. We read because my father has books, thousands of them. We are not a family that goes on vacation. We are a family that makes the ninety-mile round-trip to town once a month for supplies. My brother and I use books when we want to leave Wyoming. We wear out an atlas every three years. I sit on my bed and open the big rectangular book of maps on my lap.

"It's Bucharest," I tell him.

My brother looks up at me and smiles. His eyes tell me that we will go there someday. To Romania. The two of us, when we are men. He winks. He has eyes that are capable of recognizing us anywhere on the planet.

I get undressed and under my quilts. I watch his head bob to the rhythm of his writing and close my eyes. When he goes to bed, when he says good night, I lie with my eyes closed and pretend to sleep. He turns off the light, and I sink into the darkness. I can hear the purr and sputter of Libby Creek outside the cabin. The gas heater ticks and groans.

I imagine the panic and pain that must have sizzled through the horse. Apparently, *my* horse. Socks. I see the strand of wire wrapped above his hoof, barbed, working with the efficiency of a primitive chainsaw, working faster the harder he struggled. I wonder how long he suffered before he got free of the snare. I wonder if he felt relief, or if he looked down at his hoof and knew that he was ruined. I twist under my bedding and cannot sleep.

Sometime in the middle of the night I get up and kneel by my bed. The linoleum is cold, damp; it feels like the flesh of something old and dead. I sweep an arm under the bed until I find the rifle wrapped in an army-surplus blanket and pull it to me. Its blued, steel barrel is as cold as an unburied pipe.

I set the desk lamp on the floor so I won't wake my brother and fill the rifle's magazine with shells, bolt them back out, wipe them on the front of my T-shirt, reload, and close the action. I lean the gun by the door and get back into bed. I can't get warm. I feel as cold as the linoleum, as the rifle barrel, as the job I must somehow do in the morning. I think of slipping into bed with my brother but know I will wake him. I love the sound of his even breathing while he sleeps. I clench my teeth and concentrate on the rhythms of my brother's breath. I pray to hold firmly, in one whole piece, until it is light. Before dawn I dress in the dark, take up the gun, and start for the corrals.

My parents' cabin is dark. I stand at a window and squint in at the dining table. The hour before dawn seems to me always the coldest of the night. My eyes water, and I flex and fist my fingers against the seams of my leather workgloves. Inside the cabin a propane heater softly illuminates a corner of the room. Yellowed shadows struggle against a line of hanging work coats. A brown-and-white cat named Monk is balled on the seat of a fabric-covered chair. The rifle slips loose from where I have tucked it against my arm, and I heft its weight back into my body and move away.

I stop again where the corrals meet the side of the barn. I listen. I am fond of the sound of horses in the night. The lifting of feet. Stamping. The clicking of their iron shoes against rock. They mouth one another's withers and rear and squeal and whirl and shuffle and cough and stand and snort. There is the combined rumblings of each individual gut. They sound larger than they are. The air tastes of horses, ripples as though come alive with their good-hearted strength and stamina.

I give Socks a half can of oats, break the skim of ice that has formed on the water trough, and catch Bird to ride. I saddle him under the lights of the tackshed, speaking to him softly. It is the first time he's been touched in seven months. He watches every move I make, rolling his eyes until the whites show, mouthing the bridle's bit. When I make the final pull on the latigo, the seat of the saddle rises as though I've shoved the oat can under the skirt of its back. Bird's ready to fire. Ready to bust the night-chill out of his bones.

I turn him in a tight circle several times, and while he pivots through the last turn I step into the stirrup and let his momentum swing me securely into the saddle. He stands absolutely still for just one breath, snorts, and starts to buck. He's never been very fancy in his tantrums, and I manage to keep his head pulled up and out of the rhythm of his clumsy plunges. The crow-hopping stops as abruptly as it has begun, and he steps out stiffly, as though only now come fully awake. I spur him into a trot for the quarter mile down to the mailbox and back and step off. He stands like a gentleman, his ears up and alert. I slide the rifle into the saddle scabbard. The horizon has just started to lighten. Bird and I can still see our breaths in the morning air, but our blood is hot. I return quickly to the corrals and halter Socks.

Socks has never offered to buck. He's fourteen and has given me nothing but work. He's a rangy bay whose legs run white from his knees down. Without being bred for it he's naturally gaited and one of the smartest horses about terrain I've ever ridden. He studies the ground like some horses study cows. He moves with the same sure ease over loose scree, through downed timber, in fast water, over open ground. If I give him his head after dark he invariably brings me home, stepping in the same prints he's made on the ride out. As one of our hands has said about him, he's the kind of horse that comes early and stays late. I can hardly look back at him as he haltingly follows Bird and me. A step, a pause to gather his weight in his hindquarters, a step. At times he groans so mournfully that I turn in the saddle, prepared to watch him die. The waking knot of panic comes alive again in my gut, rises in my throat. I swallow. My throat burns, my mouth tastes of copper.

I've expected Bird to be impatient and fight the bit for the whole trip, but perhaps there is a communion between animals that I do not understand. I wonder if they find a community in one another's miseries. Bird walks as though he is picking his way through a field littered with cactus and broken stone. He looks back so often that I have to continually rein him back onto the trail. When Socks's breaths come in rasps Bird stops completely, refuses to move, stands with his head hanging low, as though listening.

Traveling the three miles to the bait-ground takes us four hours. By the time we get to the little meadow where I intend to kill him, Socks is almost dead. His eyes appear glazed, as though grown over with bluish cataracts. He sways as he stands. The swelling has spread to his shoulder and chest, and he wheezes without the effort of moving. I pray he is so deeply in shock that he has forgotten he is a horse, forgotten the taste of clear water. I think that a lesser horse could not have made this trip to be killed. A lesser horse would have died tangled in the wire. I feel he has made the effort for me.

I tie Bird in the trees and walk quickly back to Socks and unsnap his halter and let it drop. I'm in a hurry. There is a chance that he can endure more. I know that I cannot. I chamber a shell, sight quickly, and stop his struggle before he can respond to the sound of metal slipping against metal. He falls, kicks once, and is still. The gunshot's report echoes against the opposite side of the valley. A magpie starts up and will not stop his squawking.

The shot and the immediate presence of death spikes through Bird like a lightning strike. He circles the tree where I have tied him, snorting, glaring into the middle distance of every direction, sawing against his leadrope. I drop the empty halter by him as I pass and keep walking through the spare timber. When I get into the creek it is over my knees and my boots fill with the icy water. And then I am out and struggling up a sharp embankment and into a nest of pine boughs heaped around and over the crude pole frame that acts as our blind.

A thick downfall keeps the whole affair held against the hillside, and there is the noise of Kitty Creek to further separate it from the meadow. If there is a breeze it reliably sweeps down this tight drainage and holds the hunter's scent away from the bait. It is a fine place to sit and raise a rifle and kill a bear.

I stare at the reddish brown mound seventy-five yards in front of me. I have killed Socks in a good place. Close to the timber that borders the meadow. A bear will feel safe in his approach. Far enough into the meadow that a hunter will have a good shot. And then I remember that I should have cut a window in his gut. Sawed through his hair and opened him to decay. A sore that coyotes and ravens can worry. A place that will help him rot. My father will be disappointed. I think of my father's disappointment and remember the ruined leg. The smell of the leg will attract a bear. Socks has gotten a head start at decay. I have an excuse. I wonder suddenly why I am not crying. I think a boy would cry. I think maybe

I have begun to be a man. I feel only quietly blunt, and desperate. I feel as though I want to stand and run, but do not have the strength. I tighten my chest to exhale, and suck at the air to reinflate. Again, and then again. My eyes water, but the breathing helps. It is my only weapon against the release of the thing that struggles inside me. A small fight. I fear that if I allow myself to empty I will be filled only with the regret of what I have just done.

I look down at the rifle that lies across my knees and think of the bear hunters that pay us for this. They come every spring and fall. Usually from the East. More recently from the Midwest and South. Professional men. Lawyers, executives, doctors. Not bad men. But men who believe in trophy. They are hard men to respect. In hunting camp they drink every night. They stagger out of the dining tent and fall to their knees and vomit and wipe their mouths on the tails of the new shirts they have bought for hunting bear. In the mornings they suffer the shits. When they are drunk they tell us about fucking their wives. They tell us about fucking women who are not their wives. They tell us about fucking the men they are in business with. Not all of them. But the drunks and the braggarts are the ones I remember. Every fall I sit behind the woodstove in the tent and watch them. They only look my way to ask for a dipper of water, or to send me to their sleeping tents for cigarettes. I do not think of them as men. I think of them as big, loud Scouts—overweight and balding children. I imagine that they come to us to earn a bear badge. Not to kill something ordinary that can be eaten, but to kill something extraordinary that is capable of eating them.

I slump against the hillside and look up into the scatter of sunlight through the pines. I think of our hunters' nervousness in this and other blinds where I've sat with them. When it rains they smell of excitement and they smell of fear. They ask what it is like to kill a bear. They ask how others have done the thing. To the sounds that magnify with the dusk they ask in a tight whisper, "What is that? Is there something out there?" There is no whiskey in the blind. And I am not just a boy sitting behind a stove. Now I am a boy who's watched bears die, and they have not.

I tell them that seeing a bear for the first time is like hearing a rattlesnake for the first time. I tell them that there will be no mistake. Sometimes a man moans. Most men just sit and stare. A few smile a terrible smile. They are the ones we do not accept back. There are limits to any profession.

My father tells our hunters to take out the ball of the shoulder with the first shot so that the bear cannot charge. Simple instructions to ruin bone and flesh. He tells them to never shoot at the head, that a grizzly's skull will deflect their bullet. I have no way of knowing if they remember. Some make good shots. Others fire wildly. Some bear are wounded, and we track them and kill them up close where they have curled to die. Some fall where they feed, across the body of the horse. A few have healed themselves, tracked us, become wilder and more dangerous.

My immediate future looms suddenly and vividly real. Within a week a bear can be killed here. That bear might die atop the body of the horse I have just shot. Socks. The skinning of the bear will fall to me. I think that perhaps I might then cry. I promise myself to try. Cry while I twist and lever one dead thing away from the other. Cry while I strip the furred skin away from its flesh. I think of the rank smell, the maggots, the blood gone dark and thick. If it is a boar and the hunter knows the peculiar anatomies of animals, there will be the matter of the bone around which the bear's penis grows. Bear bone. Dick bone. Joke bone. The hunter will want that solid bone. I will knife the muscle away and scrape the thing clean. And then I will take the rolled hide up in my arms. The horses will shy in apprehension as I approach them. The hide will be heavier than it appears, and it will stink. A packhorse might snap its lead-rope and run wildly into the timber.

The hide will be made into a rug. The rug will be mounted against a wall. I have just killed a horse so that a man can display the hair of an animal in his den. We often receive pictures of a bear hide nailed to a wall. The hunter stands in front of the thing holding a drink, his legs wide, smiling, looking as though he will be called to dinner shortly. Sometimes his wife poses with him. I have often wondered what ultimately happens to those trophies. I imagine them older, dusty, lackluster, insect ridden, making their way to garage sales, or into trunks littered with mothballs. I imagine them as a gift to a favorite son. I imagine them as proof that a man came West and had an adventure.

In the years that my family has guided hunters we've killed two or three bears each spring, and again in the fall. No one has been mauled. The deck seems stacked. I flex my feet against the insteps of my wet boots. I have just killed a horse and my only punishment is cold feet.

My father has loaned me his copy of the Lewis and Clark journals. I have read that when they traveled through parts of Montana they flanked their party on both sides with several men who did nothing but kill bear who posed some threat. I look up again at Socks's brown body. I do not think that a bear will come here to harm me. I think that a bear will come to eat a dead horse. Because he is hungry. I do not think that he will brag about the thing to his sow. If he knows he is in jeopardy it will not excite him, make the meal more tantalizing. He will run. Or he will not show himself at all. I wonder about the bears who come and are killed. I think that their souls must be disappointed to be killed by a thing who does not even have a solid bone in its penis.

I run my thumb along the length of the rifle's barrel and think that there are boys who play baseball. Boys who ride bicycles, not horses. Boys who complain about having to mow a yard. I have a friend in town who watches a television show titled *Zorro*. He practices snapping a small whip and longs to own a sword.

In the magazines my father gets each month I've read that there are boys who do not go to school because they have none. Hundreds of thousands of boys who starve. Boys who beg. Boys who spend their days in prayer. I have traced the outlines of their countries with a finger, holding the atlas open on my lap. And I know that someday I will no longer be a boy. Someday I will be a man, perhaps with a son of my own.

I rewade the creek and sit on the bank and empty the water from my boots. Bird has settled and nickers as I approach. The day has warmed. Squirrels chatter. Raven-shadow occasionally blots the trail before us as we move home. It feels good to have something alive and warm beneath me. Bird's ears are pricked, his gait loose, he seems alert to every movement. He stops unexpectedly on the bridge over the Shoshone and stares down into the water. I strain to see if there is a moose, or otter, or fisherman. There is nothing. Only sunlight on water. I smile and feel ashamed that light makes me happy. I tap Bird's sides with my spurs, and he moves ahead. It takes us less than an hour to return to the corrals.

There is a note from my mother tacked to their cabin door telling me that she has had to help a friend who lives farther up the valley. That I will find enough in the refrigerator for a sandwich. That she loves me. I eat and then strip and soak in their tub, half napping. I dream that I run wild in a forest. It is a common dream. My feet grip the earth with certainty. The earth yearns for my touch, arches against me. I lie down upon the soil to feel its care for me, and imagine that I am recognized, that I am held dear. I think that I will fall in love with a girl who is raised on this same wilderness. I do not think I will fall in love with a girl from a city. And then I come fully awake and sit up in a tub of tepid water. I stare at a clock on the shelf by the sink. It is almost four. The yellows and golds in the pine walls catch and hold the afternoon light. It will be summer in six weeks and there will be water in all the cabins, and I will move into the bunkhouse with the older cowboys.

I'm in the tackshed oiling saddles when my father comes home. He has picked up my brother from school, and my brother runs ahead of him and stands shuffling in the doorway of the building. He carries his books and when he can think of nothing to say opens one and stares at the page as though he needs to find out what next to do. He is worried. He wonders if we have grown apart in a day. If I am less a boy, and he more alone.

"How was your report?" I ask him.

"It was great." He snaps the book shut and smiles. "Thompson's Labrador had pups."

"Did you see them?"

"No. Dad says we can go down this weekend. Pete says he's saving us the one that came out with the cord wrapped around its neck." Relief shows on his face. I am still his brother.

My father joins him in the doorway. They lean into its separate jambs and watch me work the neat's-foot into the leather.

"He tell you about the dog you're going to get?"

"This weekend."

We all nod.

"You got an early start this morning," my father says.

I look up from my work. "I'm not good at waiting," I say.

"I can understand that," he tells me. "I'm no good at it myself." He lights a cigarette, and we watch the smoke mute and slide in the last slanting light of the day.

GREYBULL

"How long's that going to take you?"

I lever myself out of one of the fifty-five-gallon oil drums we use to store grain and stand holding two filled coffee cans of oats. I have the last rotation of horses tied in the stalls, and these two cans are the last I have to deliver. A bay in the far stall whinnies.

My father stands in the barn's doorway. He wears laundered, pressed jeans and a silver-belly gray hat. The hat is free from sweatstain and horseshit. The hat's crown catches and holds the morning light. It is the hat he wears to town. His hands are clean. His thumbs are hooked in his pockets. His shirt blouses in a slight breeze. Its pearled snaps come bright and dull as he shifts his weight.

"I'm almost done," I tell him.

I walk into the stalls and squeeze between the hot, impatient bodies of the unfed pair. Their heads are turned together at the ends of their halterropes, their noses nearly meeting, their large dark skulls rising up like a pair of bodiless wings. My father steps into the granary. The horses' rhythmic chewing echoes off the low ceiling as would the sound of a troop of drunks staggering on gravel. Bars of sunlight leak through the weathered board and batten barnside and hatch the row of horse rumps. Grain dust and motes of powder-dry manure hang in illuminated scrims in the walkway behind the horses. A pair of slate-blue butterflies falter in and out of the blades of light. A horse snorts. Another coughs. The barn cats scrabble above us in the loft. A speckled roan spraddles onto the toes of his back hooves and pisses. The smell of hot urine spikes through the general scents of grain, animal sweat, the tang of pine needle and manure. It is the third summer I've wrangled horses for my father. I'm fifteen, and five-foot-three. I've been up since four. My body still vibrates from the twelve miles I've ridden gathering this bunch off night pasture.

"You had your breakfast?"

"Yes, sir."

"I thought I might go over to Greybull."

"What's in Greybull?"

"A horse sale."

I come back into the granary, drop the coffee cans in the half-filled barrel of grain, and slide the cover on. The horses stamp their feet against the thick board floor, and the sound echoes in the stalls, into the loft, against the tin roof, rebounding in weak resolution. They snort. They chew. They sneeze. Their tails work the air alive against an excitement of flies.

"I didn't know we needed horses."

"You didn't know you were going to grow hair under your arms either, but there you are." He lights a cigarette, snaps the wooden match in half, and flicks it back through the granary door. "I'm thinking the price might be right."

"How do you know what the price is going to be?"

"I won't unless I go. You want to come, or don't you?"

We've shipped our spring bear hunters off and don't expect the first group of summer tourists for a few days. The river is risen too muddy to fish. The banks are collapsed, the rapids choked with the commerce of timber torn away and turned downstream. The feeder streams, also too swollen with runoff to allow us very far into the mountains with a pack trip. There will be mostly day rides. I nod and look to the shifting horses in their stalls. "As soon as this is over," I say.

My father backs his pickup to a two-horse trailer. I straddle the tongue of the trailer and guide him back under the hitch. I lower the hitch onto the ball, plug in the brakewire, and drop the safety chain over the ball. I wipe my face dry of sweat with a shirttail and get in the cab. "I need anything?"

"Unless you learned how to play something musical I guess you don't. The radio's decided not to work."

"It hasn't worked in a year."

"This year?"

"Yes, sir."

"You're sure?"

"Since Ted winched the tree over the hood." We both look to the crease that folds diagonally across the truck's hood. The paint is flaked. The hood freckled with pocks of rust, the antennae snapped off into two inches of jagged stub.

"Funny what you forget to notice," my father says. "Damn shame neither one of us can carry a tune."

I hate the racket an empty trailer makes pulled over the ruts of a dirt road, like dragging some wheeled barrel ready to come apart at the staves. On the two-lane it whistles out behind us. I forget it's there, empty or full. If we return with the weight of a horse on its floor it will produce a sound solid and thrumming and primitively musical.

My father drives into the morning glare. The bug-splattered windshield spackles the light across our chests. The side windows are down. The treaded tires whine. "We don't get a lot of chances to be together," he says.

"We work together."

"When we work together I guess I'm your boss."

"What are you now?"

"I'm your father." He turns with a half smile. "Why don't you pay attention today and see if you can notice a difference?"

My father's shirt is unsnapped at the cuffs and fallen down his forearms. The mink-brown hair at the backs of his hands and wrists catches in the wind and morning light. I look to my wrists. Rub my palms against them. There is only a slight blond fuzz. He thumbs his hat back away from his face. "It's going to be hot today," he says. "Summer's finally got here."

"It's not like we didn't expect it."

"I guess it's not," he says and turns to have a look at me. I know that our faces appear alike: same jaw, same forehead, same eyes. I've seen photographs of him as a boy, and they look as I would look dressed in unfamiliar clothes. Our similarities have always surprised and unsettled us both. He turns back to the highway. I study the profile of his face. There are streaks of lighter skin at the corners of his eyes, where he has tightened his face, squinting into the day's work. His cheeks are smooth shaven and browned. He puckers his lips, sucks just once at the air, and rests his left arm through the windowframe. In another month the air will be choked with cottonwood fluff. It will drift against the crook of my father's arm. It will swirl in the cab as flakes of desiccated snow would swirl, but now the air is only sweetened with the specks of lesser pollen.

We break out of the forest and onto the straight drive through irrigated pastures toward Cody. The valley widens. Foothills rise in the aquamarine and grays of new sage growth beyond the alfalfa-green squares of cultivated land. When we reach the reservoir it is stained with an alluvium of mountain silt where the river enters it, smooth and struck silver and green in the sun and rising to our right as we weave along the ledge of highway, through the bare rock tunnels in the canyon.

Cody is busy with out-of-state license plates. I stare out the window at plump men in short pants and women in halter tops, shorts, their midriffs bare. They seem foreign. Sunstruck. Stunned by vacation. Their children follow in their parents' shadows. They are out of their element, all of them. When we stop for a light they stare with bland indifference. They seem to be people bred solely for utility: I think of them as bands of balded cattle. I feel predacious, superior, glad for work on the land.

East of Cody we have another hour to Greybull. It is still morning, but the air comes away from the highway in shuddering, translucent tubes of mirage. The drivers of the cars and trucks we meet lift a single index finger loose from their grip on the wheel in greeting. I've never seen a man wave with his whole arm unless trying to ward off a blow. At the horizon there is the darker rim of the Bighorns, their ridgeline churned in a froth of cumulus where the sky has ground into the mountain rock. There are smudges of bastard cloud fallen loose and ridden up and fading upon the vault of blue dome. The two-lane is straight and gray. Insects burst in patches of mustard and rust against the windshield. Fist-sized birds ride the airstream over hood, glass, and cab and die against the unexpected rise of the trailer we pull, producing the lonesome sound of a softened ball thrown against the side of a metal shed, randomly, again and again.

"You happy?" my father wants to know.

"I guess I'm as happy as I need to be." He's humming a series of single notes that he means to be a tune. "Does it matter?"

He shrugs. "It's just something that comes to mind when your radio's broken."

At the sides of the road there are alkali bluffs, struggling grassland, reefs of low-growing sage, the chalk-white soil lifted here and there into sudden blurred cones of dust devil.

"You ever been to an auction?"

"No, sir."

"You'll enjoy yourself. Kind of a picnic where everybody comes sober. You can get a soda if you're thirsty, I don't mean there's any food. Auctions make me happy even if I don't buy anything."

I nod and stare along a line of fence posts diminishing to the north in the rising crowd of sage. To the west of the fence there is a collection of raw-white Charolais bulls, mostly standing, several down to rest, one mounting another in sexual rehearsal. Their asses are shit stained. Their skins flex against the flies. They appear monumental in the sun. I think of pictures of Stonehenge I have seen. The bulls do not turn to look at us as we pass, as any scatter of broken dolmen would not turn.

"You don't have to worry about moving your arms."

I focus again on the side of my father's face. I tell him that I do not understand. I tell him I was not listening.

"You always hear about some dupe who waved to his wife or girlfriend or someone at an auction and the auctioneer took it for a bid. In the story it's always more than the man can pay."

"I never heard that."

"Well, now you have."

"I wasn't worried."

"I thought you might be. I didn't know."

The highway is crowned and the borrow ditches greened in weed from the advantage of the asphalt's slight runoff. The metal highway signs so shot full of holes they appear to be stencils of a language I haven't learned.

I put the heels of my boots against the glove box and slouch in the seat. I take off my cap and hook it over the toe of my right boot. Its bill catches in the wind. My head cools. The hair above my ears, and in a band across the back of my skull, dries stiffened with perspiration. "They just sell horses at this sale?" I ask. I realize that I don't know what to expect.

"Today's sale is mostly horses. Maybe a pen of sheep or two. I imagine some cows. A pig wouldn't surprise me."

I roll my head on the back of the seat to look to him, smiling. He looks away from the highway. Sweat has beaded on his forehead and across his upper lip. "That tickle you?" he asks.

"I have a picture in my head of getting a saddle on a pig. I don't see how the stirrups wouldn't drag on the ground."

"If I see one with withers I'll buy him for you. If he bucks you loose you won't have far of a fall."

We smile at one another. I tell him I think I'd look fine on a gaited sow. To our north a coulee breaks away in crumbling angles. Its wet bottom is spotted brown and white and black, strewn with several dozen Angus and Hereford cows and their calves.

In another mile the ashen soil is cut by a sluggish stream, and then a stack of beehives at the edge of an alfalfa field streaked with the darker greens of clover. The air smells sweet. I think of a spoonful of honey and swallow. There are cottonwood and Russian olive planted in rows for windbreaks. My eyes catch on the sharp, blockish bodies of green, yellow, and red farm equipment inching through the fields. As improbable as giant insects. Year-old stacks of weather-paled hay lean into collapse. There is a single trailer house. Several houses sided in pastel aluminum.

We don't slow down in Emblem. Population: ten. No street-lights. A building with a zip code. A roadside church. A half-dozen squat, galvanized grain silos, and more miles of irrigated farm-land, a strip of it, incongruous on this arid prairie.

A sign advertises Greybull twelve, and underneath, Basin nine-teen.

"I didn't think Basin could beat Greybull," my father says. He smiles. It is his standard joke. I return his smile because I am his son, and he expects it. "Probably had to go into extra innings," he says.

"I don't think I'd like to buy anything I might eat."

"You don't think you'd eat a horse? If you were hungry enough?"

"I'd have to be hungrier than I've been so far."

The Bighorns rise up out of their foothills as we come in under them. Their heights are pleated green in distant pine, broken with the paler green of meadow. I imagine the wildflowers I cannot see. The high depressions flash white with snowfield. Here and there the soil falls away as the last thrust of rock summits, rose and amber and flashing in the sunlight. Cloud-shadow dapples their western slope. I sit up straight and pull on my cap. A butte of blunted red sandstone breaks out of the poor and wind-scoured landscape in the middle distance. A jackrabbit lopes across the highway in front of us and sits hunched on the highway's shoulder, watching as my father slows the truck. The hare's ears fall back along his skull in our airstream.

The Greybull livestock building stands to the north of the high-way, glowing dully. Its corrugated tin sides shimmer in the heat. The building is two stories high, perhaps fifty by seventy feet, its shorter side to the highway. Several acres of pens and alleyways fall away to the west, presenting a labyrinthine puzzle of banded shadow and light. The pens are constructed of roughhewn lumber painted white, spiked up higher than the shoulders of a horse.

They appear stout enough to sort a herd of elephants. Beyond the pens run railroad tracks, and then a meat processing plant, and then the Greybull River hidden behind a flush of leafed trees, mostly olive and cottonwood.

The parking lot is gravel, rutted from a recent rain, grown up at the edges in tire-broken weeds. The pickups are mud splattered, most of them hitched to trailers, their grills and windshields uneven fields of smeared insect body. There is a row of stock trucks. A semi is backed to a loading chute. Half a dozen blond children play in the shade of a tree, taking turns roping an old roan-and-yellow dog. His eyes are glazed in cataract. His tongue lolls from his grayed muzzle. He does not duck the loop, they don't jerk out the slack. A pretty woman with red hair drawn into a ponytail sits on the tailgate of a truck. Her checked blouse falls open, and she nurses her child. She smiles. The round globe of her breast catches the sunlight. A line of men have climbed up on the pens and look out over the milling animals, pointing, smoking, laughing. There are the lows and grunts of cattle, the bleating of sheep, the sharp whinny of a horse. The ground quivers like a thick drumskin under the drubbing of hooves. The thrum of flies fills the air as would the echo of a distant siren. I climb up the side of a pen and sit on the top edge of the board. My father stands beside me, his elbows cocked shoulder-high, resting on the top board, his chin on the overlap of his hands. A man my father's age sits at my other side. His bootheels are hooked on the board under his ass, his knees splayed up level with his hips. He rests his elbows on his knees and nods into the pen. "You like him?" he asks.

"Yes, sir, I do."

In the pen is a single dun gelding. His mane and tail, muzzle, and stockings darkened as deeply brown as wet earth. So is the line that dissects his back, from his mane to the base of his tail. His ears are pricked. His face alive with intelligence. He's well muscled and put together like a cutter. His tail's been pulled short and works his hindquarters free of flies. A crow stands on his withers, turns and walks the length of his back, looking over the swell of his belly for a meal in the fresh manure. The ground and air are dotted with crows and red-winged blackbirds. They make a racket in their competition.

"Want to see him move?"

"I guess I would," I tell the man beside me.

He reaches into his shirt pocket and pinches out a small pebble, cocks his thumb behind a loop of index finger and loads the pebble like a boy would balance a marble. It catches the dun up high in the neck, and the animal spins on his hindfeet smoothly to his left, trots to the far side of the pen, and turns and faces us. He snorts. His ears vector to each of us, scanning for annoyance. The crow has lifted into the air, flapping, and settles again on the dun's back.

"Pretty, isn't he?" The man widens his knees and spits a slick stream of tobacco juice into the pen. He's unshaven, and his lower lip bulges over the wad of Copenhagen he's laid in against his lower teeth. He lifts his hat and smoothes a hand over his bald, white head.

In the background we hear the public address system remind us that no consignment is too large or too small to appreciate. I tell the man that I don't own a cat that moves as well as this horse. He nods. "You going to bid on him?"

"I don't know."

"He'd look good under you." I smile and admit that he might. The man spits again. "Course he'd look good under me, too."

In the air, above the insect buzz and static of bird argument, we hear the market report for lambs, breeding ewes, breeding bucks, slaughter ewes and bucks, goats large, goats small, weaner pigs, sows, boars. We hear yesterday's quotes for bred heifers, heiferettes, cutter cows, utility cows, steers, bulls, cutting bulls, horses light test.

"You ready to get out of the sun?"

I look down at my father. "Yes, sir," I tell him. I have another look at the dun and climb off the pen.

The entrance is built into a corrugated add-on at the building's west side. The screendoor is clotted with flies. They rise and fall, like a damp black cloth against the mesh as we enter. My father stands at the buyer's window, and I stand before a wall of ribbons and plaques presented for nearly every variety of prize animal. Two walled ramps rise into the building, and I follow my father up the one to our right.

The ramp opens halfway up a curving stack of bleacherseats built around three sides of the interior. They rise from the building's floor into the eaves. Before us, below us, at ground level, is a blockish half-mooned arena. Its floor curls up in fresh amber woodchips. The arena does not taper at the ends as a crescent would, more a bent alley of ground, opening through a gate at either end. Livestock is run in one side, out the other. We can look down into the auctioneer's bay. There is a window squared out of the east wall at the arena's concave side. Behind it a room-sized shed is built onto the main building, bracketed by the runways that feed and empty the arena. Inside there are two men seated over microphones and a woman standing behind them fingering through a sheaf of papers. She wears a sleeveless blouse, and her arms are muscled like a wrestler's. The air feels cool, damp. There is laughter and echo upon echo of swirled conversation. The seats and walls are painted white, the trimwork and supporting poles an inkpen blue. There are perhaps one hundred and fifty people spaced throughout the place, thickly along the rail. The colors of worn denim, faded corduroy, and work-stiffened canvas dominate. Shades of blue and brown everywhere. And the bright primary colors of chain-store shirtcloth.

There is a knee-high stack of carpet samples where we have come out into the seats. "For your ass," my father says, and takes one. I leave them for the older men. I figure my ass is fine. My father sidesteps to the middle of a row and sits. We are centered between floor and ceiling. There are five-gallon buckets spaced at the ends of every other row, half-filled with sand for butts and spit. A big man wearing bib overalls and no shirt enters at the end of our row and kicks the sand-bucket ahead of his steps. It skids to a stop short of my father's boot. A black-and-white border collie bitch follows at the man's heel. The bleacherseat squeals when the big man sits. The dog curls between his feet, tucking her nose under her tail. "Morning, Jesse," he says. My father nods. There are matted curls of gray-tipped hair cushioning the man's shoulders, grown up the back of his neck and down his arms. "What's got you out of the mountains?"

My father lights the man's cigarette and then his own. "Thought I might buy a horse."

The auctioneer repeats the prices for slaughter cows, high cutter and boning utility.

"There's some good ones coming through here today. Tom Holman's brought over some colts that know their business."

"Lost three to winter pasture."

"You looking for three?"

"Not all at once."

"That your boy?"

"One of them." My father introduces me to the big man and leans back so that I can shake his hand. His name is Evan. The dog's name is Grace. She raises her head when she hears her name and then settles. The man's hand is wet. Sweat drips on my father's thighs from his forearm where he reaches across. I smile and wipe my hand on my jeans and squint up into the lights. There are three broad-shaded floodlamps and a few banks of florescent tubing. The auctioneer tells us that domestic wool is trading active at steady to five-cent-higher prices. Some, bellies out untied. Mostly in poly pack bales. Some, skirted and classed in poly bales. Greasy fob.

On the wall to the sides and above the auctioneer's bay are advertisements for feed stores, banks, ag supplies, truck dealerships, meat processing. The bay is bordered with a single strand of Christmas lights.

A numbered lot of Angus bulls are brought through and sold. They're drowsy, dusty, their noses slick with snot. I think that Angus might be a good name. I whisper the sound of the word, and then my own name, and then Angus again. My father says, "What's that?"

"Nothing," I say and nod toward the bulls. He watches me. I search the crowd for someone I know. Most of the men are middle aged or older; there are a few young couples with kids younger than me. A little boy below us stretches out on the bleacher with his head in his mother's lap. The smell of men and animals, of sweat and shit and urine, of cigarette smoke and coffee, is strong as a meal brought hot from an oven. This big shed is warming. A single woman laughs like women laugh late at night coming out of bars. The general conversation rises in pockets of clatter, crests, recedes. The auctioneer barks through the PA system as though trying to rouse some retired marching band. The woman's laughter has settled to a girlish giggle. Her body jerks with an occasional hiccup.

The auctioneer tells us that compared to last Friday, slaughter cows are fully two dollars lower, the bulk of receipts for bred cows, and cow and calf pairs. Demand and buyer attendance good. Supply 15 percent slaughter cows, 5 percent feeder cows, 80 percent replacement cows. The little boy sits up and leans against his mother. She pours some coffee from a thermos and holds the cup while he takes a sip. A block of heifers sells low. The auctioneer pleads. The bald man who thumbed the stone into the dun's neck is propped against the entrance to the rampway. He nods. I nod back. He bends low to his right and spits into one of the white buckets.

"We'll have a horse sale right along with our regular sale every month from now on," says the auctioneer. He's a pale man with a black hat and a water-blue bandanna tied loosely at his throat. His face shines with sweat. He looks like the cowboys who work for us look the morning after a three-day drunk. He sips from a white mug and winces as he swallows and then leans into the microphone. Evan tells my father that he's a replacement auctioneer. "The regular guy let a bull kick him in the hip. He's staying home until he can walk without puking." There are two signs on the wall to the replacement auctioneer's right. The first reads: *All guarantees are between buyer and seller. We act as agents only.* The one below it: *Not responsible for accidents.*

A thin man rides the dun in through the gate. He bends down over the saddle horn to clear the overhang and then straightens in the saddle with his toes turned out. He keeps the palm of his right hand pressed against the horn and reins the dun in tight circles. The little horse moves as smoothly as water running down a drain. First to the left. Then to the right. The thin man does not look into the crowd. He keeps his chin tucked and his back straight and in the middle of the horse.

"Fifty dollars," says the auctioneer. "I have fifty, and five, now five, and sixty. There's sixty. Give me sixty-five."

The bald man nods. The woman with the boy and the thermos of coffee looks back, studying the crowd.

"You have money?" my father asks.

"Yes, sir."

"Let me see it."

I reach into my pocket and take out my savings. The money's rolled and snapped tight with a rubber band. My father's eyes widen in obvious appreciation. It's a big roll. "How much is there?"

"Eighty-nine dollars."

Evan leans forward. Grace is up with her chin on his knee. "Looks like a lot more," he says. Grace begins to pant.

"It's all in ones," I tell him. "Feels better in my pocket that way."

Evan nods and rests his hand on Grace's soft head. She rolls her eyes up the length of his arm.

"You want this horse?" my father asks.

"Yes, I do."

"Then I'd stick that wad back in my pocket and go to work if I were you."

"Sixty-five, sixty-five, I've got sixty-five," sings the auctioneer. "Who's going to give me seventy?"

I raise my hand, and the woman behind the auctioneer nods and taps him on the shoulder. "And five," he says. The bald man looks my way. The blue and red stripes in his shirt seem to pulse. Dust and cigarette smoke blur the ceiling. I take off my cap and wipe my forehead with the back of my sleeve. I wonder that the building has heated so quickly. The bald man puts one finger in the air.

"Seventy-five's in, and now eighty." The auctioneer is looking straight at the woman below me. The thin man is backing the dun, releasing him, backing him again. "Holman trained, Holman guaranteed. Five years old and firing on all cylinders. Where's my eighty?"

I raise my hand.

"There's eighty. Now five, five, five, where do I have eighty-five?" The woman shakes her head, "No." The bald man puts a finger in the air. "And ninety."

I bid the ninety, and the bald man takes it to ninety-five. He tongues out his wad of Copenhagen and spits it into the butt bucket and pinches in a new chew. He winks at me and lounges back against the rampway. He looks like he just got cleaned up for dinner. "One hundred, looking for a hundred, one hundred dollars," sings the auctioneer.

"Take it to the son of a bitch." My father leans in against me.

"Who?" I've forgotten he sits beside me. I look at him as though he is a stranger.

"That winking son of a bitch that can't come in and sit down."

"Where's my one hundred?"

I nod.

"And five."

The bald man smiles and bids.

"I've got the five. And ten. Is this a sound horse, Tom?"

The thin man nods and spurs the dun into a lunge and stops him in a skid.

"Now," my father whispers, and I raise my hand.

"There's my ten," sings the auctioneer. "And now fifteen. Who's got fifteen? Looking for fifteen."

The bald man bids. My father swings his leg against mine. I take it to one hundred and twenty before the auctioneer can make the offer.

"Twenty. Twenty. Twenty. Got twenty. Looking for twenty-five."

My father winks at the bald man. I wink, too.

Grace has climbed into Evan's lap. He strokes the length of her back, and when he grins the flex of his face seems to flare his ears. I look back for the bald man, but he's gone. I search the backs of the heads in front of the rampway looking for his hat.

"Twenty. Twenty. I'll take twenty-two and a half." The auctioneer looks to the woman with the kid, but she's pouring another cup of coffee. "Twenty-two and a half. Going. Twenty-two and half. Going." And he snaps his gavel and sings, "There's a one-hundred-and-twenty-dollar horse." The muscled-up woman points me out, and the auctioneer tells the crowd, "Sold to the boy in the blue-billed cap." The thin man looks up into the bleachers and nods.

My father stands, and when I don't he hooks me under the arm and lifts me to my feet and gives me a push. Evan sidesteps out behind us.

In the rampway I tell my father that I don't have the hundred and twenty dollars. I tell him the eighty-nine is all I have.

"I heard you the first time." He lights a cigarette. Evan drops Grace out of his arms, and she runs ahead as though she's looking for work. I take the wad of ones out of my pocket and hold it up as evidence. "I'll loan you the rest," he says, and asks Evan if he needs a ride to town.

"My rig's in the lot. I'm going home and take a nap."

At the buyer's window the woman smiles at my father as I count out my savings. The bills are damp and stained from being in my pocket for nine months. My father writes a check for thirty-one dollars and centers it crossways on the top of my stack of ones. The cashier shows me where to sign the bill of sale, and I fold the thing carefully and put it in my shirt pocket. I snap the pocket shut.

"How do you feel?" Evan asks.

"Lighter," I tell him, and he laughs.

My father backs the trailer to the south side of the pens where Tom Holman has unsaddled the dun. The horse stands slick with sweat and shines like a river rock. He's tied up short to a post. "There son, that's the man, there son," I say as I walk to his head, running my hand along his side. He feels electric. His body humming from the showring. I stand at his shoulder and move my hand down between his front legs. He lips the collar of my shirt.

"That's a good horse," says the thin man. "You treat him right and you two ought to get along fine."

"Yes, sir. Thank you."

"This boy rope?" he asks my father.

My father swings the trailergate open, and it flashes in the sun. "He throws a good horse loop in the corral. The only times I've seen him rope ahorseback was to catch the dog or his little brother."

"If he wants to learn, this gelding can teach him."

"You listening?" My father stands holding the gate open.

"Yes, sir."

The thin man looks down to me. A bead of sweat runs the ridge of his nose, and his sideburns are feathered damp. "This horse bucks once or twice in the spring. Usually to the left. If that's not all right I can take him back now."

"I'll watch for it," I tell him.

He nods and extends his hand. "My name's Tom Holman. In case you have a complaint." I shake his hand, and he turns and shoulders his saddle and walks away. I pull the halterrope free and walk the dun into the trailer and tie him off. When I step out my father swings the door shut, and a bull snake ropes straight up out of the pigweed and falls against the crests of spurge, moving fast.

"Goddamn," my father shouts. He's holding on to the trailer and jerking like a current runs through it. His face is caught between surprise and a smile. "I thought I was snakebit."

We watch the snake move away. He's big, more than four feet, brought liquid and bold in the heat.

My father smiles, but sucks at the air. "My legs got airborne before the rest of me. I feel like I jumped my knees through my lungs." And then, "Now would be a poor time to laugh."

We drive into Greybull and park along the curb at the A & W. My father gives me two one-dollar bills, and I go inside and order a malt and a fish sandwich and an extra container of tarter sauce for my fries.

When I'm back in the truck my father asks, "You want to eat here?" The dun stamps on the floorboards of the trailer.

I tell him that I've seen enough people today. He says he has too.

We stop at a bar in the center of town, and my father leaves the truck idling, his door standing ajar. I dip a fry into the tarter sauce and hold it against the roof of my mouth. The tang spreads until the hinges of my jaw feel like they might cramp. He slides back under the steering wheel and hands me a plastic cup of bourbon and water.

"Try not to spill that in your malt," he says and smiles. His hat is pushed back on his forehead.

I nod and balance the malt on one knee, his cup on the other, and he drives to the river and parks the truck. I set my lunch on the hood and step the dun out into the grass. We settle in the block of shade the trailer throws and watch the horse graze. He's careful not to step on his leadrope. My father sips his drink. He swirls the ice cubes against the sides of the cup.

"I'm raising you to five dollars a day." I look at my father to see if it's a new joke. He's turned his hat on its crown in his lap and leaned his head back against the trailer. His eyes are closed. I've been getting a dollar a day. A full-grown man is paid four hundred and fifty a month. He levels his head and looks at the river. "You're worth it," he says.

"I'll work harder," I tell him.

He turns to me. "If I wasn't satisfied I'd have fired you back down to just being my kid."

The dun snorts and kicks up at his belly with a hindfoot. I bite into my fish sandwich. The batter has come away from the fish and sticks to the bun.

"Course this all starts tomorrow. We're on vacation today." He takes another sip from his cup, swirls the ice, and leans his head back again. "I'll take what you owe me out of the raise. Lunch is my treat."

The dun folds his legs and rolls kicking at the sun. "Fifty dollars," I say, because that's what I've heard men say when a horse rolls: that a horse is worth fifty dollars every time he rolls.

He rolls again. "One hundred," my father says. The dun huffs and rolls once more and stands and shakes. "Looks like you got a bargain."

"Did you know the bald man?"

"The one bidding against you?"

"Yes, sir."

"Not before today. Why?"

"Just wondered. It's just something you think about when your radio's broken."

My father smiles and drags his sleeve across his forehead. The trailer ticks in the heat of the unclouded sun. "What are you going to call him?" he asks. He nods toward the horse.

"I was thinking, Mud. Or, Mouse."

"Because of his color?"

"Yes, sir."

"Either one'll work when you need to cuss him. Besides lighter, you feel any different?"

"I'm feeling bigger, I think. Like I'll wake up tomorrow and my clothes will be tight on me. Like I might have to buy new ones."

"I know how that feels." He stands. He holds his hat in his right hand. He tips back the last of his drink and scatters the ice by the trailer tire. He throws the empty cup in the bed of the truck and reseats his hat. "It won't happen overnight," he says.

The dun brings his head up just level with his chest and studies us, chewing, ears flicking, his eyes as dark as his forelock. I wonder what he sees. I wonder if he can hold us clearly in his mind, looking from glare into shadow.

JOHN AND JACK

"He's my partner," says John. He drapes an arm across my shoulders and glares at the dozen young men who lounge above us along the top rail of the corrals. They all wear chaps and spurs. Clean shirts. Their chaps are unbuckled from the bottoms, up to their knees, and sweep and flap in the sunstruck air. They rake the rails with their rowels, and dust sifts from their boot seams. Their initials or their families' brands are cut out of thicker leather, in red, gold, or green, and sewn to the wings of their plain brown chaps. Half of them wear a single leather glove, tacky and stained with resin, on their left hands. They're lean, older boys, all of them; easy in their bodies. Their hands, and the halves of their faces that shelve down and away from their hat brims, are weathered, darkened by the sun. Hair feathers over ears and shirt collars. Not one of them has a fresh cut. A black-headed boy lifts his hat, splays his fingers, and palms his hair back away from his eyes, reseating the hat before the hair falls forward, thick and disobedient as a crow's wing. Their eyes are clear and expectant. None of them is older than twenty-two. Only three have been out of Wyoming—on mere roadtrips to Montana and South Dakota.

John tightens his grip on my shoulders, holding me as a man would his favorite son. He spits to his empty side and thumbs his hat back from his face. The length of me could straighten completely and still pass under the pit of his arm. I'm short and stocky—compact. I've prayed for a burst of growth, but have no faith that cosmetic entreaties are honored. And neither my mother nor father is tall. That works against me.

I'm a year too young to compete in this rodeo. When feeling particularly insecure about my size I repeat what I've heard a short man say: "I'd be six-foot-eight, but I went to root." So far no one has asked me to prove the brag.

I'm fifteen, and John is in his middle forties. He's tall, and hook nosed, and clean shaven. He's a man thoroughly involved in his own livelihood; not jealous of the lives of other men. He sleeps soundly and works doggedly when awake. He knows horses, the good ones, the ones gone edgy and mean. He works horses with an easy confidence, the way a preacher works a congregation. He's a man as nearly capable drunk as when sober.

John and I share a bunkhouse and the same responsibilities each summer. When he drinks from a glass or cup, or is mounted and holding his bridle reins in his left hand, his left elbow juts out oddly and away from his body at a severe right angle; held nearly level with his shoulder. The first summer I lived with John I drank and rode in exactly the same way—with my elbow in the air. And then one night I watched him come out of the bathroom without a shirt and saw the fist-sized chunk of muscle gone from the back of his left arm. "The Second World War," he'd said when he caught me staring. I was too young to have gone to war. I lowered my elbow. That was four years ago. I am still too young. I hold my elbow naturally to my side but have not stopped watching John. I study his every move.

He calls me Little Man, and I consider it a vast compliment. He doesn't refer to me as a boy. He expects me to do the same work he does, and is patient enough to teach me what I do not know. I have much to learn.

I stand next to John and look past the older boys to the end of the corrals. Jack has come out of the parking lot and stands in the sun, where the corrals turn and angle toward the creek. He leans against the corner post. He is my friend, my age. He goes where he wants, does as he pleases. I think that if he'd choose to test the rules and ride a bareback horse he'd be allowed. I know that none of the older boys would try to stop him. I do not think the men would try. I smile at Jack. He nods back.

I look up at John and smile. He returns my smile. The expression involves his entire face. Everything makes him smile. Tying up the back leg of a horse who doesn't want to be shod makes him smile. Whiskey makes him smile. He smiles when he eats. Against a wind. He smiles in the darkness just before he falls to sleep. The mountains make him smile. I've never seen him lost or completely unhappy.

Today we're at this one-event rodeo the Rimrock Ranch stages on summer weekends. Bareback riding. A small rigging that crudely resembles a cocked suitcase handle is cinched to the bucking horses' withers. No hackamore. No halter. No saddle. Nothing to get tangled in and dragged. The rider simply hangs on to the rigging, lays back, and spurs the animal over the points of its shoulders as it tries to buck out of its flank strap. None of these horses or young riders will be featured on the cover of rodeo magazines. This is the bottom rung of the amateur ladder. Like an impromptu kitchen wrestling match. A classroom. A place to gain confidence.

I've ridden down the valley with John in his white Chevy. The big, heavy car takes the bends as though propelled by a sail, as though it rides on water. When I am in John's car I feel held away from threat; when I am with John I feel able, and that the world is dense with possibility.

John sips from a pint of Ancient Age and drives loosely, giving the car its head. "You sit a horse okay for a kid," he says. He means the statement to be reassuring.

"No one knows that," I tell him. I can't keep the whine out of my voice. It's generally agreed that a Rimrock contestant has to be at least sixteen. Plenty of our own horses buck and are unable to jar me loose. I imagine my chances to be as good as the older boys. In fact, I imagine I might win. I imagine that I might be the youngest boy to ever win. I sit rigid on the car seat, my body knotted from the disregard I believe I have suffered. "No one's going to know whether I ride worth a shit," I add. I turn and stare out the car's side window.

"*You* know you've got the good stuff," John says. He smiles and drinks from the bottle, replacing it between his legs. His elbow comes up high against the car's window when he drinks. He settles it on the armrest. "*I* know what you've got." He's trying to comfort me. I work up a tight smile, but it is as useless as a smear of fresh paint on an otherwise weathered building. I am raw with self-pity. John pops a wooden matchhead into flame with his thumbnail and lights a Pall Mall and cracks the window. He flicks the match out of the car. He works a flake of tobacco to the tip of his tongue and spits it toward the floorboard.

I flex my body against the seat, my arms against my sides, my feet hooked under the seat. I relax, and flex again. I can feel the blood flush into my face, and hands, and feet. I like the feeling. I know that I am strong for my size. I'm anxious to grow into the expanded strength of a man.

John coughs. "You're the only audience you're ever going to get," he says.

The road is cut through a thick stand of lodgepole pine, the sun high and ahead of us, the car full of quick, moth-sized shadows, skittering and strobelike. "I don't understand," I tell him. I watch the shadows in my lap, on my belly and arms. I really don't understand.

He sweeps his arm, the one holding the bottle, across the dash, indicating the landscape out the windshield. "Handsome day, isn't it?" I nod. "Goddamn right it is. And you're sitting there pouting over something you can't help. You understand that, don't you?"

"I guess I do."

"Feeling sorry for yourself and a quarter'll buy you a cup of coffee. Think about it." He takes another pull on the bottle and levels the car as we sweep out of a long curve.

I look up into the faces of the older boys. They're watching John. A few of them glance to me, wishing they were me, wishing

John had his arm around their shoulders. In half an hour they'll be bending over the chutes built into the far end of the Rimrock's corrals. They'll be laughing, helping cinch the bareback riggings tight, giving one another advice, seating their hats, nodding their rides out in front of the gathered dudes, pulling flank straps. "Fall back from this little bastard when he comes out," they'll advise. "The gray horse ducks under himself to the left." "Keep your toes turned out." "That tall blond-haired girl's smiling at you, Hank," one of the boys will tease. "Try to act like you know what you're doing. Keep your thumb out of your ass." But right now they're watching John and me; I'm the entertainment. A few of the bolder dude girls have eased into earshot. I've miraculously forgotten that I won't be riding a bareback horse.

John squeezes me tighter, beaming. Everyone's excited and mostly sober. Some of the more timid girls have come up behind us, giggling. I turn and smile. John clears his throat. "Little Man here and me, we're going to pool our resources and go into business together," he says. I have no idea what he's talking about, but swell at the thought of being included in his plans. I try to imagine the business we might start. I have seven dollars in my pocket. It represents my entire savings. John drives the eight-year-old Chevy, sleeps in the bunkhouse, and takes all of his meals at the lodge. He owns his own tack and a duffel stuffed with clothes that outfit him through all four seasons. His only extravagance is the thirty white shirts he keeps starched and folded into a box in the trunk of his car. The shirts are in case he gets a bartending job in the winter. He prefers winter bartending over winter cowboying. The shirts are also for the time when he owns a bar. It's his dream. I know I'm too young to be useful in a bar.

"We're going to open a whorehouse," he announces. He says it loud enough for everyone to hear. I look up at him. He doesn't look like he's kidding. He holds his eyes wide. "Think of it," he demands. There is real urgency in his voice. Everyone thinks of it. Images come clear in their minds. Several boys fidget uncomfortably on the rail, raise their eyebrows, look sideways to the dude girls to see if anyone's shocked. My smile takes over like a bucking horse. I can't control it. If I smile any broader I'm afraid my eyes will be kicked shut, that I might damage my face. There's a lot I'm too young for, but apparently opening a brothel with one of the best cowboys in the valley is not one of them.

I look toward Jack. His arms are folded across his chest. I cannot see his face. He is staring down at his boots.

John shuffles a bit. There is a hint of apology in his voice when he speaks. "We're slightly shy on assets though," he says. He pushes the brim of his hat back farther from his face. He looks down at me and winks, but the older boys don't see it. When he shows them his face he's all serious, concerned. He clears his throat. "That's why Little Man's agreed to do some fancy hand-work until we get enough saved to have his teeth pulled."

The older boys bob at their waists in laughter. One of the boys has fallen backward from the rail. The bold girls laugh too, the timid ones ease away, whispering, confused, trying to sort out the chain of events that will lead to our capitalization. John squeezes my shoulder harder, but it only feels like pressure, like a dentist digging at a tooth after your mouth's gone numb from the anesthetic. I shrug out from under his grip and walk as fast as I can toward the creek, toward the shelter of the trees that border the creek. I won't give any of them the pleasure of seeing me run. I'm sweating, and I step out with each foot unsurely. It feels as though I'm reaching for a next stair that isn't there. Every thought has drained into my blood, become red, and hot, and fallen to the simplicity of muscle. I suck my cheeks in between my teeth and bite down hard. The prettiest girl here was bent over laughing, gripping her knees. Laughing at me. I hate being a boy.

I weave my way down one side of the creek, unspooling through the strew of boulders, cottonwood, downed timber, juniper, pine, and sage. I walk a quarter mile before my embarrassment is paid out and I am back in the world, aware of my breath, separated from the clenching and unclenching of my heart. I blink hard against the sunlight. The world seems to have come unusually sharp with color.

I back against a large cottonwood and slide down until I'm sit-

ting, leaning against its gray and rutted bark. I stretch my feet toward the creek and close my eyes. I think I might lie down and
sleep; I feel that suddenly sapped of vitality. There is the slap and
suck of the creek. That is what I hear. And there is the smell of cottonwood. The smell of the water-glutted trees is so strong that I
open my eyes and look behind me, thinking my mother is there,
and then remember that she never comes to rodeos. The trees' odor
is that sharp: the odor of a woman who has worked out in the sun,
her hands in her garden. The smell is a mixture of earth, sweat,
sun, soil. I look to my sides. I am alone. There is a bonnet of cooler
air that the cottonwood's leaves have protected, and held, and excited. It falls to the water, closely jacketing the trunk, covering me
like a damp cowl. I close my eyes again.

I think of the story John has told me about his parents. He has
said that his parents got caught away from their cabin in a blizzard
and froze to death when he was ten. That is the story he tells. He's
told me he wrapped himself in their bedding. He says he was too
confused and numb to keep the fire going. He's told me he could
hear his mother singing to him that night, that he felt her hands
on him, her touch like ice. He has sat on his bunk and curled himself over his knees, whispering, and told me that her breath froze
against his face and made it impossible to open his eyes. He's told
me he wasn't frightened. A neighbor found him the next morning,
snowshoed out with him held bundled high against his chest,
thawed him, raised him. "It's a hard story to hold in my mind,"
John has told me. "Like a dream is hard to hold. I'm only telling
you so I won't forget it altogether."

A cowboy who's worked with John has told me about John in the
Second World War. The man has gone over the details about the
wound that keeps John's left arm held high, and a story about
John's wife running off with another man. He's said that John's
wife took their infant son to be raised by a stranger, her new lover.
These are not stories I hear from John. I think the parts of his life
that he doesn't put into stories wash vague in his memory, become
finally forgettable. I think he cares mostly for the memories that
help him smile.

I smile. I think I should have seen the joke coming. I think that if I were older I would have. I decide not to care about the older boys. When I am sixteen I will win first-place money. The pretty dude girl will go back to some place in the East and have nothing but a story she will whisper to her friends. No one had a camera. That is what I think. That is what I will remember. This may not even be a story I ever tell.

"That's not the funniest thing I've ever seen." Jack sits beside me. I have not heard his approach. He's come down the creek with the noise of the water. He pulls his knees into his chest, wraps his arms around them, and stares at the channel of white and steel-blue water shifting over stone.

Jack is my height, but outweighs me by forty pounds. He is as lean and muscled as some sea mammal. I have seen pictures of dolphins. Jack reminds me of a dolphin. There is no fat on him. There is no part of his body that he does not use. His legs are so stout, so striated with muscle that he has to buy jeans with a thirty-six-inch waist to fit over his calves and thighs. His mother takes in their waist by six inches. His forearms are as thick as my neck. He is a boy of such vigor and confidence that when he moves from one place to another, men and women turn and stare. I've watched them. I've watched people lose themselves watching Jack cross a street. His body and his innocence are his gifts.

"What's the funniest thing you've ever seen?" I ask.

"Last summer when you squinted up through the slats in the hay loft floor and the pack rat pissed in your eye." Jack wears a ballcap and a clean white T-shirt. His eyes are brown.

"You thought that was funny?"

He grins, still staring at the creek, hugging his knees, and nods. "I wake up at night and laugh about it. I can't believe you let a rat piss in your eye."

He nudges me with a shoulder. He squints up into the whorl of swirling cottonwood shadow above us, as though he hears rodents there, in a loft. We laugh.

Jack opens two beers from a six-pack at his side and wedges the other four behind a rock in the creek. We each take a sip. The beer is warm and sour and weedy as a bog. Jack squats on his haunches, gouging at the soft, moist soil with a stick. "You don't have to take that shit," he says. He turns to me, serious now, the stick driven into the ground like some boundary stake.

"What shit?"

"Being made a joke of. That's what shit."

I think that Jack is waiting a year to ride bucking horses so that we will both be old enough together. I look to the creek. "It was just a joke," I tell him.

"Tell that to the bunch of needle-dicks rolling on the ground laughing. I don't think something's funny unless everybody's laughing."

"John was just having fun. He didn't mean anything by it."

"They weren't laughing at him, were they?"

I feel again the limits of being a boy. It seems like an apprenticeship that will never end. John is the man I want to become; Jack is the boy I want to be now.

On a bet I've watched Jack walk the length of a football field on his hands. I've watched him stand in the lodge kitchen, place a dime between his boots, spring into a tight backflip and land again, each foot exactly to the sides of the dime. When boys from other towns arrive in Cody to go to school they fall under Jack's protection. They are invariably boys with thin arms, thick glasses, and clothes that their older brothers have worn threadbare: boys who do not fit. It does not matter. Their first friend is Jack. His friendship gives them time to settle unharmed.

Jack takes off his cap and circles his hand on the top of his head. Earlier in the summer—on a wager orchestrated by the older boys—I shaved Jack's head. Smooth as a river stone. He immediately looked thirty. His voice seemed to drop an octave. We borrowed John's car and drove to a roadside bar in a town where we knew no one. Jack walked into the bar like he was just thirsty. He ordered a case of Coors and a fifth of Southern Comfort, paid for them, and walked out unchallenged. It was a bar we'd tried in the past with no success. I keep his head shaved. Jack doesn't want to be a boy either.

We drove out on a dirt road north of Cody. We parked by the twenty-foot-high C loosely cobbled against the side of a hill with whitewashed stones. It's been put there so that airplanes can identify the small Wyoming town below them. We left all the car doors open with the radio tuned to a rock station. We drank and reeled in the sage. We closed our eyes and weaved separately against the wobble we felt in the earth, and then Jack vomited. I've seen plenty of men do the same. I never vomit. I've tried to make myself vomit but can't pull it off. John says it gets the poison out of your system if you're able to get sick. I always feel worse than Jack the next day.

I fell asleep across the car's backseat, and Jack curled in a depression on the downwind side of a knot of sage. When we woke the moon was set. We stood in the dark and pissed and stared at the pattern of streetlights across the river in Cody, and then up into the scatter of stars. We were dry-mouthed and quiet. The radio was off. We opened fresh beers and drove upriver to our summer jobs. Jack wrangles horses at Shoshone Lodge, five miles closer to the wildness of Yellowstone than my parents' place. When we went through Cody we saw a cop parked west of town, past the Dairy Queen, asleep in his car. We smiled and tipped up our cans and drank. We felt invisible to rules.

There are some nights each summer when the loneliness of not quite being a man wells up and makes sleep impossible. I dress in the dark and slip out of the bunkhouse. John has never asked me where I go. I saddle the flighty colt I've kept in to wrangle on and ride in the dark to an opening in the timber halfway between Shoshone and Holm Lodge. Sometimes Jack is there. We share cigarettes and sit alone in the night smoking, waiting for dawn and another day of activity. We talk about having our own horses, what we will do when we are out of school. We talk about pussy. Sometimes Jack is not there, and I sit in the dark. Sometimes I talk to myself.

Jack leans forward and plucks a small green stone from the water. He rubs it dry with the pad of his thumb. The stone dulls in the air. His hand drips and glistens like a fist of quartz. I breathe in deeply and slacken another notch into relaxation. The air is still cool next to the tree.

He turns to me, his hand open, holding the flat green stone. He searches my face the way I've seen him search the night when we have been out and heard the coughs, huffing, the shuffle of pads and claws as some large predator passed. I smile. He nods and lowers his eyes. He skips the stone into the water and laces his fingers together around his knees.

A mosquito lands on his forearm, working her legs against his skin. When she bites, Jack flexes his arm, the muscles gripping, and holding the little insect's proboscis. We watch as the hair-thin bug swells with blood, unable to release, finally exploding in a tiny blossom of red. Jack licks a thumb and wipes away the blood and insect parts. He leans forward, pulls two beers from the creek, and hands me one. We listen to the water.

Out on the slope of sage to the east, three small puffs of cloud cast shadows as dark as ponds. The rest of the landscape seems smacked solid in the heat.

Earlier in the summer we'd hitchhiked to a party in Yellowstone Park, along the Firehole River. John has told us that if he could pitch a tent to cover the park he'd have the biggest bedroom in the world. The girls outnumber the boys by ten to one.

We're the youngest at the party by four or five years, and conspicuous—most of the young men and women are from big midwestern and eastern colleges, come west for the adventure of a summer job in the mountains. They clean the cabins and hotel rooms in the park. They empty garbage cans, clerk in the gift shops. This night along a wild river is part of their vacation.

We stay at the edge of their conversation and laughter, and walk into the forest when we have to piss, far enough away that their voices sound only like a slide of brittle stones. We stand in the shadows, away from the bonfire. We drink cautiously, aware that we are out of place. We are careful to become the last two drunk. We hope that by the middle of the night we will look older, perhaps exotic. We have come because we are boys, and the girls outnumber us ten to one.

It is not even midnight when a large blond boy walks to us. He struggles to maintain his swagger in the soft, uneven duff. He is a handsome boy. He wears a University of Michigan sweatshirt. I guess that he plays first-string football. I guess his major does not require him to learn a foreign language. He is six inches taller and fifty pounds heavier than Jack. "Having a good time?" he asks. He is filled with keg beer. The mountain air and press of girls have swollen him.

"Sure," says Jack. He smiles and glances behind the boy. He is choreographing the fight. He pictures himself against three or four pairs of fists. The blond boy has no idea he is already a broken thing. I take a step to the side and drop my beer. I scan the knot of gathering boys, looking for where there is trouble and where there is none. These are big boys. Even if they are drunk and clumsy and slow, if I am careless I will go to the hospital. I know that Jack does not like to fight, but that in a fight he is sudden and precise. I know he won't run.

"I hear you're stout." The boy's arms hang stupidly at his sides. I cannot believe how little he considers his knees, or groin, or throat. I wish we had not come.

"My friend's had a rat piss in his eye." Jack makes the statement flatly. The girls, and a few of the boys with some sense of irony, snicker. Jack looks to me and grins. His eyes flicker to a darker boy who stands to the left and slightly behind the blond boy. The darker boy is edgy, standing sideways, offering little of himself. I nod.

The blond boy snorts. "Is that supposed to be funny?" he asks.

"It's supposed to be a fact. Like me being stout." Jack bends at his knees without taking his eyes from the bigger boy and sets his cup of beer on the ground. I take a step away to flank the darker boy. He and Jack are the only two to notice.

"I can kick your ass."

"That hasn't happened yet," says Jack, but quietly, slowly. It's obvious that he's not boasting. He turns up the bill on his cap so that he can meet the bigger boy's eyes. He smiles. A smile completely without threat. He just smiles, appearing silly under the green crescent of the turned-up bill.

The bigger boy glances back to his friends and snorts. His girlfriend moves a step toward him. She seems uneasy. She looks toward where I stand. She whispers her boyfriend's name, but he has turned back to Jack. "You don't think you can get your ass whipped?"

"I just said it hasn't happened yet." Jack allows this as though it truly puzzles him. And then he unexpectedly asks the boy, "How much do you weigh?"

The boy hesitates, perhaps worried that he might be inaccurate. I think only his mother and coach have asked him the question. "Two hundred and twenty," he says.

"Then you don't want to do this."

"Do what?"

"Fight."

"Why wouldn't I?"

"Because it won't be what you expect." Jack has made the statement with the firmness of a man. I don't think he is repeating something he's heard. I think he is honestly telling us all that the world is littered with surprise. The blond boy's girlfriend touches his arm, and he turns to her; when he turns back, Jack is lying on the ground in front of him. Jack grins up into their faces. "Step in my hands," he says. He holds each hand, palms up on the ground, his thumbs pressed to the outside of each shoulder.

The blond boy laughs. "You're a crazy little bastard," he says. Already something has happened that he did not expect.

"Just step on my hands. You've got the rest of the night to kick my ass."

Because the request is made without threat, and because the crowd has pressed forward with interest, the blond boy steps onto Jack's palms. "Now what?" he asks.

"It'd probably help if someone stands to the side and steadies you."

The blond boy laughs. "Who do you think you are? Mighty

Mouse?" The other boys laugh, and the dark boy steps up beside his friend. They have become curious. They're athletes and know the impossibility of pressing more than two hundred pounds of live and unsteady weight into the air. They know that arms pinned to the ground, with only the muscles of the chest to bring them forward, are useless. And then the blond boy rises. The darker boy steadies him. Six times, up and down. The last time held up, Jack's arms at full extension. Jack lowers him carefully, and the boy steps off Jack's hands, and Jack stands as though the ground has pushed him to his feet. He has brought his cup of beer with him. He takes a sip.

The older boys step back. Their girlfriends move closer to them. The big boy is embarrassed. "You're an asshole," he says.

"You're just weight."

The blond boy furrows his brow. "What?"

"Weight." And Jack drops him like he is just that, weight, with one single punch to the middle of his chest that no one even sees. The boy's air and consciousness leave him at the same time. We both square off to the darker boy, expecting him and the others to charge. But they don't. The big boy's girlfriend steps forward and hands Jack another cup of beer. She says, "Thank you for not hurting him." Jack nods. The darker boy nods. The girl kisses Jack on the cheek. We are all just drunk kids in the dark in a wilderness. I think that Jack was the only one who knew that the fun could stop.

A red-headed boy pours his beer on the ground and asks if we need a ride to the east entrance. We tell him that we do. He wears a tie-dyed T-shirt, his hair drawn into a ponytail. He lives in Cody. I've met his younger brother.

He backs his pickup to the fire, and his girlfriend gets into the cab. Jack and I climb over the tailgate, and sit against the cab, finally lying down on the metal bed to watch the shifting stamp of stars against the night sky. It's an hour's drive. We pound on the top of the cab when only a few miles into the national forest, and he drops us by the side of the road.

"I wouldn't have been much help," he says. "There were too many of them." We shake his hand and thank him for the ride.

We walk in from the highway to the bunkhouse where Jack sleeps. It is only two in the morning. We don't have to gather horses until four. We've collected fresh bottles of beer from a pool in the creek and sit at a wooden table playing cribbage. Fifteen two, fifteen four, and a pair is six.

"Thanks for backing me up."

"I didn't do anything," I tell him.

"You were ready to. I wasn't there alone."

Jack takes off his shirt. The front of his right shoulder is swollen and purple, black and yellow. "Something gave," he says. It looks like some bright snake is coiled under his taut, white skin.

"When you hit him?"

"When I lifted him." He moves his cribbage peg and holds his beer can against his shoulder. I shuffle the cards. "I thought I might have to stop," he says.

"But you didn't." I deal the cards.

"But I thought I might." He slides his forearm across the table until it presses against mine. Each of our wrists are notched against the other's elbow. He blows on the tip of his cigarette. The paper and tobacco flare. He rolls his arm slightly away from mine, making enough space to stand the cigarette on its filter between our arms, and rolls his forearm back against mine. "So we'll remember," he says. We fan our cards open with our free hands and play. The smell of burning flesh rises above the lamplight. Neither of us looks. The pain is not as sharp as I think it will be.

✸ I STAND up into the shade of the cottonwood and flex my shoulders. I extend a hand to Jack and pull him to his feet. When we come out on the road by the corrals John is waiting for us. He sits on the trunk of his Chevy with his bootheels hooked on the bumper, sipping from the pint of Ancient Age. His is the only car that's left. Two mounted men are moving the small bunch of bucking horses up a ridge away from the corrals.

"Your ride's left you," he says to Jack. "If you want you can pile in with Little Man and me."

Jack looks up into the belly of eggshell-colored cloud, and back down to the toes of his boots. "If you've got the room."

John slides onto his feet and starts for the car's door. "Got room up the wazoo," he says.

Jack gets in the backseat.

When we turn off the dirt road onto the paved two-lane, John asks, "You drunk?" He doesn't look at either one of us. He's watching for traffic.

"No, sir," I say.

"Not yet," Jack says. He's laid out on the backseat with his heels resting on the sill of a back window. He holds his cap on his chest. His chin is tucked in, and he's sighting the landscape through the splayed toes of his boots.

John reaches into the backseat without taking his eyes off the road and hands Jack the pint of whiskey. He hums a tune that seems to be the single phrase of a melody. The radio hasn't worked since we borrowed the car and played the rock station all night. Jack sits up and hands the bottle to me, over my shoulder. I take a sip and wish for music. I wonder what it takes to fix a car radio. The radio in my father's truck has been broken for years. My brother used to joke that we lived so far up on the forest that we only got yesterday's programming.

"Talked to Glen at the Rimrock," says John. I hand him the bottle. "He says he's anxious to have you two try out a bareback horse next Sunday. He says he's got a pair of snakes that are likely to toss your bony young butts on the ground."

I look into the backseat. Jack has put his cap over his eyes. "What do you think?" asks John. "Think you might, or are you going to let me down?" He looks at me, and then into the rearview mirror.

"Next Sunday would be fine," I tell him.

"Fine by me, too," says Jack.

"Then it's settled." John brings the bottle to his lips and his left elbow rises up against his side window.

That evening John and I run the horses up the valley, leaving them to settle, fan, and fill their bellies in the dark. We ride side by side on a logging road back to the corrals. It's been a long day. We've run out of conversation. In the last sodden light of the evening I watch his face relax under the brim of his hat. He looks tired. He knows I am watching him. He whistles through his teeth—just a tune to accompany the footfalls of our horses, the creak of our saddles.

Someday I will be as old as John. I wonder if he's seen any part of his life approaching. I don't know how to ask him. I wonder how much of his past he remembers. I wonder if he heard the bullet before it tore the back of his arm away. If he was really saved by a man on snowshoes who took him in. I wonder if he remembers the scent of his wife. If it makes any difference.

I try to remember the way I was when I was two, or four, or six, or twelve. I can only see the boy I have been told about. I think that it is possible for me to remember who I am only when I hold myself against the way my family sees me, and John and Jack. I know who I am with horses, but I do not know how they see me. I think that I am complete only in my dreams. I remember my dreams. I vow to always remember my dreams.

I look to John. It is darker. There is just his silhouette. I picture my dreams as a line of silhouettes. I picture my dreams as a line of ghosts. I cannot see their faces, but I feel their eyes are on me. I feel them smile. I watch them nod their heads together and imagine they gossip about the man I will become.

I close my eyes and move with the rhythm of my horse. I hear whispering. The whispers tell me stories. I see Jack working as a lineman, leaning away from the top of an Alaskan power pole. I see myself driving to the Billings airport, to pick him up when he returns home for his father's funeral. I daydream John as an old man tending bar in the VFW. I can see him clearly with my eyes closed. He does not recognize me. I'm grown. I drink only soda water, occasionally a shot of bourbon. The room smells acrid. The air is hazy with smoke, humid from the pool of spilled draft beer on the floor behind the bar.

In the dream John wears a starched white shirt, as white as new snow. As white as the blizzard in which his parents died. I wonder if he still feels his mother's hands and breath on his face. Hears her singing. He's hatless. His hair is thinning and gray, streaked as white as the shirt. His face is gray. He's not whistling, but he smiles. His eyes are distant, as though skimmed with ice. He does not tell me, but I know that his last wife fell asleep with a lighted cigarette and burned their trailer and herself to the ground. I can see it in the way he holds his arm when he serves the customers.

"You asleep?"

I open my eyes. It is dark. I know John still rides beside me only because of the sounds of his horse, the bare gather of light in his hat, and off his teeth. He's smiling. "No, sir," I tell him.

"Dreaming about riding bucking horses?"

"I was," I tell him. It doesn't seem to be a complete lie.

"Usually better than the actual ride itself," he says. "Sometimes you fall off hard. Sometimes it happens even when it shouldn't. You just don't see it coming."

I nod, but I think it is too dark for him to see me. There is a new moon. I feel warm, in the right place at the right time.

The horses stop at the corrals and bob their heads to pull some slack in the reins.

"I think I'll ride upriver," I tell him.

"Say 'hello' for me."

"I will."

"You have anything you want to talk to me about?"

"I guess I don't."

"Good night, then."

I ride to the clearing in the forest. I sit at its center and stare into the black vault of the sky. There are high clouds and smeared patches of Milky Way come vaguely opalescent in the cloudgaps. My horse grazes beside me. The smell of broken grass and pine is strong.

It is an hour before I hear Jack's horse in the timber. He stops the horse beside me and steps down and sits. He lights a cigarette and hands me the pack. "Do you think you'd ride a bucking horse next week?"

"I think I would," I tell him. "What about you?"

"I think we'd probably win first and second money," he says and describes a circle in the black air with the tip of his cigarette. It's too dark to tell, but I think both of us nod. I hear his neck move against the upturned collar of his jacket.

"John says 'hi.'"

"'Hi' him back."

My horse sparks a shoe against a rock. We both turn to the sound. And then simply, perfectly, without announcement or explanation Jack starts to sing "The Ballad of Pecos Bill." It is the only song he knows by heart. He sings every verse. It is a song about an orphaned boy raised alone by wild animals.

TOMMY TWO

The boards are pine and fir, and rough cut. Their irregular widths are fitted together to form a floor made smooth and gray as soapstone by sixty years of scuffling boot leather. The floor is worn down in troughs—from front door to stove, from front door to toilet—and still, at its thinnest measures three solid inches of lumber, spiked to joists as thick as men's necks. There is no give. The paper-thin cracks between the boards have silted tight with granules of soil, sand, ash, and manure. The mixture has sifted in, swollen with the frosts, sifted again, swollen again, bound itself into the wood's grain as mortar would.

The interior, walls and ceiling, are tongue-and-grooved fir. They once received a single coat of shellac. The varnish is worn back to the raw wood in banks of smudged shadow above the beds. It's peeling in fragile golden leaf-shapes—orbicular and reniform—the entire lengths of the corners, from floor to ceiling, and along the baseboards. There are shelves, two chests of drawers. Underneath each shelf there is a two-inch dowel for hanging clothes. There is one set of bunk beds and two twins. Three wooden chairs act primarily as nightstands. There is a sprung easy chair pulled to the wall by the stove. Its position is exact: an inch closer to the stove and it would ignite. It absorbs and throws off heat as though it were a fifth tenant. Its skirt retains a hint of the bloodred and purple-paisley pattern its fabric once held, but the arms are worn to the frame, and its back and seat are patched with canvas.

Sometimes, in the evenings, a man will sit in the chair, pull off his boots, line them with the other boots at the back of the stove, and ease into the hot canvas and fall asleep. It is my job to make sure that the only thing in the cabin on fire is the stove. I get up and pinch the lighted cigarette from the sleeping man's hand. I jack open the lid on the stove and drop the butt in. I take a blanket from the man's bed and cover him. If he wakes in the night he will stand, wrap himself in the blanket and curl on his bed. It has happened that way dozens of times.

This is a one-room cabin for exhausted men. I live here in the summers with the older cowboys. We sleep and bathe here. Our work is done outdoors. On occasion a man will stay in all day, but he will be sick, or badly hurt and too stubborn for a trip to the hospital. If he is strong enough, and the day is mild, he will get up and open the door so he can watch the sun on the pines and sage. He will not want a door between himself and the sound of Libby Creek shifting on her bed of ordinary stones.

There are two windows of six handblown panes in the sleeping room, a smaller four-pane arrangement in the bathroom. The bathroom window is hinged at the top and can be wedged and held open with the pine stob we keep standing in a corner. There is no screen. All of the windowpanes are imperfectly blown, lumpy, swirling with prisms of light when sunstruck, gauzy in shadow, casting distorted sideshow reflections in the night. The door is made of six vertical planks with a wooden latch that falls into a wooden hook. To enter from the outside we pull a leather thong that lifts the latch and the door swings open.

In the bathroom there is a cold-water pipe that comes to the sink, shower, and toilet. The bathroom is one step up from the rest, added on, and sports a flowered linoleum floor. I have wondered about the linoleum. It is only a couple of years old. I think it was laid because of the imperfect men who have lived here. The linoleum has sunk in spots, and I imagine the wood floor underneath it piss stained and rotted. There is a mottled mirror over the sink, and over that a naked forty-watt bulb. No one spends longer in the bathroom than he has to. Gordon and John sit on their beds to brush their teeth and walk outside to spit off the porch.

There are no curtains. No plants. There is a calendar advertising a saddle and tack shop. Our sheets are changed every two weeks and the bathroom fixtures scoured, the linoleum mopped. I keep the main floor swept, and because I prefer clear smears of rainbow, the windows washed. And I am always the last to sleep. I lie in the dark, listening to the stove tick, the wind in the flue, the creek, the sounds of sleeping men. I know their coughs and groans. When they mutter and moan in their sleep I know if their dreams soothe, or if they frighten. If a man gets up in the night I can distinguish the whisper of his bare soles on the floor, one man from the other, with my eyes still closed. This is my home. I have no concerns in a broader world.

In the mornings I swing my feet into the dark chill of the cabin and onto the grain of the wood floor. I sit on the edge of my mattress and reach to the seat of a straight-backed chair pulled to the head of my bed. I take up the shot of cheap whiskey left on its seat for me, swallow without thought, swallow because I have done so since I was fifteen. It is the initial step in my morning's regimen. The whiskey thrashes to my stomach like a drowning wasp. Every morning the whiskey makes me grimace, makes my eyes water; brings me awake with fire. I am sixteen. It is several years before I learn that all boys are not treated to a pubescent eye-opener of sour mash. I am allowed the bottom bunk because I start the morning fire in the potbellied stove.

I squat in the dark with my toes on the big square of tin slid under the stove, my armpits hooked over my kneecaps, and feel for the kindling, the box of wooden matches. I open the stove and stir at the ash with a stick of kindling, digging for coals. We burn softwood, and there are rarely coals unless John or Gordon has stayed up late reading or drinking by the fire and tending it. But that is not usual.

Every night I feather half a dozen pieces of kindling with a long, useless knife nearly the size of a machete. Phil bought the thing in Nogales, Mexico, last winter from a woman he thought beautiful. When I shave back the sides of the kindling, so that they bristle in curved strips no thicker than a match, I wonder what the woman must have looked like. I imagine her eyes and smile bright as flame.

In the mornings I light the first piece of kindling, turning it in my hand until it has caught all the way around. I do not need paper or kerosene to start a fire. I make a small heap of the feathered sticks and dried pine cones in the stove and sit in the chair for just the moment it takes for them to render a thin film of coals. And then I add a piece or two or three of sap-speckled stovewood and I am back under the covers of my bed. I can tell from the sounds of burning wood if I will have to go back to nurse the fire.

When I am in bed I light a Lucky Strike cigarette, smoking drowsily, feeling the stove warm the belly of the cabin. The wood pops and sputters. The men start to come awake: Gordon, in stages of coughs and turnings; Phil uncoiling slowly, his body going rigid in a series of stretches, and then languid, finally propping his head and shoulders against a pillow, lighting a cigarette; and John all at once. These men are all older, in their late forties and fifties. Someone gets up to piss. The linoleum in the bathroom is always cold. The heat rises in the stove, and the flue groans and ticks. If the boots lined behind the stove are not yet dry they begin to steam. I still think of the scent of men as a thing combined of wood smoke, tobacco, pine, whiskey, leather, and horse urine. It is four in the morning and solidly dark. Once one of us has turned the bathroom light on it is left on and casts a weak, flesh-colored column of light back into the sleeping room. We dress in this light.

Every morning John stands at the sink and cups handfuls of water against his face, and sits on the edge of his bed toweling his neck, rubbing his eyes, working the cloth around his ears. He sleeps in his shorts and a T-shirt so stretched from wear that it blouses across his frame like a stained drapery. His arms and legs are gray as the floor, his forehead gray because he is never out without his hat. The part of his face that falls below the hat's brim, and his neck and hands, are brown, lined, weathered. He gets into his shirt and snaps its front and cuffs still sitting. He throws the towel back into the bathroom.

Gordon pulls on his jeans and stomps his feet into his boots. John stands to pull on his pants.

By four-thirty we are buttoned into our flannel and denim and corduroy, all four of us, and shuffling in our heeled boots down the ruts and humped boulder-backs of the two-track to the corrals. John always asks for a match. Gordon always blows into the bowl of his hands and asks if anyone has seen his gloves. We smoke and slap and hug at our sleep-starched bodies. The temperature at this altitude has struck the moisture from the air, snapped it evenly in beads across soil, grass, pine needle, wildflower, aspen leaf, and the acre oval of horse manure in which we start our work. Until the middle of June there is a skim of frost along the tops of the corral poles.

We put the light on in the tackshed and shoulder our rope halters, our bridles and hackamores. John steps a foot up against his saddle's fender, where it sits on its rack, one foot at a time, and buckles his spur leathers.

Phil coughs and shivers. "Wish I could have taken a shit," he says. "I always feel more acrobatic if I can manage a good shit."

"That colt you ride might jar it out of you."

"And he might not, too." Phil's bent over buckling his chaps. He looks up, working the buckle behind a knee. He smiles.

John drags his saddle and pads to the edge of the deck and stands the saddle on its fork. He steps into the dirt and dried horse-shit to grind out his cigarette. Gordon shoulders past him into the corrals. He drops his saddle on its side by the gate to the round corral and folds the hairpad and saddle blanket on top of it and blows into his hands. There is no wind. There is silence. The songbirds and squirrels are still asleep.

I bring the big electrical bulbs on at the barn. They flood the corrals with light. The colts we train by utility move nervously, like young, violent men in the yard of their reformatory. We walk

them down. We corner them, trick them into bit, bosal, and headstall before they can remember that it is the first part of our sleight
of hand that will land us on their backs. We don't raise our own
horses. We buy most of them at auction, and they come with their
owner's bad habits. It takes time, but we work them quietly,
steadily, and they slowly begin to trust that they can survive in the
world. Most of them buck because their hearts have been broken,
and most of them mend. We lose only a few each year to their his-
tories.

Gordon's colt shies and backs into the side of the barn and
squats and springs into the center of the corral. He trots the
perimeter of the corrals, and Gordon walks after him and steps in
front of him and turns him against the rails and steps in front of
him and turns him again. Back and forth. Shortening the pendu-
lum of his swings toward escape. He talks to the horse. His voice is
calm. When the colt has wound down against the round corral he
stands and trembles, and Gordon puts a hand on him. He strokes
him. He moves to his head, talking evenly. The horse is a four-
year-old, an ash-colored gray, his muzzle, legs, mane, and tail running to dark slate, and he's been nearly ruined. Gordon slips the
bridle's headstall over his ears, and the colt steps his front feet together like he's been hobbled. He tucks his chin into his knees and
lowers himself almost to the ground. He's been tied and beaten in
the head, and there's not one of these three men who don't hope to
be locked alone in a room with the man who mistreated this animal.

Every morning we hear Gordon make the same oath. "I'll kick
the sorry son of a bitch hunchbacked," he says. "And he'll stay that
way too. I'll kick the bastard into a Quasimodo-Mickey-Mouse-
looking son of a bitch. Permanent."

Gordon buckles the bridle's throatlatch and steps away from the
gray colt, and the colt pulls back against the reins, whistling, snorting. Gordon walks in a circle with him, talking, giving him the
time to remember that there is no pain.

The gray stands, lifting his front feet, first one and then the
other, as though the ground is hot. He leans back against the reins,

keeping them taut. Gordon walks down the reins and holds a hand against the horse's cheek. Just that. And talks to him. The colt still stamps at the ground, but he is quieting.

Phil's got his horse saddled and standing fast, his ears pricked forward, interested in Gordon and the gray. He turns the colt at the far end of the corrals. To the left. The right. Backing and releasing him.

He stands his horse and hooks a leg over his saddle horn. The horse is heated enough to steam. He is a paint, and he lifts his chin and bobs his head to slacken the reins. Phil lights another cigarette and watches Gordon take up his saddle blanket and hairpad and spread them on the gray colt's back. We all suppose his steady gentleness will save the horse.

John's horse is the one we might lose. We bought him from a brutal man who had him too long. Most mornings John has to tie up a front foot just to get him saddled. He stands quivering in the round corral, swelling himself with fear. He's a big horse, and strong. John seats his hat, drops the foot, and swings into the saddle. Every morning it is like some storm has touched down and spun through the corrals—the unexpected sort of storm that twists the sides from trailer houses and threads garden hoses through the trunks of oaks. John claims that when this horse bucks he can feel his fear. He says he's not sure he can reach to the bottom of it. It worries him. He says the big colt's fear sometimes works into his own legs and rises. He says he can feel the fear grip his chest, tighten his throat.

The colt does not buck from anger or for exercise. He bucks to tear himself apart. Every morning is his single-minded attempt at suicide. He doesn't care who he takes with him. He has bucked into the rails. And he's fallen. And he's gotten up screaming, and bucked again. When he finally tires and settles, he staggers, and blinks, and shakes his head, and steps high as though walking out of some narcotic bog. John has stayed with him for three weeks. After the morning tantrum he helps the colt through an hour or two of cautious work, but we all know it is only a matter of time before the horse cripples John or himself. It is only a matter of time before he comes apart on the side of the mountain and falls over the face of a rimrock, or into a puzzle of downed timber. If he doesn't show some improvement in another few weeks he will have to be sold.

This is my second year on the line-backed dun I call Mud. He's fast, short coupled, and smarter than most boys my age, certainly smarter than me. He seems to accomplish everything I put him to with the easy energy of a child. He is that naturally and innocently athletic. When I am alone in the dark, in bed, I think of this horse with reverence. I think of him as I would think of some quietly earnest priest. He owns that kind of authority. He allows me to ride him through an act of grace. He defers to me in partnership. He snorts and circles as I swing on top of him. If he bucks it will be for sport, because we are both young. When he bucks it is an expression of his joy.

"Here comes your cat," Gordon says. He's on top of the gray. The horse stands and bobs his head and strikes at the ground.

I'm bending down from my saddle to open the gate. I see the cat clinched to the top rail of the gate as I swing it out. Mud sees him too and nickers softly in his throat. The cat lays his good ear back against his skull, and the barn lights flash in his single eye. I straighten and turn to Gordon. "He's not my cat," I tell him. Gordon smiles. I hold the gate away from Mud.

The cat's name is Tommy Two. He's black and white and furred in patches of healing second-growth. His body is a trophy of combat, scabbed, crippled, one whole ear and eye, both on the left side, gone, and what had been the middle-to-end segment of his tail. We all agree that he is nominally a cat. None of us would be surprised to hear him speak. Hear him curse. John and I think he was a pirate in another life; a brigand fallen down the reincarnational ladder. When I look at Tommy I no longer see a cat. I see an outlaw—a dangerous and fugitive midget—stuffed into the skin of a cat.

Each morning he wakes early and swaggers from his squalid nest in the barn and strolls the perimeter of the corral on the top rail. He settles on the sawed-flat end of a post to see if any of us will be killed by our horses. His whiskers twitch in the hope of being sprayed with blood. He has lately become interested in the violence of John's early summer colt. He is democratic about pain. He doesn't care which one of us gets hurt, only that there remains a chance for real gore.

This morning he is up a few minutes late and caught on the gate. He yawns his eye shut, and bows his back and sprays the gatepost, and walks to the center of the gate and sits and yawns again. He seems above most catlike behavior—except for the killing and eating of mice. He does not, however, torture them to death as the mainstream of barn cats do, but simply finds them, eats them, and shits them. He does not lick himself clean. He has other cats perform his toilet. If they refuse he hurts them.

Mud arches his neck and stretches his nose to the cat. Tommy Two stands and grinds his scarred forehead—the size of my fist— into the horse's soft muzzle and arcs his body along Mud's chin.

His father, Tommy One, was eaten by coyotes. John saw it happen and claims there is at least one bitch coyote on this mountain that will not order cat again for supper. According to John, there was a cup and a half of coyote left at the site of her meal.

"I had a loop made and could've roped the bitch to show you the beating she took," he told me, "but I stepped down to search the area for living chunks of T. One." There weren't any. "If he hadn't lost his footing I think he could have whipped her ass."

Mud sidesteps and allows the gate to swing in against him and does not shy. Tommy Two walks back past me and mounts. My denim jacket and yellow oilcloth slicker are rolled and tied behind the saddle's cantle. He stretches his length along this roll of outer-gear, and digs his claws in against the saddle strings. The dun-colored colt looks back to see him secure before he will take a step forward. Only then is it safe to use my spurs.

I swing the gate open, and John's colt walks out sideways and onto the dirt road. He blows and boogers and ducks at the rocks and clumps of brush that are taking shape out of the gathering light.

Gordon reins the gray colt around Mud and Tommy and me and

spurs him into a trot. He still hasn't found his gloves but knows better than to try to pet the cat. Tommy will let Mud lip his ear and snort against his belly. He'll wind between the horse's legs, rub against his shins. On a good day he'll tolerate some affection from me. He prefers to be stroked against the grain of his fur. He likes it rough. I've never heard him purr. No one else can lay a hand on him.

Phil and Gordon ride ahead. John and I follow. We will ride together on an abandoned logging road along the valley floor, and then fan apart, climbing through a web of game trails, tracking the hundred horses we have turned out to graze through the night. They will have splintered into small bands, feeding as families, and we will find them, bring them together, use them, and turn them out again in the last light of the day.

It is rare that John, Phil, Gordon, and I are all together on the ranch. It is usual for two of us to be out on a pack trip. The two left to work the ranch take riders out for an hour, or two, or half a day. But it is early in the season and the creeks are too swollen to cross, so we all work the day trade and wait for the water to go down.

Two miles up the valley I turn Mud into a tight cut with a spring at its head. Tommy and I are fortunate that Mud owns the gait of a more expensive horse, and we slide quietly through the trees. The cat stands on the roll of jackets and leans into me. His head is pressed into my side, above my right kidney, for a forward look at the scenery. Our eyes water in the near-frosted air. Our blood is warming. It is still half an hour before the sun tops the ridge.

I find three old, brown geldings at the spring. They are always together, never climbing very high off the valley floor. Kid horses. Docile old gentlemen that remind me more of dairy cows than horses. If we don't find them they come in by themselves, nickering for grain. We don't bother to bell them. I start them back down the trail and put Mud up the spine of a sharp and shattered ridge of loose shale and foot-deep stretches of slippery pine duff.

Each man and horse dissect the drainage, riding separate ridges, and push the horses we find down. Always down toward the creek.

This is a wilderness area. There are no fences. When we are out of fresh track and can hear the faint ringing of bells only behind us, below us, we start back, gathering horses, gathering momentum, always coming down.

To do this thing will require of Mud a shaman's dance. Every morning. The trails we ride are made by elk and deer. He will shift his shape in ways that flatland horses never learn. He will uncoil through a maze of tumbled downtimber with the grace of a snake, and do it fast. He will plummet down a slope of scree, his ears laid back along his skull, as perpendicular to our angle of fall as his momentum will tolerate, and catch in a patch of loam to turn against his force of weight so drastically, and magically, that I have this summer, and last, twice been left sitting in the air.

Mud grinds up the ridge and into a group of six horses standing in a copse of stunted juniper. Two palominos, a paint, a bay, a blue roan, and a black: Jim and Tim, Puzzle, Secret, Freddie, and Bird. Bird's been belled. This bunch will take a day off if they can. They stand still as partridge, and when I ride into the edge of them and slap my coiled lariat against my chaps they flush as partridge would, down the ridge. Mud stays on top of them. We dive straight down through the popping of limbs and scatter of stones. When Mud judges that their momentum will carry them to the valley floor, he pulls up and works a diagonal slant of trail to regain his altitude. I look back into the face of the one-eyed, one-eared cat. He has come loose and flops back along Mud's rump. He holds fast with only one fist of claws and breathes through an open mouth of yellowed teeth. We're all out of breath. I reach back and pull Tommy tight against the cantle and lean forward to take my weight off Mud's kidneys.

I think that it is circus riding we do, unable to be shown, an act that can't be booked, because of the limited size of tents. And I am never sure I like it, honestly like coming each morning to so many edges of pain and fear.

The ridge crests and flattens into meadow and crests again sharply where it knifes into the side of Sleeping Giant Mountain. There are more than a dozen horses grazing in this small and accidental park. They lift their heads and watch as Mud, T. Two, and I circle to their uphill side. The trail curves away north, and turns, and ascends through the crack in a face of volcanic stone. There are no fresh tracks. If there were I would start this bunch down the ridge and follow the tracks and drop east into the Goff Creek breaks—a series of slashing ridges that form the head of another drainage—and bring what stock I found out to the river and upstream to the home corrals.

The horses start to move away from us slowly, still grazing, the two belled leaders striking out a tinny melody in the soft, gray light. There are scraps of tattered cloud below us.

I hook my right leg over the saddle's horn and spin the rowel of my spur. I light a cigarette. It is so still the smoke gathers under the brim of my hat. I spit the flakes of tobacco from the tip of my tongue and look back up as the sun clears the horizon and strikes the spines of the high ridges, bringing them golden, rose, and white. The glare off the rockface of Sleeping Giant hurts my eyes.

Tommy Two stands and arches against my back and growls low, like some bigger and cornered animal might. Mud and I turn to look at the dog coyote that has stepped out of a patch of timber into the grass. His fur bristles henna, bronze, brown, and steel in the morning sun. He looks to his sides to reassure himself that he has room to run and then steps slowly along the base of rock, dropping into shadow, falling below our line of sight.

I stub the cigarette out on the sole of my boot and drop my foot back into the stirrup and touch Mud ahead, in behind this last bunch of horses. T. Two has flattened out to better grip my slicker but still watches our backs. He produces a base growl that hums at the bottom of my spine.

The horses line out along the trail, flashing in the sun, warming, moving down country. I whistle once through my teeth and slap my chaps. They are stretched out, walking fast. I know where they will break and scatter off the ridge, and absorb the six I've found lower down and started toward the creek. All of their bells will clang together. I will think the sound a cheap advertisement for a morning Mass. I pull my hat tighter on my head. It has taken us an hour to climb to this height; we'll strike the valley floor in under ten minutes. We'll beat the sun to the creek.

I lay back in the saddle, back against T. Two, and Mud brings us off the ridge. He squats, and springs away from his hindquarters in the loose shale. He comes straight down, and turns in a series of improvisational switchbacks to avoid a stand of rimrock, and straight down again. We hit the deep, watery grass of the valley floor at a dead run.

There are two feeder ridges that meet at the creek, in a small uneven meadow. The twenty horses I've gathered break into this open place at a jarring lope, ducking and shouldering one another, kicking into the air, steaming in the high grass, slicing into thirty more that John has thundered off his ridge. We meet behind them, in their slight rise of dust. I sit straight on the mud-colored colt. I've shaken three coils of lariat down. There is a rawhide popper on the lariat's end, and I snap it in the air and laugh, and John laughs too. There is no happiness like the pounding of so many horses into one. I imagine I hear the horses laugh. I think it every time. I think that running is the way a horse may laugh out loud. When I am older I will believe that following in their wake has filled me with the inconsolable joy of animals.

John snatches his hat and waves it above his head. His thin hair lifts in the chilled air. He's grinning like he's been to town. I turn in my saddle to return John's smile, and Mud feels me shift and ducks his head and steps to the side and out from under me. I roll in the wet grass and come up sitting, and staring into the receding face of a pirate cat. Tommy's riding high against the cantle, his blunt tail curved above his back. He does not look sorry for me. He looks satisfied and proud of having stolen my horse.

I stand and spit out a quid of dirt and grass and feel for blood. There is none. I stamp my feet and find my hat, and it occurs to me that I am getting paid for this and Tommy Two is not. John trots back to me, leading Mud. I watch the faces of the man and horse and cat and am happy, and know that I do not ride for money. I ride because I can, because it brings me out with others of my kind.

"I'm glad to have seen that for free," John says. He's smiling. The horses stamp, breathing hard, their heads turned away down the valley. "Pointy-assed as you are I thought you might hang up and snap something off."

"I'm fine," I tell him, but avoid looking into his face. I take the reins and step into the stirrup.

"Try not to kick your cat loose," he says.

"He's not my cat," I tell him, and I swing my leg high over T. and rein Mud in beside John's colt.

"Gordon'll turn 'em into the corral," he says. I nod.

We hold our horses to a walk, and the sun reaches into the valley and slaps it apart in a puzzle of sunstrike and shadow. For more than a mile we ride through blocks of glare and cooler, darker pockets of night-air. The soil has been farmed ahead of us by the discs of a hundred hooves, and the scent that rises is damp, and acidic and familiar. T. Two reaches out with a single paw and rests it for fifty yards on John's right hip. He stares ahead, between the horses, and then pushes back and walks out onto Mud's flat rump and sits and stares behind us into the morning light.

Gordon and Phil have already grained twelve horses and turned them back into the corrals and have a second dozen tied in their stalls. The horses mill and pace. They snort and roll and shake.

Mud swings in against the corral poles and stops, and T. Two steps off. He twitches his nub of tail and snaps the fur along his back and starts for the barn. Mud nickers, and the cat stops and turns. He sits for a moment on the end of a post, looking back at us, and yawns, stretches, and starts off again.

Gordon lifts his hat, works his hair into a mess, reseats the hat, and folds his arms on a corral rail. "You've got dirt on your head," he says.

"Mud got out from under me."

"You hurt?"

"I guess I'm not."

He grips the rail and pushes back into the corrals, against the arc of his back, stretching. "Your feelings hurt?"

"I'm fine."

He looks up and smiles.

John and I unsaddle our horses and hang our chaps and spurs in the tackshed. We halter the next shift of twelve horses and tie them in the barn and spill a coffee can of oats in each of their wooden grainboxes and walk up to the lodge for breakfast.

My mother and Gordon and Phil and the cabin girls are at the table. My mother looks up from the paper she reads. She smiles. "Are you hurt?" she asks.

"I'm fine."

"How's your cat?"

"He's not my cat."

She nods and looks back to her paper.

After breakfast I heap the kitchen scraps—bits of toast, sausage, ham, pancake, all daubed with syrup—on a platter and carry it into the loft of the barn. I sit on a bale and watch as the barn cats swarm the plate. Tommy comes out of the shadows and sits and watches them too. When he approaches they scatter and writhe, mewling at the perimeter of his reach. He eats a nub of sausage. Laps at the syrup and takes up the largest scrap of ham and returns to the shadows. The cats edge back to the plate, watching as they eat.

That summer it rains predictably in the late evenings, after we have run the horses up the valley to feed, and I climb into the loft and listen to the drumming on the corrugated tin roof. I feel right for adventure. I dream of travel, of independence. I invent words, whole phrases, and mouth them, and pretend I am speaking some exotic language that I do not know.

If we turn the horses out before the sun is down, I keep the doors swung open. They face west and align with the setting sun. The evening light slants through the stand of pine along the creek and quickens in the aspen leaves. When I hold my hand out it flashes rose, and smooth. The hay bales mute soft as bricks of gold. The smell of pine and sage has grown heavy in the day's heat and hangs heavy in the loft.

T. Two sits to my side and stares into the dappled light. He tucks his legs under his gut, and his eye blinks, and he sleeps. If I rest a hand on his back he does not move away. Once he rolls to his side to give me a chance at his belly. I tell him of the places we will travel. I speak to him of adventure. I say aloud the names Blackbeard and William Kidd, and draw a skull and bones in the hay-dust that lies thick on the floor. I tell him we are buccaneers. Cocaptains. I tell him to keep his powder dry. He curls in his sleep and flexes his feet.

I read from the *Articles of a Pirate's Life: If any man shall offer to run away, or to keep any secret from the company, he shall be marooned, with one bottle of water, one small arm and shot.* Tommy lifts his head and squints. There are flakes of hay stuck in his fur. He rolls in the dust and stands and does not shake or preen. I close my eyes and imagine that I feel the lift of a heavy sea. "They'll never overtake us," I tell him, and pull him onto my lap, and he does not struggle to get away.

One evening I take two cans of beer I have stolen from the cook. I pour half of one in a shallow bowl, and Tommy laps and sneezes until the bowl is dry. My legs are stretched out in front of me, crossed at the ankles, and he works his forehead and ears and muzzle against the sole of a boot. He curls against my thigh and goes to sleep. I feel his spine flex and fall. All summer long he has gone out with Mud and me. The exercise has worn away what little winter weight he had. He snores as Gordon snores, but not as loud. I cross my arms on my chest and sleep.

When I wake it is dark, and the cat is gone. I crawl on my hands and knees and feel for the open square in the loft's floor. I climb down the ladder, bark my shins in the granary, and walk out into the night. The horses snort and skitter in the corral. There is no moon. I shuffle up road with my hands out, hoping they'll find the trunk of a tree before I walk into the thing. When my footing starts to rebound I steer back onto the hard-packed road. I bump into the bunkhouse and still am unable to see its walls.

I pull my boots and pants off on the porch and lay them by the door when I step inside. There are no creaks in the floor and I'm in bed without a sound. There is the ticking of a clock, and the sounds of the men asleep.

"You in the barn?" John asks. He whispers. I think that if I turn on the light I would find his eyes closed, his face relaxed.

"I fell asleep."

"I feathered your kindling."

"You didn't have to."

"You do something all the time it becomes a chore."

"Thanks."

There is just the clock, and the quieter rustling of the creek. I close my eyes.

"You worried?"

"I wonder about things," I tell him. "How my life might turn out."

"Your life'll turn out the way it wants."

"Have you done everything you thought you might like to do?"

"I guess I haven't." I hear him turn in his bed.

"I think T. Two does what he wants. Maybe all the time."

"He might. I'm not an expert on the lives of cats."

"I'm just wondering."

"Well, you might wonder if you want to look as beat up as he does when you get his age. Good night."

"Good night."

Before Labor Day, the last week of August, Tommy Two does not walk the rail to ride with me. John sits a new and impatient colt, and it is still too dark to search the barn. It does not occur to me to call out his name, and I spur Mud out, and he humps and breaks into a sloppy trot. We move upstream. The air is dry and still and brittle. John turns to look at the back of my saddle and then just straight ahead.

I put Mud hard up a slope and stop to let him blow. I feel alone, unbalanced, and reach behind, across the top of my slicker, but there is nothing there. I have grown accustomed to the cat's hard, warm body pressed against my back. Mud moves as though there is lightning in the air, and bucks off a ridge that can break us both.

At the bottom he stops, and turns and eyes the empty roll behind the cantle and whinnies. The yellow surface of the slicker is scratched, and gouged and torn.

When we've brought the horses in I search the barn. I find his nest, and it is cold, and after breakfast leave table scraps that the common cats devour.

"He's dead," says John. He's come up behind me in the barn. He pops a matchhead with his thumbnail and lights his cigarette. "There's a new generation of coyotes grown," he says. "One of 'em probably didn't believe the story about how hard T.'s father was to eat." I look to him and nod my head.

That's the way it could be, I think. The way John sees it. It would be the way to bet.

That night I get up from my bunk and dress and stand out on the porch. It has rained, and the air is chilled with the first false hint of fall. The moon is full, and the rocks along the creek shine in the night. I go back into the bunkhouse and pull my blanket off my bed and wrap it around my shoulders and walk back into the night.

I climb into the loft and call his name. I open the doors and let the moonlight in. The other cats rustle, but stay away. I stretch out in the hay with the blanket pulled to my chin. I clasp my hands behind my head and close my eyes and listen to the creek.

Before I sleep I see him hitching to the Gulf of Mexico. The picture is clear. There is no mistake. He lounges in the well of a convertible's downed top, the wind catching in the cup of his one good ear. I see him signed aboard a cargo ship, respected by its crew, mousing out its hold for work. On moonlit nights I see him sleeping on the open deck. He's nestled in the lap of a drunken sailor. An old man and an old cat. They rise and fall against the sea. The cat bows his neck and grinds the scarred fist of his forehead into the heel of the old man's hand. I smile with my eyes still closed. I can see the hand. It is calloused, and broad, and smells of fish and sun and rum and salt.

ADOPTING BEAR

I'm not sure of the exact time. It's dark. There is no wind. The night presses down dense with cold. I remember last night's moon as nearly full, as nearly a harvest moon. It had risen up round and amber. It had risen even before the sunset, and for a moment, when it pulled wholly away from the horizon, struck the pale horses in a flash of opalescent light—the moon to one side of them, the sun to the other—they stood stark and shadowless. For just one moment.

I blink into the cold night air. I can't see the walls of the tent or my breath. It is that dark. I shut my eyes and shift in my sleeping bag. I suppose I've come awake in the black slice of night between moonset and dawn.

When I need more sleep my shoulders ache and my heart shifts, and occasionally flutters, as though I have stepped off a cutbank and into the air. I tighten my shoulders and chest and relax. My whole body feels thick and steady and strong. I flatten a hand against my abdomen and push, and there is only the comfort of a half-filled bladder and gut. I am rested. I do not have to piss or shit. I do not have to dress and light a lantern and shuffle to the canvas outhouse we have built in the trees behind the tents. I'm thankful for that. It is late September in Mountain Creek, and the grass is grown waist-high, and it is well below freezing. Walking out in the night means wading through the frosted grass stems, soaking my jeans and boots.

I don't know why I've come awake. I listen for horses. I do not hear their bells, their steps on the frost-stiffened ground. I listen harder. I listen for a bear. I listen for the huffs, snorts, the coughing of a bear come into camp. There is only the deep silence of the night. I imagine a bear standing quietly by the side of my tent. A grizzly. Waiting. Aware of me. The thought of a bear thrills like a horror film escaped from its theater. My own murder stands vividly in my imagination. The dark night grinds down hard. I imagine a bear's small, dark eyes watering and intent in the cold air. I imagine a bear's nostrils flexing, breathing in my scent, its gut grumbling, whining for the taste of me. I think of a bear's teeth, its claws. I listen for the clicking of teeth. I think of the thick, dish-shaped skull—the brain inside that skull anxious for extra prehibernation calories. I pinch my chest, the back of an arm. My body seems soft as lard. I think of myself as food. I pull my woolen watch cap more tightly against my head—over my ears and eyes—and curl my face into the throat of my sleeping bag. I am wearing long underwear—top and bottom—and socks. My jeans and shirt are rolled against my feet at the bottom of the bag. I breathe in the warm, familiar scents of my body and stained clothing—a mixture of woodsmoke, leather, and horse. I think again of the thin canvas wall of the tent. It is black inside. It is black outside. If a hungry bear stands in that blackness the smell of me could draw it against the tent wall. I think of a grizzly's nose pressed against the tent. I think of its mouth watering, scrims of thinning drool sheeting from its black lips. I pull my knees into my chest and flex and imagine my body as unalterable as a knot of steel. I nearly laugh. I've become too old for bullshit fantasies of invincibility. I am now sixteen. I know that if a bear wants me for a meal it can open and spill me as effortlessly as an actual can of beans.

Last fall, a few miles from camp, one of my father's guides was badly mauled by a grizzly. She was only a four-hundred-pound sow and wounded and allowed to sicken overnight, and still she came very close to killing the man. The man's name is Bert Bell. He is not in camp this year.

Bert and the wrangler were tracking the bear's bloodtrail through several inches of new snow. The wrangler is not much older than me and has red hair. My hair is blond, tinted red in the sun. The red-haired wrangler shot the bear off Bert. I wonder if that information has entered the hearts of all bear. I wonder if red hair raises a flag for vengeance.

The sow was weak, dying, and lay up behind a downfall, waiting for them. Bert said that when the wind shifted, he could smell her. I think she waited for the men to come so close because she was almost dead, because she was numbed with despair, and still she covered the thirty yards to Bert before he could shoot and knocked him off his feet and bit into his left side below his ribs. I curl up tighter in my bag. I grip my left kidney. I think how lucky Bert was that the bear was so weak he could get her jaws open and away from the soft parts of him and feed her his hands until the red-headed wrangler shot her twice and she slumped and died. The wrangler's name is Dave. He is not in camp this year either.

My sleeping bag is spread on a raft of finger-thick pine saplings cut to length and nailed into a stouter border of poles. The whole affair stands off the ground on two-foot rounds of fir, one supporting each corner. There is a layer of hairpads between the poles and the sleeping bag. And the bag is wrapped in a canvas tarp that grows white in the night with frost. I am warm and comfortable, and set off the ground level with the jaws of a bear. I realize that when I imagine a bear waiting for me outside my tent I am not just after the excitement of a rehearsed accident. There is a part of me that expects an accident, a mauling—expects to be eaten. There is a part of me that does not believe I will die easily.

Claude is in the tent with me, in his sleeping bag. There are the two of us. It is too dark to see him, but he is there. He is five years older and has been out in the world. He has been to Vietnam. I can hear my heart beating in my ears. If I turn my head it seems to deepen the sound, and the throb of my blood echoes in my skull. I turn on my side and listen to my heart and wonder if the war has made Claude brave or empty. I have friends whose brothers have come back from the war. Some are reckless. Some are quiet. All of their voices are different, hollow, echoing. Sometimes they will stop and listen to the sound of their own voices. They know something has changed.

Claude does not talk to me about the war. He has not been back quite a year. He still can't believe he was gone from home so long. I do not know if he is afraid. Maybe I am the only one afraid. I wonder whether getting older will give me more, or less, to fear.

I think of the first dead bear I ever saw. It was skinned, its naked corpse remarkably like that of a large man's. My horse scented the thing and shied and bucked and threw me. When I think of that bear I flush. I feel it is a crime to kill them, and my family makes its business from their deaths. I have been taught that all crime deserves punishment.

When I was eleven one of our hired men drove me to a landfill on the edge of Yellowstone in the middle of the night. We sat in his pickup with the lights and heater on and watched twenty grizzlies scrabble for the choicer bits of garbage. It was a degraded scene. The bear were quarrelsome and greedy. They fought for scraps of decomposing rot, bluff-charging amid the scatter of diapers, cans, and plastics. They did not seem like bear. They seemed just a convention of fat, squalid drunks. I squinted hard to blur the scene. It was a trick to keep me from crying; to keep my notions of them unspoiled.

At eleven it was my ambition to be a bear. I wanted to join their clan. I envied them their power and speed and impunity. I thought of the two- and three-year-old boars as older, wilder boys; as a pack of savvy bullies that prowled my neighborhood. I stretched up against the trees they used for scratching posts. I pawed through the ruin of decaying downed timber they had rolled and broken searching for grubs and mice. When I found their track I slipped off my boots and socks and stood barefoot and silent where they had stood. I did not pare my toenails. In the fall I ate wild berries. I expected to learn the language of bear, but I only learned to love them. Now, when the sun is up I am still their friend. I still imagine that I can stand with a foot in their world. But at night I know I am slowly growing into a man. I am afraid that a bear will find me out, judge me. I am afraid that a bear will kill me for the traitor I am.

On a night late into the third hunt last fall a grizzly swung through camp, stood on the log rolled to the back of the cook tent, stretched up to its ridgepole and ripped down the rear wall. None of us saw the event, but we heard the immediate screams of the cook. He slept on a bench at the back of the tent. He slept with a high-caliber rifle my father had loaned him. He was an affable old bachelor, a drunk, and starkly frightened of bear. A bottle of whiskey and the rifle helped him sleep.

We rolled out of our own tents and ran toward the sound of his screams. We had pulled on our coats and boots. Most of us ran bare-legged. My father had on only his boots and hat and a white T-shirt.

When the gunfire started we dove onto our chests and crawled in the snow. The old man spun inside the ruined tent shooting the rifle into the air as fast as he could bolt the cartridges into its chamber. The shots were high and uncommonly effective in destroying the canvas roof. I had never seen a rifle shot at night and was amazed at how far the flames licked out of its muzzle.

When the cook emptied the magazine my father and a guide muscled him to the ground before he could reload, and the rest of us lit lanterns. I thought the incident hilarious, and was barely smart enough to choke down my laughter. I walked into the timber, smirking, and held my light down to the bear's tracks stamped in the snow. I bit the insides of my cheeks. Each paw print looked large enough to drop my hat through. I stared into the darkness past the cast of lantern light and listened. All I could hear were the sobs of the old cook and the men speaking in whispers as they set up his bunk in the dining tent and lit a fire in the stove.

The cook has been dead for nine months, since last winter. He had gotten himself out of the mountains and died when all of the bear slept and could not witness his death.

I listen harder for the bear who I imagine waits for me. I hold my breath. There is only silence. I worry that I am a coward. I worry if I am bitten and pawed by a bear that I will scream—that I will beg. I worry if I am eaten in the night that my soul will become confused and lost to the darkness.

I have had my driver's license for just six months. It will be four and a half years before I can legally walk into a bar and order a beer. I am anxious to have a chance to fail. I want to show the world that I can stand up under the weight of failure. And there are other considerations. I am worried that I might not prove a good lover. I haven't been with a girl who's had any more experience than I've had. There has been no one to ask.

When I was thirteen and Claude was eighteen we wrangled horses together. He was a state wrestling champion. We used to wrestle on the bunkhouse floor until my face and arms and knees were wood-burned enough to make me quit. I think Claude is good in a fight, but I was not with him in Vietnam.

"You awake?" It's Claude. I hear him turn in his bag. I tell him that I am. "What are you doing?" he asks.

"I'm thinking about bear."

"You think that's why you're awake?"

"I don't know."

"What time is it?"

"Four or five, I guess. You thinking about bear?"

"I am now."

We listen to the night. There is only the sound of our breathing. Because it is too early to get up and go to work I tell Claude about a book I have read. It is about the Blackfeet Indians. I tell him about a Blackfeet bear knife. I explain that the knife has a double-edged blade and the jaw of a bear for its handle.

"Both sides of the jaw?"

"Just one side I expect. There weren't any pictures."

I tell him the bear knife indicated the power of the man who owned it, and that if another man, a warrior, asked to purchase the

knife, and it was agreed upon, the two men would purify themselves in a sweat lodge, and then sit together naked in the lodge of
the man who owned the knife.

"Why?"

"I don't know. That's just what it said in the book. I guess the
knife was sacred."

"Then what?"

"Then the man who owned the knife would crawl around his
lodge four times. He'd growl like a bear and paw the air and snap
his jaws. Then he'd stand up and hold the knife by its point and
throw it as hard as he could at the man who wanted it."

"They both still naked?"

"I guess. What difference would it make?"

"It would make a difference to me. Then what?"

"If the man caught the knife it was his. Its power too."

"Shit." Claude is quiet for a moment, and adds, "I wonder how
many times the guy didn't catch the knife."

"It didn't say. Would you do it?"

"I might," he says. "I don't think I would have a while ago, but
now I might."

It's the end of the story. I can't think of another. Sometimes I
wish Claude would talk about Vietnam. In less than two years I
will register for the draft. The war is each year expanding. I have a
theory that my blood will not clot in the hot, wet air of a jungle. I
do not feel like a blessed boy. I want to be an old man, but do not
feel a whole lifetime away from dying.

Claude struggles out of his bag and pulls on his boots and a
denim coat and digs in his duffel and finds a flashlight and steps
out into the night to piss. He does not walk into the trees to the
canvas outhouse we have built. He stands on the other side of the
tentflap. I can see his silhouette through the canvas.

When he comes back in he is huffing against the cold. He pulls
off his jacket and boots and slips into his bag.

"Would you fight?" I ask him.

"A bear?"

"If he was on you? Like Bert, last year?"

"I'd run," he says.

I tell him that he cannot outrun a bear. It is something that we both know. The information is so common that it's become a joke.

"I wouldn't have to," he says. I've set myself up for the fall. "I'd just have to outrun you."

We do not laugh out loud. We smile.

I gather the horses in the dark before dawn. The grass is sweet and deep, and they have grazed the meadows along Mountain Creek and are no more than a mile from camp. Phil and Claude saddle their horses by lantern light and ride their hunters out in the dark to hunt an elk. The bulls are nearly three weeks into their rut. They are red eyed and incautious. Their necks are swollen. They circle their harems and bugle and drool and fight.

Gordon walks his hunter to the bait-ground just a quarter mile from camp. They will sit in the blind in the gauzy dawn-light. The bait has been worked two nights by a bear. They will try to kill this bear. The hunter's eyes are wide in his face. He does not look to have had much sleep.

I stay in camp. There are five twelve-by-fourteen sleeping tents and the larger cook and dining tents. The big tents face one another, with a canvas canopy draped across the space where their ridgepoles meet. I sit on the flat end of a round of fir and watch the cook. I drink a cup of coffee. I would be in school if Claude had not come out of camp three days ago with a pack string and the young man his age from Tennessee my father has hired to wrangle horses. The Tennessee man got drunk and drove south. Claude woke me at the lodge in the middle of the night to repack the horses with fresh supplies and trail them back to Mountain Creek. It is not the first fall I have missed school to take the part of a new man who found the high mountains too wild.

It is not fully light when I hear the shot. A lantern hangs and hisses from the cook tent's ridgepole. A single shot, and then another. Just that. The sounds come in sharp and swelling—I can feel them solidly in my chest. I look up at the cook. He is the dead cook's replacement, a sober man, in his fifties. He is bent over a pan of frying bacon. He stops and straightens and cocks his head. We listen. There is the sputter of bacon. A stick of wood pops in the stove. There are no more shots. I pour myself a second cup of coffee.

In half an hour Gordon and his hunter walk into camp. They are stepping away from the ground as though they want to break into a trot. The hunter is sucking at the air. He is a small man. He had been bucked off his horse a week ago and bruised his shoulder and cannot seat the stock of his rifle solidly when he fires and the gun's scope jumps up and digs out silver dollar–sized divots from his forehead. He is too excited to care. His forehead is freshly bloodied in two overlapping discs above his right eye, and blood has run into the eye. He drags the sleeve of his jacket across his face. "He charged," he says. He still has not caught his breath and will not sit. His right heel is lifted off the ground, and the right leg bounces against the ball of the foot. He looks down at the leg. He lays a hand against his thigh. He cannot stop it.

My father stands with them outside the entrance to the tent. "Wounded," I hear Gordon say. "A grizzly," he says. He stares down at his boots. He grips his rifle above the trigger-guard, holding it at his side. He steps away and points the gun into the timber and thumbs the safety on.

My father nods. He smiles at the hunter. "Let's have something to eat," he says. He sits by the hunter and cleans and bandages the man's forehead while he eats his breakfast and settles.

It is midmorning, and I am chopping wood when Claude returns to camp with his hunter. Claude's hands are bloody. There is blood splattered on the front of his chaps and the folds of his shirt at his belly. They have killed an elk.

Two hunters have already gotten their elk, and the quartered animals hang cool and stiff in the trees behind the tents. After lunch we will pack in the newly dead animal.

The cook is boiling potatoes on the stove. I am stacking wood by the stove. I think I will be sent with Claude. I am glad to be away from school. I am not thinking about wounded bear. My father steps inside the tent and asks the cook to pack two lunches. "Get your jacket," he says.

"Now?"

He nods.

When I return with a jacket he hands me a sacked lunch, and I undo three buttons on my shirt and slip it inside. My father takes up his rifle and bolts it open and chambers a shell and puts on the safety. Gordon stands by the side of the tent, where the enameled washbasins hang from a pole. His rifle is balanced across his shoulders, his arms draped over the thing, breaking across the barrel and stock, his forearms hanging loosely in front of the gun.

Gordon is a big man. Over six feet. More than two hundred pounds. When his arms are dropped to his sides they hang nearly to his knees. His canines are sharp. I've sat in the bunkhouse with him when he tells a story and gets excited. He slobbers, his jaw works faster than his speech. He is a reason to believe in evolution. I think if he were naked and laid out in a meadow that he would look like a dead, skinned bear.

I follow Gordon and my father to the bait-ground. We stand beside the blind. I can see the hump of the baited horse at the far end of the meadow, thirty yards in front of us. I hear my father click the safety off his gun. "Did he charge?" my father asks.

"He just turned and looked at us," Gordon says. He says the bear is hit once, he's not sure where, that the hunter's second shot was after the bear was gone.

We walk single file along the fringe of the meadow to the horse. The horse was a big-boned paint we called Samson. He looks now to be just a large, sodden, and unfinished puzzle. Part of his neck and shoulder are eaten away. The hide hangs in tatters and scallops over the wounds. His belly is opened and the bowel broken and scattered in the matted grass. His hindquarters and back are mounded with dirt. His lips have drawn away from his yellowed teeth. The eye socket on the upturned side of his head has been pecked hollow. My father puts his toe to a length of gut and turns it. Maggots writhe, glistening in the bright air.

"Here," says Gordon, and I turn to him. He is kneeling ten feet past Samson. He pinches a clump of grass stems at their base and brings his fingers up their length and opens his hand. His fingers are slick with fresh blood. He stands and walks a few feet into the timber. "And here," he calls back to us.

"You feel ready?" my father asks.

I look to the dead horse and to Gordon squatting in the trees. I nod.

"Do what Gordon tells you."

I nod again. He thumbs the safety on and hands me his rifle.

"You have any questions?"

"No, sir."

"You can do this."

"I know I can." I look up at him.

"No you don't," he says. He smiles. "Tonight you'll know. Don't be bashful about using that gun."

"I won't."

He cups a handful of shells out of his pocket and lays them in my palm. The tips of his fingers brush my palm. I have not inherited his hands. My hands are my own.

"You'll hear him," he says. "Or smell him before you see him. It'll seem like it's happening all at once."

I have put the extra shells in my breast pocket and stepped back away from my father. Gordon comes out of the timber and stands. He wipes his hand on the right thigh of his jeans. "You sending the boy?" he asks.

"That suit you?"

Gordon looks to me, to the rifle I have tucked under my arm. He runs his tongue against his teeth, from one side of his mouth to the other. It makes his face appear to have a life of its own. He smiles and nods and looks back into the timber. "You think we've waited long enough for that bear to want to die?"

"What do you think?"

"I think we have."

"Get back before dark."

Gordon looks at my father. "You can count on that," he says and turns and walks away. I follow him.

The ground is wet, pocked with week-old patches of snow, and the bear's tracks are plain everywhere except in the open meadow grass. For the first hundred yards the stride is exaggerated and then settles, the pawprints just two feet apart. Each track has pressed an inch into the ground. The hindprints are nearly a foot long and half a foot wide, but the ground is soft and moist, and they are smeared. The foreclaws extend two inches ahead of their tracks and have gouged into the earth. There are sprays of blood every thirty or forty feet. That's all. No pools or clots.

"He's a big bear, isn't he?"

"He was when we shot him." Gordon does not turn. He walks. And he stops to listen.

I come up beside him at the edge of a twenty-year-old burn. It is grown up woolly in seven- and eight-foot-high spruce, so thick that it appears we are stepping out into a lake of green water. "Take your safety off," he says and moves into the copse. I can hear him breathing high in his chest. He has to part the boughs with his rifle's barrel to step ahead. The trees press in against us on all sides. I know that if the bear is in here that he will kill us. I am afraid that I will lose Gordon in the crowd of trees. I follow so closely that I step on his heels.

I hear a noise behind me and turn my head and there is nothing, and I hear it again and turn and identify it as my hair brushing against my jacket's collar. There is a rushing in my ears. My skin itches, and I think I would be more comfortable if I could step out of my body and pull it along behind me. I bring a hand under my jacket to hold against my chest. My shirt is soaked with sweat. I can smell myself. I can smell Gordon a step ahead of me.

He stops and I bump into him and we listen, and he farts and we both jump sideways in the soft growth and raise our rifles chest-high. We smile, but we don't laugh.

"I hope this isn't the last stupid thing I do," he whispers.

I nod.

"If something happens, try not to shoot me."

I nod again.

My father has told me that if a bear has me on the ground and is chewing on me that it is best to play dead. I have practiced with my brother. I have drawn myself into a ball on our cabin floor, and he has poked and stabbed at me with a garden rake, but carefully. And still I flinched, and when a tine scraped my neck cried out.

I think of the times I have been kicked by horses, bucked off on rocky ground, had them fall out from under me. I've taken more than a hundred stitches, seven broken ribs, a broken wrist, concussions, and had my top front teeth sheared off level with the gum. I have suffered none of it quietly. I do not think I am brave enough to play dead.

We move out of the burn and walk its edge and find where the bear has come out. The tracks lead into a stand of old-growth timber. Gordon sits on a downfall and takes off his hat and raises his right arm at the shoulder and rubs his forehead against the muscle in the front of his arm. His face is covered with sweat. "Good thing we didn't spook a grouse out of there," he says. "If we had I think I'd have shit my pants." He looks at me harder. "You okay?"

"I'm not sure I am."

"What do you say we go out around there on our way back?"

"Even if we kill him?"

"Even then."

We track the wounded bear for two miles in open timber. We go slowly. When my weight settles into each step I feel safe, for just that instant, but when I lift a leg to step again, know that everything can change. Just that quickly. From one step to the next.

We find less blood. And then we find it rarely. The bear's stride is lengthening. We kneel at a spring where he has lain down to cool himself and drink and pack his wound with mud. The boggy ground is gouged and torn. It is midafternoon.

"I think he's pissed," I tell Gordon.

"I think I would be, too," he says.

We scramble up through a broken escarpment. There is only a spot of blood every hundred yards like some bright blossom of lichen. For the last twenty feet we have to sling our rifles over our backs and climb with our hands. At the top there is a dusting of snow, and the track is plain and lengthened into a lope. We follow it for a quarter mile and find no blood.

Gordon looks into the sky and sits and brings out his lunch. "I think this son of a bitch is getting well," he says.

I sit down beside him and take a bite from my sandwich, but my mouth is dry and tacky, and I spit the bread and meat out. Our rifles are across our laps.

"You scared?"

"I wish I weren't." I look at him.

"Wish in one hand and shit in the other," he says. "See which one fills up faster."

"You scared?"

Gordon pulls back his bread and pokes at the square of elk steak inside his sandwich. He presses the bread back together and takes another bite. "Getting eaten ranks low on my ways to go."

"Below drowning?"

"Below damn near everything. Maybe above being burned to death."

I put my lunch back in my shirt.

"We'll ride up here tomorrow and see what we can find," he says. He looks behind us. "I don't think this bear's hit hard enough to die."

We angle down off the rimrocked ridge and skirt the overgrown burn and cut our trail on its far side. We walk fast, but it is evening, nearly dark in the timber, and we are still a half mile from camp. Gordon stops like I've seen a dog stop at the end of its chain and kneels, and I kneel beside him. There is the track we have been following and on top of it the prints of our boots, and over those, here, and then here again, are the newer tracks of a bear. A grizzly. The same grizzly. Gordon stands and stares into the timber. He is holding his breath. "He's circled around," he whispers. He looks down at me, and his face is pale. "He's tracking us. He's done running."

We move away from the trail into lighter timber. I think I might break into a sprint. I can see myself running, feel its release. I do not run because I do not want to get ahead of Gordon, be killed between Gordon and camp. I feel watched, but when I look to Gordon he is looking behind us.

When the lodgepole and spruce open into meadow we walk in the thigh-deep grass and watch the border of trees to our sides, in front of us, behind. I blink each time I turn my head. My head wags from side to side. I think that if I am staring and blink that the bear will charge in that instant of blindness and be on top of me. I listen. The forest is loud. I remind myself to breathe.

I think of a bear's thick, wet teeth piercing my muscle and scraping down the length of a bone.

Squirrel-chatter works in my spine like electricity. I think of my bones splintered in the snap of a bear's jaws.

I take a step and then another. I imagine the taste of my blood. I imagine the taste of me on another animal's tongue.

We work in and out of the timber between small meadows, away from the trail, every step taking us a few feet farther to camp, toward the voices of Claude and Phil and my father, to lantern light. It is almost dark. I cannot make out the plaid in Gordon's shirt. We do not even speak in whispers. I think of an ear, an eye, my scalp peeled away from my skull.

We stop and we listen, and then we move again. I can hear the thrumming of our hearts without stopping, even above the sounds of the forest. When I think of it I take out my sandwich and drop it behind me and walk away. I think of chunks of muscle stripped from ligaments; my blood staining a bear's coarse, silvery fur. My blood on a bear's nose. In his nostrils.

Even when we see the lighted tents just one hundred yards away I do not feel safe. I know that I can be killed just here, this close, drug down and my neck snapped with the smell of woodsmoke in my nose. I know that a grizzly's paw is powerful enough to swat down a bull elk. I have seen it happen. I am watching it happen even when I am standing under the flap of the cook tent and the men are staring at me and Gordon is standing behind me.

"You find him?" my father wants to know.

"He found us," says Gordon and pushes past me and sits by the stove.

The men watch as I bolt the cartridge from the chamber of my father's gun and stand the gun in the corner of the tent and turn and walk out of the tent and stand under the canopy and stare into the darkness.

Claude follows me and stands beside me and hands me a mug with an inch of whiskey in the bottom, and I drink and cough.

"Just sip it," he says and goes back into the tent, and I take a step into the darkness, away from the safety of the light and the voices and laughter, and start to cry. I do not sob, but it is a while before I can stop, and I go to my tent because I want to keep my face away from the men.

I am still awake when Claude comes into the tent and gets undressed and puts out the lantern. I ask him if he thinks Gordon and I are lucky to be alive.

"Do you think you are?"

"Yes, I do."

"Do you feel alive?"

"*Very* alive."

"Like you don't want it to quit?"

"Yes."

"I know that feeling," he says and turns in his sleeping bag and goes to sleep.

The horses are close to camp. Their hoofstrikes vibrate on the skim of cold ground. I can feel them stepping in the frozen meadow a hundred yards away. I reach a hand out and hold its palm against the tent's canvas. The material is cool and flexes. It is tougher than my skin, but cannot keep out the cold. I turn my back to the tent wall and curl in around my gut. I feel drowsy. My body wants to sleep. I shake my head and listen to the night. I do not want to die in my sleep. I want to be awake; I want to cry out.

❈ IN JANUARY my brother and I are out on snowshoes above the lodge. We are plodding an angle up an exposed ridge to gain altitude, to have a look at the country, because we are young and bored with the inside of our cabin. The snow squeals under the rawhide webbing of the snowshoes. It is late in the day, and our shadows fall away from us as gray and blue as gunmetal.

We stop to catch our breaths and squint into the distance. Our eyelashes freeze and stick together. We blink to be able to see clearly. Our nostrils are frozen to the posts of our noses, and we breathe shallowly through our mouths.

The sky is one primary blue. There are no clouds. It is well below zero and the air glitters crystalline with minute particles of ice so light they will not fall. There is only snow and the blue-black patterns of evergreen.

Libby Creek is below us and under a foot of mottled ice. I look toward the river. The brush willow are just leafless spikes of soft ocher. There are banks of chokecherry and rose hips.

It is January, and for fifty miles in every direction the earth is pounded silent. I think of bear, think of them buried in their dens around me. I think of the blood-warm burrows of bear—the big boars curled to sleep, shifting to scratch and smack their jowls. I close my eyes and can see the milk-filled sows wintering their fatness against the appetites of their cubs. I think of them asleep beneath the snow.

I look up the ridge. I look for bear. I imagine their breaths condensing, rising in slim spires, from unexpected flues—from their quiet homes.

My brother turns to move away from me. A bayonet he's bought at the Army Surplus Store in Cody hangs from his belt. It slaps against his leg. It is as long as a machete.

"I'd like your knife," I tell him, and he stops.

The request is unexpected. He stares at me. He is thinking of the things I own. He is making a trade in his mind. Our breath is frozen and hangs between us. I tell him the story of the bear knife. He takes the bayonet out of its thin metal sheath and holds it in the cold air. Its blade is dull as stone.

"You want me to throw this at you?" he asks.

"I think I do."

He smiles. And then he snorts. "Why don't you just wait," he says. "In a year and a half you'll probably go to Vietnam and get killed anyway."

He sheaths the knife and starts down the ridge. I wait until he is in the trees along the creek, and then I follow.

WINTERING

I drive home to northwestern Wyoming with the car windows down. I do not play the radio, or sing, or whistle. I listen to the wind. I do not speak to the wind. I have had to explain myself too variously, too specifically. A gas station attendant in Thermopolis asks if I want my oil checked, and I turn and walk away from the man. There have been too many questions. The wind asks for nothing. I have worn away from conversation, television, music, even laughter. I want to be in the mountains, hold myself against them noiselessly, and mend—inside and out.

I have just graduated from college, and my legs ache as though I've been required to stand for four years, thigh deep, in a pool of December river water. I've been told that brain matter does not experience pain. I have no way to assess the damage there. My legs throb so badly I wish at times to lose them. I grimace when I take each step.

I rub my thighs as I drive. I reach lower and squeeze my calves. The muscles feel swollen, thick, cramped. I suck at the wind. I wonder if tennis shoes would have helped. The thought makes me smile. I own a pair, but wear them exclusively inside a pair of waders when I go fishing. I did not fish in college.

On the flats south of Meeteetse there are antelope. Two, and then three bunched together. The sage is grown up to the animals' bellies, lush aqua and muted grays. The antelope look to be boats bobbing in the chop of a northern sea. Boats without fishermen. Boats of beauty, their bowsprits carved into pronged horns, catching the sun, simply drifting.

Some of my classmates wore hiking boots; the kind of boots that a climber might purchase to tramp through the Himalayas. Most of them had bright-red laces. I thought they looked ridiculous. I did not see myself as a climber, or for that matter, a walker. I saw myself as a young man temporarily afoot, without a horse. I wore what I have grown up wearing. I wore cowboy boots. The college was in Laramie, Wyoming, so that was not unusual.

What was unusual, for me, at least, was the concrete: sidewalks, parking lots, roads, paved squares. My legs have lengthened off-road. They are accustomed to soil, wet and dry, the plush of meadow grass and pine needle. Four years of college on concrete has nearly crippled me. Graduate school would have likely landed me in a hospital. I limped away from Laramie swollen from my lower back to Achilles tendons. I did not attend graduation. I packed the car and did not look back.

I stop the car outside of Cody. The sun is setting behind Rattlesnake Mountain. There is a low scatter of exaggerated cumulus come bronze and mulberry and vermilion. I sit on the road's shoulder and close my eyes and breathe home air. The wind lifts my hair and releases it against my forehead. I feel the mountain's presence as palpably as a change of season.

For the next two months I work odd jobs—shoeing horses, building fences, some carpentry. I live with my parents. I am not good company. By the end of July I find a job managing Elephant Head Lodge. It is not far from where I grew up. I think that if I can make it through to the end of summer, watch the aspens turn and the tourists turn for lower land, that I will be all right. Only a month or two of smiling at strangers, and I will drain the water out of the cabins, strip the beds of linen, get the horses on winter pasture, and put up a *CLOSED* sign. Two months, I think, and I will be out of the business of interaction, and in the mountains alone.

I dream of January. Of dusk at four in the afternoon. Of the careful, slow pace of below-zero living. I imagine that I will wrap myself in winter: five months of gauzy light; the sweet stultification of the cold. I close my eyes and think of the creeks and river capped with ice. And the snow. Day after day of soft accumulation. Snow that will blunt all noise to whisper. I imagine that walking on snow will mend my legs, massage my psyche open to a pliant balance.

By the first of September the tourists are thinning, and it freezes two nights in a row. In the mornings I hear a bull elk bugle. My excitement gathers. I feel the momentum of my prayers for solitude gaining mass. Fred Garlow calls.

He wants to know if I will caretake a ranch. He tells me an eastern couple has bought a place, built a lovely home, and wants a man to watch it.

"Just watch it?" I ask.

"It's the Four Bear. There's some wild horses."

"How many?"

"I haven't gotten close enough to all of them to make a count."

"What do they want done with them?"

"They want them kept wild."

"Isn't that Olive Fell's place?"

"She sold it. She's got life tenancy. So do the horses. She's been up there forty years by herself. With only the horses. I don't guess she wants company any more than you probably do. The place you'll be living is a mile away."

"I have a job," I tell him.

"This one's better. It's year-round, and there's no dudes in the summer. Tell me you'll take a look."

"When?"

"Tomorrow."

I meet Fred where a dirt road breaks off from the two-lane that runs from Cody to Yellowstone and get in his pickup. He drives alongside Jim Creek for a quarter of a mile and then switchbacks up a sage and sandstone ridge for another two miles. We rise off the valley floor slowly. I step out to open a wire gate. "I can see into the park. That's thirty miles," I tell him.

As I walk back to the truck I keep my eyes toward Yellowstone, watching a mass of storm roll off the Continental Divide.

"We get up by the house, you can have a look into the Southfork. Over the top of Table Mountain. You won't want for scenery."

The switchbacks become tighter, steeper, the roadway canted. "Think this gets slick?" I ask.

"I think it can be a soupy son of a bitch. There's a lot of bentonite. If I were you I'd stay home when it rains, or you'll have gumbo to your hubs. It's the shits getting stuck going downhill."

We top out under a log home built on an exposed knob. Floor-to-ceiling windows flash on three of its sides. Fred squints into the sun, looking up at the house. "That's Olive's place. She got a crew of Finns down from Red Lodge to build it for her in the early '50s."

There are ravens perched on the peak of the roof.

"I've never met her."

"I imagine you've heard that she killed a couple of people. A lady who lived with her one winter, and a hired man."

"I've heard that about everyone who lives alone."

"I was with the bunch that rode this place. We found the body of the woman."

"I heard she died of exposure."

Fred spits out his window. "When you're dead, you're dead. If you die outdoors in the winter, I guess you're exposed."

The road curves along the uphill rim of a bowl for another mile, ending against the lower bulwarks of Jim Mountain. "This whole basin'll come up in wild iris in the spring," he says.

I nod. I try to imagine splashes of purple and pale blue pocketing this open, tan landscape. The new home is sprawling and angled and looks to be a broken escarpment fallen from the palisades that rise above it. It is constructed entirely of wood, native stone, and glass. Sage and wild grasses grow to its sides. Fred steps out of the truck. "This is it. Something like eight thousand square feet I'm told."

"They expect me to keep it clean?"

"We can probably get one of those services in town up to clean it. I think the folks that own it will be out for only a month in the summers."

Fred shows me the walk-out basement apartment where I will live. Its south-facing windows let in so much light I pull down the bill of my cap.

"Are they good people?"

"Who?"

"The new owners."

Fred pulls at an ear. "I like 'em better mostly than people I've known all my life. If I didn't, I wouldn't have hauled your butt up here."

I trust Fred. I've known him since I was a boy. I've heard him dismissed in town because he's Buffalo Bill Cody's grandson, but consider that just bullshit from gossips with enough spare time to worry over their neighbors' lives. The old cowboys who have worked with him estimate him honest and a first-rate hand.

The upstairs of the house is quiet and crafted with the care of a church. The walls are hung with Russells, Remingtons, Wyeths, Bierstadts.

I stand in front of a huge Wyeth canvas. "This one of the reasons they need someone on this mountain?"

"One of 'em. These things aren't reproductions."

We leave the house and walk west into the shade of the pines and cottonwoods that border Jim Creek. There is a set of corrals and several small, dark cabins. "Olive used to live in one of these until she got enough money for the house out on the ridge." He sucks at his teeth and hitches up his pants. "She's kept this ranch together without any help. I guess by selling her drawings in the Yellowstone stores. And some paintings. I don't think I could have done it."

"How high are we?"

"Over seven thousand feet."

We walk back to the truck. I step onto the rise of a boulder and away from Fred. The day is starkly clear. I can see thirty miles to the east, twenty south, and forty west. Without turning I can feel the mountain of Forest Service pine and spruce silently against my back. I imagine I can feel it contracting, cooling, preparing itself for darker, colder months. My legs ache, but the pain is manageable.

"What do you think?"

"You been up here when it blows?"

"You'll get some wind. It'll drift."

I look back toward the basin we've skirted to get to the house. It drains west into Jim Creek. I imagine a westerly wind sweeping it clean, burying the road tucked under the fringe of its eastern skyline.

"If it snows early and stays, I could be in here from November to March. I've just got that little '52 Scout."

"There's a storeroom next to the apartment in the basement. And a chest freezer. I wouldn't let you come up here without putting five or six months of food away. There's a phone if you get hurt or feel chatty, but you might want to say your good-byes."

I step down off the rock. "I'd be alone?" I try not to look too eager.

"I imagine you'll get all the alone you can tolerate."

I turn away from Fred and smile into the searing clearness of the day. "It'll take me a week to find a replacement unless the guy I'm working for has someone in mind."

"Make a list of the groceries you think you'll need. There's a washer and dryer in the house so you'll be able to keep what clothes you've got laundered. I've found it helpful to overestimate on the toilet paper, aspirin, potatoes, and beans. You a hand with the bottle?"

"I guess I wouldn't bring any. I've already been in a poor mood for a couple of years."

We get back in the truck, and Fred lights a cigarette and thumbs his hat back away from his face. "I'll call Olive and tell her you're coming up here. I'll let you introduce yourself. She doesn't hold up well under company. You understand?"

"I don't know that I do."

"If you get real lonely she probably won't want to go dancing."

My father tells me flatly that what scraps of sanity I have will be gone by February. "A caretaker?" he asks and shakes his head. His voice rises. "You went to four years of school to be a caretaker?"

"It's not a career choice. It's for the winter."

"It's a job for old drunks or crippled sheepherders."

"What about Christmas?" my mother asks.

I tell them that I think the coming weekend would be a good time. We exchange gifts on Labor Day. They give me a down vest and a pair of lined workgloves. I've framed a drawing of a bear I've made. My mother hangs it in their bedroom.

"I hope it works out for you," my father says. He's settled from the shock of my announcement. We shake hands. My mother gives me a hug. She holds her hand against my cheek and stares into my eyes until I look away. She kisses me, and hugs me a second time. I tell her I plan to unplug the phone at my new home. She looks down to the kitchen floor.

"I'm not mad," I tell her.

"I wish you were."

"Why?"

"It'd be easier for me to understand."

"I love you," I say, but it doesn't feel like enough.

She nods. Her arms are folded across her chest. I hug her, and her arms drop and hang between us.

I drive up the mountain the next morning. The fall is holding, the days warm, the nights chill, the trees are beginning to turn, their leaves ripening to bright yellows, golds, and russets.

I park next to the house and stand out of the Scout and can't believe my luck. I seem above most of the world, above all traffic. The air is as blue as lapis. It will fade to the color of frost in a few short months. I have been offered a home where winter will last. The snow will remain untracked until I walk it. I unpack my clothes, snowshoes, my saddle, books, a typewriter, and a week's worth of groceries.

I lie in the tall grass in front of the house and stare into the still and flawless sky. The earth is warm. I fall asleep and wake in the late afternoon. It does not occur to me that my fantasies of solitude are naive. I do not know, for instance, that fantasy and intent, at a high, lonely place, work themselves against the conjurer's mind, their edges knapped sharp and dangerous as obsidian knives. I do not know how permanently I am cutting myself away from the life I have lived, and that at altitude all wounds heal slowly.

I fix a light dinner and go to bed after sunset. I wake in the night and walk out to sit under a waning gibbous moon. The air is cool, dry. There are no insects. Owl-sound loops through the half-light like the warming reed section of an orchestra. The yips and howls of a pair of coyotes bring clear the face of a friend killed in Vietnam. His expression is one of surprised wonder. I lower my head and pray that his soul finds comfort and give thanks that I was not chosen to go to war. My breath sounds loud as the stirring of spruce boughs. There is a faint light in one room of Olive's house, and that is all. The insubstantial moon has set. The stars come brighter. I go back indoors and sleep the rest of the night.

I wake early to an alarming and constant scream. I do not say to myself, "Those are the screams of a woman, or bear, or horse." I say nothing. I can feel my heart quicken, and rev. I think for a moment that the earth is quaking open, that I am caught in the jaws of some vast accident. I leap from bed and pull on my pants and boots and run from the house. I run getting into my shirt. The sound seems supernatural, as maddened as the shriek of an angered god. I run toward it because I am convinced I cannot escape.

My mind plays through its brief catalog of casualty. There is the scream of a man pinned under the broken and dropped block of an oil rig—a scream of intense pain and bewilderment—a mountain lion shot through the bowel, a male bald eagle broken and falling in what I imagined at the time was a lost fight for family or sex. I know them now as just one sound: a sound that strips muscle from bone and leaves the listener merely skeletal and vibrating, stark and white as an ivory tuning fork. I run faster. I think of some crazed anchorite laboring against the weight of his solitude. I think that that is what I might find. I think of the scream as simply prayer gone wild, uncaged, sheering a man away from his passions.

The scream pulls me toward its center, contracts and loosens my tendons and ligaments, jerks my knees high into the air, makes me generally elastic with fear, and fast. It is not a matter of wanting to witness the source of the sound. It is a matter of wanting to make it stop.

I do not know it is a horse until I find her. A wild mare, gone delirious with pain.

She has gotten into the cattleguard closest the house—all four legs of her, snapped at the knees. She has thrashed while she's screamed, and blood runs from her nose and ears and barely from an eye she has beaten loose from its socket. Her leg bones have torn through her flesh, and work as she struggles like the jagged teeth of some beast feeding on her from the earth, stopped from rising into the air by the iron bars on which she lies. She is losing her fight to live. She breathes hard between screams, her mouth slick with a pink foam, her one good eye rolling white, but glazing rapidly in shock. I think she must have fallen into the thing at a run.

The sight of her turns me faster toward the house. I scrabble in my duffel for a pistol. I find the thing and grip it as though it is the neck of a rabid dog. I grip it hard because I am alone and know what I am about to do. I make my second sprint to the mare. Her cries are deeper. The ground shivers with them. Birds fly toward me in confusion. Prairie dogs scatter in a panic to avoid the slaughter they believe she heralds. I reach her, breathe in once to steady my lungs and heart and fire into her head. I have to shoot her twice, she is that determined in her struggle, and then I walk into the sage and sit. I drop the pistol in my lap and hold my palms against the earth. My shirt is unbuttoned, open, hanging at my wrists.

I begin to howl, perhaps because I am alone. It seems my only adequate response. I do not worry that I will be heard. I howl until I am out of breath. I look around me, blinking. I wonder if any part of me has gone with her, broken through the thin and penetrable surface that holds us away from our individual deaths. I grip my head and chest and thighs with my hands. I make sure that I am still here, complete. I sit quietly for half an hour and then walk to the house. My legs feel weak. My mouth is dry and tastes like steel. I do not feel like eating. I button and tuck in my shirt and pull on a jacket. I find a log chain and bucksaw and back my little four-wheel-drive to her body.

I saw through the ruined bone and tissue and hide at her knees, work her legs from the cattleguard and lay them in the back of the Scout. I pull the length of chain to her. I loop it around her neck, hook it snugly under the ridge of her jawbone. I circle the free end over the trailer hitch and ease out in the lowest gear. The chain bites solidly, her head holds fast, and I drag the amputated corpse a mile from the buildings. I slide her into a deep ravine and toss her legs on top of her. In a week she will bloat and rot, and the eagles and ravens and coyotes that catch her scent will come to this steep place for a meal. When I drive back across the cattleguard the tires slip in the apron of blood-soaked ground.

I make a pot of coffee and stall for time. It seems that I've done too much all at once. I check my watch. It isn't yet midmorning.

I walk toward the creek hoping the sound of water might settle me. I find two weathered sheets of plywood and several stockgates leaned against the back of a small barn. I wire the plywood over the cattleguard and put in a gate. I do not want to trap another horse. This one is enough.

Fred comes at the end of the week with his pickup bed heaped with canned goods, flour, beans, toilet paper, and two hundred pounds of packaged and frozen meat that he's packed with ice and wrapped in a tarp. He pulls a trailer, and we unload three riding horses and tie them to the buck-and-rail fence and carry the supplies into the house. "Thought we might get some fence mended before it snows," he says, and later, while we are saddling the horses: "Those cattleguards don't work worth a damn if you board 'em up."

"One of Olive's horses got in it."

"I saw the bloodstains. You get it out yourself?"

"With a chain. I had to kill her."

"Olive see it?"

"She wasn't there."

"That doesn't mean squat. She bought herself a telescope with some of the money she got for this place. I've looked through it. She can see the color of your eyes if she wants to."

"Then I guess she saw it. She hasn't called."

"I don't think she would."

We ride up the creek, climbing out on a ridge that borders the Forest Service. There are three hundred yards of fence down across the crest of the ridge. We reset posts and stretch new wire where it's needed and untangle the spooled mess of wire that the elk and feral horses have walked down. Fred stays the night. We finish the fencing the next day and load the riding horses into the trailer. The days have remained clear. The evening light is soft and grainy with a late hatch of flies and mosquitoes. I ask Fred if he wants dinner.

"I'll eat in town," he says and lights a cigarette. "You all set?" he asks. "Now'd be the time to think of what you might need. There won't be enough work to keep you busy."

"I brought some books."

"I hope you don't mind reading them twice."

"I don't. I think I might try to write."

"You have plenty of paper?"

"I guess I do."

"All right then." He gets in his truck. I don't know that I won't see him again until spring.

Within a month, a rain and two wet snows fade the mare's blood to rust, to ocher, blending it finally into the dark, brown ground. Her scream remains. I am sure I hear pieces of it each day leaked from the side of the mountain. It comes out edged and brittle and wracked as the morning it tore itself loose from her, the mare, a bay, a horse unused to the inventiveness of men. I grow accustomed to it. I think of it as bright red. I hear it as a melody that accompanies my isolation.

In October the phone rings. It is the first time, and it is before dawn. I do not know what time it is; I have put my watch away in a drawer. I get up in a panic. It is a woman's voice. "Are you the man in the house?" it asks.

"I suppose I am."

"I'm Olive Fell. There's hunters up by the spring. The one over on the east corner."

"How do you know?" I've found a lamp and turned it on. I'm settling.

"I scoped them. I want them run off. There's no hunting here."

"Right now?"

"I'm an old woman. My legs aren't up to it."

"Yes, ma'am."

The hunters are a local man and his midwestern cousin. They wear camouflage clothing and sit their horses as sluggishly as clods of pond mud. The cousin has sprinkled himself with cologne. I smell him when I step from the Scout. They are belligerent. They are trespassers and indignant that they are caught, but they keep their rifles in their scabbards. They claim they don't know they're on private land. I tell them I've found where they've cut the fence to ride onto the place. I take their names and ask them to leave. I escort them back through the opened fence, then bring up the wires and splice them together and staple them solidly to the posts. They don't say they're sorry. They tell me to go to hell.

When I get to the house the phone rings again. It's Olive. "I should meet you," she says.

"All right."

"After lunch. The day's been ruined anyway. Those men give you any lip?"

"Yes, ma'am."

"Thank you."

"It's okay."

"They kill anything?"

"Not that I saw."

"Thank God for that. And thank you for boarding up that horse trap." She hangs up.

When she opens the door she shakes my hand right away and then turns and walks into the kitchen. I follow her because I don't know where else to go. She is only about five feet high, has short red hair, her body plump and speckled. I guess she is in her seventies. She wears blue tennis shoes, blue denim pants, a short-sleeved blue fishnet undershirt, with a denim tunic pulled over it. Also blue. The pants and tunic are boxy and appear homesewn.

"You want some tea?"

"I'd drink a cup. How did you see them in the dark?" I ask.

"I saw their headlights. Where they parked and unloaded." She puts a kettle to boil and turns and looks me up and down. She folds her arms across her chest. "I never killed anybody," she says.

"I believe you."

"You don't have to."

"I know I don't."

"I don't have guests, but when I do they have a hard time not asking. The only one who doesn't want to know is my brother, and he doesn't visit."

"I've been in his flower shop in town."

"Usually takes me about a week to get over seeing somebody. Like when the man hauls hay cubes up for my horses. That's why."

"Why what?"

"Why I don't have anybody in." The kettle whistles, and she turns back to it. "Do you know why you've come up here?" she asks.

"I want to be alone. I think I might like to write."

"That'd be a tough way to make a living." She turns back to me with our cups. "You've found a good place to try," she says.

We take our tea into the living room and satisfy ourselves with the view out of the three walls of windows. The sun catches on every surface in the room. It is like standing inside a flame. There is a painting on an easel by the fireplace and tables mounded with prints. She shows me her studio. She takes a shoebox out of a drawer and hands me letters to read. They are from Georgia O'Keeffe and John Steuart Curry.

"I went to the Art Institute in Chicago," she says. "I thought once I might like to marry Mr. Curry."

We talk until it is dark. She turns on a floor lamp in the living room. A bobcat sidles out of the darkness and into the soft, yellow lamplight fallen out the windows on the west side of the house. He rubs his muzzle against the glass. Olive walks to the window and holds out her hand, making a clucking sound with her tongue. The cat grovels against the sill, his eyes half-closed. The light catches in her hair and glows lightly against her freckled arms. "This seem unusual to you?" she asks.

"I've never seen a bobcat act that way before. Did you raise it?"

"No," she says and kneels by the window and presses her hands against the glass. "I've been up here a long time," she says. "I've never hurt anything. It makes a difference."

"I can see that."

"I don't use the horses either. They've gone three generations wild now. Before I could afford a car I'd walk down to the road and get a ride to town."

She pulls herself away from the glass and goes into a storeroom and comes out with a small harness. "I used to wear this," she says. "I'd hook it into a sled and pull my supplies back up the mountain. Soled my shoes with worn tires, wire, and horseshoe nails. Art doesn't pay. You hungry?"

"I guess I am."

"You better get home then. I don't have a good appetite. I mostly just pick. Mostly at night."

I return our tea cups to the kitchen. She is waiting for me by the front door. "You're a good boy, aren't you?" she asks.

"I haven't gotten in much trouble."

"I hope you get your writing done. I hope it makes you happy."

"Thank you."

"I'll call if I spot any more hunters."

I look toward the telescope set up in the living room, facing northwest. Toward the house where I live.

"I was thinking about unplugging the phone," I tell her.

"I'd appreciate it if you'd wait until hunting season's over."

"Thank you for the tea."

"I won't spy on you."

"Ma'am?"

"I just watch the land. It takes some watching. There's a lot of it."

"Yes, ma'am."

She calls once more on Halloween and again the first week in November. Both times she has spotted hunters. Both times I find them and ask them to leave. I tell them they are on private land. I do not tell them that they are interrupting the lives of private people.

The week before Thanksgiving, hunting season ends. I call Olive and tell her I'm going to disconnect the phone cord from its wall jack. She says she understands. I call my mother. She tells me she loves me. She asks if I have plenty of food. I tell her that I do not want to run the risk of communication. She says that I've always been the way I am, that I shouldn't worry about having gotten worse. She says that she will always love me. I hang up and look around the room. I've taken precautions: no radio, no television, no record player, no chance to be tempted back to lower elevations. I vow that I will not lose altitude. My legs tingle. They're stiff. The pain only comes now in the middle of the night.

Every day I walk, and watch, and write on a pad balanced on my knees. I have been hired to guard against frozen water lines, theft; to keep the buildings heated so they will not constrict to thirty-five below. My days and nights are my own. The snows come and drift and close the road and leave me satisfied and unsurprised. The freezer and pantry are full. I come indoors to eat and sleep and bathe, and for the warmth. The days grow shorter. I feel the earth yaw back away from the sun. The raptors, the coyotes, and the grown-fierce, inbred horses are my company. There are fifty-two of them. I have made a count. They prowl the ridges blown free of snow and congregate in the mornings at an automatic feeder housed in a shed below Olive's house for their daily ration of hay cubes. They fight among themselves. The mares. The uncut studs.

I have seen them, twice before the snow, catch a coyote out too far from cover and encircle the quick gray dog. By the sheer force of their numbers they vector every angle of escape. They bare their teeth and lay their ears along their skulls, and strike with their front hooves. They hack the little predator to a mess of trampled bone and pulp. It has made me feel fragile and clumsy to watch them. I feel they blame me for the lost mare. I know they hear her last cries of pain, as I do, daily.

I think it skitters in their minds that I can go the way of a coyote. When I walk out through the sage they become curious, rapacious, swarm around me. Half a dozen times I've bounced an armful of rocks off their sides, and waved my coat above my head, and bluffed the mob of them apart. But when the cold pushes the songbirds south and freezes the fist-sized stones into the mountainside I become more careful where I walk. And when the snow is waist deep, I walk out on snowshoes in the night with only my mooncast shadow to watch my back. Just the two of us, safe, scribing a blue-shadowed trail across the drifted snow.

There are a few weeks of dislocation, and then I line out and write sixteen, sometimes twenty hours at a stretch. I will at times, the best I can gauge, sleep a day and a half and wake in the night and wash and go to work. I make stories. They become true. They become my history. I forget that I have lived on lower ground. I sit and watch the land. Time leaches out of me into the snow and wind, loses its rote and civilized boundaries, becomes a whole and seasonal thing. I grow more comfortably wild. I eat when I am very hungry. I watch the mountains at the horizons for complete revolutions of the planet and observe myself grow increasingly quiet, and more gentle. The untamed lives that surround me move closer. At times, mice, and once a squirrel, sit on my knees, not altogether

comfortably, but they come that close—or, I to them. When lonely
I write myself a guest. I speak to him, and he speaks back to me.

I wonder about madness. About definition. I try to summon my
mother's face, my father's, my brother's, the girl I thought I'd loved
just a year ago, but they seem too far away to reimagine. As though
they have all died, and I am left without their photographs. My
body remembers emotion and demonstration, but vaguely: anger,
affection, even caress seem blunted to my memory. They come as
soft tappings on a roof—that disparate. I find that I cannot put
heat or perspiration to the few recollections that rise and fade. I
wonder if I am to become a man who knows only bobcats and coyotes and hawks. I wonder if the feral horses will someday see me as
benign, forget that I am foreign. But I have mostly come past
worry. I am content. I am smoothed by the constant work of wind
and snow and the dark, cold nights. I feel the season turn in me as
tumblers in a lock, leaving me open to the earth. It does not happen all at once.

In the shortest part of winter I become sick. The days are
stunned with cold. It is perhaps the end of January. I am not sure
how long the sickness lasts or what brings it on. I remember eating
from a swollen can, knowing better—I cannot remember why. It
was a stew. Bitter and tasting of metals. Mostly I remember the
darkness, and the gauzy, brief periods of light that come up full
and fall. Three of them I think. I am sick for three days and nights.

I make a nest of towels, a pillow, a quilt on the bathroom floor. I
drag them there and vomit into a bucket. I kneel at the sink and
sip water from my cupped hands. I struggle on and off the toilet,
and lie again on the floor, and shiver and toss against the fever. I
am not certain when I sleep. I do not know if I dream. There are
times when it feels as though I am falling down a well. There are
visions, starkly colored hallucinations. When I think that I might
die it does not frighten me. Death does not seem so far from here
to there. I reason that madness is simple release, an entrance, an
acceptance of my own peculiar struggle. There are hours of sliding
dislocation into color and shape. There are chords of sound. I be-

come convinced that I am only an audience and that there are watchers watching me. I am too young to imagine that I have seen the face of any god, and far too young to know that enlightenment shifts and fades. And then I think I sleep.

I feel the mountain throb with the sounds of a dying mare. Her last and desperate scream of pain works in and out of me. Scours me. Loosens childhood memories. Shatters thoughts of the future. Suspends me in each moment, remarkably without sentiment. I wake in the night and am able to walk to my bed.

On the morning of the fourth day I shower and sip some broth. I walk out on the frozen ground, careful that the wind does not blow me east. I feel that insubstantial, and that elemental.

It is two weeks later when I see Olive out and crowded by her horses. They duck and nod and come into her shyly. She lays her hands on their outstretched necks, their foreheads. She removes her gloves, and they nuzzle at her open palms. She is standing on the ridge east of her barn. When the horses see me approach they scatter like quail. She laughs and waves and looks up into the frozen sky. It is cloudless and starkly blue. I come toward her on a drift. Its crust sparkles and crackles, but holds my weight.

"How's the writing?" she asks. Our breaths puff and hang between us in the air, dropping as we speak.

"Better than I thought. It's cold."

"It's winter." She looks southeast and points. "I was raised over there."

"On the Southfork?"

"Between Cody and Meeteetse in a sod dugout. It was a freight stop. My father drove a freight wagon." She looks at me. Her eyebrows and lashes are frosted white. "He was a dirty man. I can't remember whether he was handsome or plain."

"What did your mother do?"

"She took his beatings. Me and my brother, too." She looks back toward the place where she was raised. "He beat us all one day until we were unconscious. Then he fell down drunk. I was the first to come awake. We were outside. It was summer. I took up a hatchet and chopped off his hand. I loaded my mother and brother in the buggy and drove them to the county seat. She filed for divorce." She looks back to me. Her face is flushed, but very calm. The thought of a man's hot, red blood seems impossible in the white and frozen air.

"Did it kill him?"

"No." She smiles slightly. "But he never laid that hand on a living thing for the rest of his life. It was a different time. Everybody knew everybody. The sheriff told me I was a brave girl. I started to paint pictures afterward. I felt that free."

"Are you painting now?"

"I don't have the same kind of concentration." An eagle circles over us, flashing in the lightstruck air. We shield our eyes and watch him spiral wider and to the west. "Do you like it here?" she asks.

"More than I thought I would."

"Enough to stay through another year?"

"I don't know."

"If you're here next winter I'd want this feeder checked. It clogs sometimes. I'd pay you for the work."

"I'm already getting paid."

She nods, and cups her hands and blows into them. "I bought a motor home, and I've hired a boy to drive it. Next winter I'm going to have him drive me to California. Arizona and New Mexico, too. I want to look at paintings. It's been a long time. I think it will help with my concentration."

"You'd be back?"

"I might not be able to stay away as long as I think. But I wouldn't want to worry about the horses."

"If I'm here I'll do it."

We search the sky for the eagle, but he is gone. "I've been worried about the horses," she says. "The winter's hard." She kicks back at the snow with the heel of her boot. "When my father was sober he was a good man," she says. And then, "You've lost some weight."

"I was sick."

"I have been, too."

Out that night on snowshoes in the moonlight I lean against a
fir to watch my breath freeze and spread. I hear a scratching by my
ear and turn slowly and find a great horned owl perched inches
from my eyes. He looks down at me and seems to nod, to say in gesture that for a man I am bending toward a rightness. That is the
way it seems to me.

I close my eyes until I can hear him breathe, and open them and
the moon has passed behind a cloud, but he's still there. He blinks
and ducks his head and blinks again. I back away and move stiffly
toward the house to warm my hands and feet. I look for my shadow
and find the thing. I laugh. The shadow shakes.

Often, toward the end of winter, I lie in bed and try to reckon
whether I have just waked from a dream of words, or whether I
have stretched myself down, having tired of a day of making stories in the cold. Once I hear an actual voice. I do not understand
the words, but it seems to matter only that I am quiet enough to
hear the text.

Close to the vernal equinox the snow is puddling at the height
of day and freezing bright at night. I wake and am sure I hear foot-
steps somewhere over me. Most of the house is built above my bed.
Fred has told me that if a thief comes he will be a professional.
The paintings are cataloged worldwide. They cannot just be sold
and hung. My mind fills with the possibility of a burglary. I look to
each side and behind me to see if I am watching, if I've awakened
in another dream.

I slip out of bed and creep into the hall. I watch in surprise as
my hand thumbs back the hammer of the pistol that it holds. I'd
fired it last into a screaming horse. I edge up the stairs and from
room to room. I hold the gun in front of me. It catches the light of
the waning moon. Each room is sliced into a thousand shadow-
scapes.

I search the house down to the last room. I stand at its threshold
convinced I've notched myself to the nub of death, convinced the
assassin-thief I know I've heard waits comfortably for me to walk
into his trap and die. I nearly piss myself with fear. I know I am

awake and fallen into the world complete. I am afraid of pain. And afraid to die.

I keep my back to the wall and ease into the room and find the man across from me. He's cornered and has raised a gun. His eyes are locked on mine. He waits. He does not fire. In the last fragment of a second before I squeeze the trigger down I realize that the man I face is my twin, and come to sack the place dressed as I am dressed, in his best white cotton underwear. I slide down the wall, and sit and stare across my knees at the reflection of myself. It is caught in the gathered moonlight of a floor-to-ceiling mirror my employers have flown in from the north of Italy. The house seems suddenly gone empty. Soundless. I cannot even hear my breath. Except for the reflection I have no certain proof that I am there.

I snowshoe out the next afternoon, two thousand feet down to a valley already free of snow. I cut the two-lane at dusk and catch a ride to town with an aged rancher known regionally for his total lack of irony.

"You been up there all winter?" he asks. His voice sounds like the bleating of an animal from some strange zoo.

"I have," I say.

"You should have seen her when she was young."

"Who?"

"Olive. Prettiest girl in the valley. Out of my league." He smiles without taking his eyes from the road, and then looks up at the slice of his face reflected in the rearview mirror. "Still is, I imagine. You get lonely?"

"I'm okay."

"Friend of mine's a plumber," he says and turns and looks at me, checking the road from the corner of his eye. "Olive called him up there a couple of years ago. Her drains were plugged. He got up on her roof to run a snake down the vent. Imagine you know how the wind blows skirting that mountain?"

"Yes, sir. I do."

"He blew off." I look at him, and he raises his brows. "Floated to the ground like a goddamn leaf. Back and forth and set down on his feet so soft he didn't have to bend his knees. What do you think about that?"

"I don't know what to think about it."

"You think the wind could swirl around and do that for a man?"

"I guess it did."

He searches my face, and snorts out a laugh. "I guess it did," he says. "You say she's still beautiful?"

"I don't think she cares."

"You don't quit caring."

"I think she has. She's the only one looking at herself."

"Maybe that's the trick," he allows.

We do not speak for the rest of the trip. He drops me at a road-side tavern at the city's farthest outskirt and waves good-bye. "Keep track of how long you're up there on that mountain," he says.

"Yes, sir."

"If you don't, nobody else will."

Inside the bar there is a blaring band, and the place is packed. I force my way to the bar and shout my order and think the noise of the people might shatter me. I tuck a six-pack of cans against my ribs and strain back through the crowd and out. A girl my age kneels to the side of the entrance, where the dark begins, and vomits. She drops to her side, asleep, and I cover her with my denim jacket and walk behind the building where there is just a ledge fifty feet across to the lip of a canyon.

I sit on the canyon's edge and stare at my boots dangling hundreds of feet above the Shoshone River. I drink the cans of pale, weak beer. The smell of sulfur rises off the hot springs that edge a bend of the river. The moon is high and on this strand of river, and in a mottled smear of cloud to the south, and brightly to the west on the white and frozen mountain where I have lived alone. I think that once the beginning herds of horses grazed this rim. I think that now there is just this bar with a dangerous parking lot at its back. The night is cool and moist.

I feel the throb of the music drop through into the porous rock on which I sit. It climbs the column of my spine—I think that night—in a single-minded effort to reconstruct me more social. There is, too, making its way into my bones, drunken laughter, voices edged in threat, murmurings of sex. I draw my knees up and hug them and drop my forehead on their caps, my eyes closed, and even though I cannot hold a tune know that what my ears hear in this sad music is the sorry harmony of a dying horse.

I am unsteady when I stand. I start upriver and away from town. My legs feel stronger with each step. I smile into the moon as though it is the open eye of a great horned owl, and I think that if I'd fired into the mirrored image of myself, they would have found the gun and glass, painted black to reflect the light, but they would not have found the place where I had gone. I hold my breath and hear the clean, red scream that holds us all as one.

WIND

This place is violent, and it is raw. Wyoming is not a land that lends itself to nakedness, or leniency. There is an edge here; living is accomplished on that edge. Most birds migrate. Hibernation is viewed as necessary, not stolid. The crippled, old, the inattentive perish. And there is the wind.

The wind blows through most every day unchoreographed with the spontaneous inelegance of a brawl. There are tracts where the currents draw so relentlessly that the trees that surround a home, or line an irrigation ditch, all lean east, grown permanently east, as though mere columns of submissive filings bowed toward some fickle pole. Little is decorative. There are few orchards. Fruit enters by interstate, truck ripened, not tree ripened. Wyoming boasts coal, oil, gas, uranium, widely scattered herds of sheep and cattle, and once, several million bison. The winds have worked the bison skeletons pink, white, finally to dust. The carboniferous forests rose up and fell and moldered under the winds, layer upon layer, pressed finally into coal. The winds predate the coal. The winds wail a hymn of transience.

On the windward sides of homes, trees are planted in a descending weave of cottonwood, spruce, Russian olive, finished with something thorny, stiff and fast growing—a hem of caragana: a windbreak; utilitarian first, ornamental by accident. Shade is a random luxury. There is nearly always at least a breeze. Like death and taxes, it can be counted on. Almost one hundred thousand square miles and a half-million residents; there aren't that many homes. Towns grip the banks of watercourses, tenaciously. Ghost towns list, finally tumbling to the east. Gone the way of the buffalo bones. To dust.

There are precious-few songbirds. Raptors ride the updrafts. The hares, voles, mice, skunks, squirrels, rats, shrews, and rabbits exist squinting into the sun and wind, their eyes water, their hearts spike in terror when swept by the inevitable shadow of predators. The meadowlark is the state's bird, but I think of them as hors d'oeuvres, their song a dinner bell. Eagle, falcon, hawk, owl live here year-round. The true residents. The natives. The gourmands. Their land-bound relatives work the middle ground. Lynx, lion, fox circle the table. Coyotes make their living where they can: as gypsies do.

Much of the landscape is classified as subarctic steppe. In Laramie a winter's evening entertainment consists of watching the gauges on the local weather channel. Thirty-below-zero, sixty-mile-an-hour winds, are standard fare. From early fall to late spring Wyoming's odor is that of a whetted stone; the tang of mineral slipping endlessly against mineral. There is no tulip festival in Wyoming. The smell of sap risen in cottonwood and pine is remembered, and cherished.

And then the winds quit. It happens on five or six days every season, more often in the summer and autumn. The sky settles as the dome of a perfect bell settles—blue, uninterrupted, moisture-less. It is nothing in Wyoming to look twenty miles in every direction, the horizons scribbled in sharp contrast at the peripheries. "No wind," we shout in wonder. We speak too loudly. We are accustomed to screaming over the yowl of air. We quiet to a whisper. "No wind," we whisper. We smile and slump. Think of the slouch that survivors effect at the end of crisis. That is our posture.

We emerge from our shelters. If it is summer we expose our soft bellies to the sun, gaining confidence, we breathe deeply, glut ourselves with the scent of sage, a stimulating and narcotic perfume. We tend our yards. Paint our homes. Wash cars. My neighbor burns back overgrowths of dried weed, heaps of tumbleweed. He mends his fence. "Nice day," he says. I've heard him say as much when it is thirteen degrees above zero. What he means is that the wind is not blowing.

The foolish become bold. They start construction projects that will require more than forty-eight hours to complete. The rest of us work tentatively. We remember we are serfs. We know the lord is only absent, not dethroned. I pass through bouts of giddiness; I cannot help myself, but like the mice and voles, I remain alert. In Wyoming the price of innocence is high. There is a big wind out there, on its way home to our high plains.

I celebrate the windless days with small chores. I right the television antenna—clamped to a ten-foot section of inch-and-a-half galvanized pipe, and wired to a corner fence post—bury a neighbor's dead dog, till a garden, shake rugs, sit naked on the porch when the sun is high, standing to piss over its rail, admiring the perfect arc, reminded, as a kite remembers in fits, that gravity does exist.

The truly damaged remain indoors. Weeping is more popular than the local radio stations. And there are those who need to mourn. Ambulances roll. Marriages that have maintained their dangerous union only by the grace of catastrophe, like climbing partners roped together on a bad slope, fastened for survival, tensed against the common beating of the wind, begin a free fall. The bride and groom slip unbalanced, scramble into argument, and fall separately into affair. In the quiet between winds the air grows lively with wind-agitated argument. Many would have divorced years ago in a more languid place.

And we make love. Passionately. Feverishly. "The sky is not falling! The sky is not falling!" We shed our clothes and embrace.

My wife earned a degree in mathematics. She doodles graphs on her napkin while she eats. She intends to gather the state's birth statistics, to chart Wyoming's children back to the moment of each individual conception. She bets she will find the majority of the populace conceived during our brief troughs of windlessness. In Casper, Cody, Lander, couples grip one another in release, in celebration of the lull. "Can you hear them?" she whispers. I worry about her; she did not grow up under this wind. Every year she presents herself leaner. Taps her pencil and does not write, becomes more desperate for emotional vacation. I stay away from her when it is quiet. I have no desire to add to a new generation of survivors.

I have a friend in Phoenix who considers living in Wyoming, especially in the winters, a symptom of low self-esteem. He tells me this over the phone. But his case is largely predicated on temperature. Our below-zero weather gets the lion's share of the press; he knows nothing of the wind. I do not know how to tell him that living under the violence of the wind is more damaging than permafrost. The flux of temperature might heave and split, but the constant winds erode, desiccate, embalm. Living bent against this howling assault resembles an adolescent life in a house of alcoholics. Brutal. Unpredictable. Dangerous. Powerless. It is no wonder that we copulate feverishly when granted a furlough. Busy hands are attached to bodies that house fretted libidos.

A good part of the year we fantasize our escapes. We appreciate that escape is not easy.

There is an eleven-passenger flight pointed each day south. It rides the overthrust of thermals that writhe against the Rockies' east slope. The locals call it the Vomit Comet. Think of a butterfly on amphetamines. Soft drinks are rarely served. Peanuts catch in the throat. I've found it more prudent to forgo the snacks and invent a mantra. No one survives the trip unshaken. Veterans of the flight arrive in Denver, stand on the tarmac, and press their faces against the cool plate glass of the terminal. They take out their driver's licenses, read their names aloud several times. The decompression is brutal. The migrating water and songbirds fly low and land often.

I would guess that a good 10 percent of Wyoming's population got to the state and stay only because the trip out seems too hazardous.

Most of us stay from a mixture of inertia and curiosity. We

spend our days watching trailer houses yaw, limbs snap, tempers crackle, sign boards and power lines topple into streets. We find it ironically lovely that the land is swept up and held and carried in the air, drifted as snow is drifted to the lee sides of sage, post, anthill, and stone. Then, too, home is where your mortgage is.

Our horses turn away, their butts to the violence, tails blown tightly between their legs, heads held low, standing hunched, numbed by the torrent, as they are numbed by a blizzard, enduring, but for most of the year there is no snow, just wind; just the storm of air. Bison faced into the wind, but they are gone. Our sheep and cattle collect in mass graves, filling ravines like haired masonry, the snow sifting into every space and crack, mortaring the block of them solidly dead.

Bars blow full by midafternoon. Men stamp their feet, as they would to jar mud or snow loose from their pant legs and boots, but they are merely grounding themselves, stomping to remember how to stand in a quiet place, unbraced. Women dance in a crowd around the juke box, together, drinking straight whiskey, on occasion baring their breasts. The pros drink their first drink fast, without speaking. They laugh, raise their brows into wrinkle, whistle as though to indicate that they have just been missed by some accident. Everyone drinks steadily—any excuse to gather indoors. Churches simply do not lend themselves to conversation or foreplay.

By early evening the men have settled into a practiced whine about ex-wives. The women's ex-husbands are usually present, with young, less-wind-damaged women. The younger women look to their sides when they speak. $R = sv^2$: rage equals sex times velocity squared. The harder the wind blows, the more tension there is. Wyoming women fight. I don't know a Wyoming woman who can't take a punch. Three rounds with the first wife is considered an acceptable mating ritual.

Sometimes a man turns and knocks a stranger to the floor. More commonly it's a friend. For sport. For exercise. He stands over the downed man for a moment, his hands locked into fists, and then steps away shaking his head, returning to his solitary bar stool, muttering. No one calls the cops. I have seen the wronged man rise from unconsciousness, wipe the blood from his mouth, and buy his assailant a drink. The wind carries both our desires and rancor east, leaving us to live from each uneasy moment to the next. Life here is constantly blown too near the bone to hold a grudge.

The bar patrons complain that their children have grown unexpectedly thoughtless. They wonder why their lives have not turned out as they imagined. They study their faces in the backbar mirrors, listen to the building groan and creak against the wind, push their hats back for a better look. They can't believe how old they've grown. Where did it all go? they wonder. Just simply downwind? They have forgotten that nature has a short attention span, has never bothered to memorize their first names.

In the winters the wind sharpens the cold to a murderous edge. Thirty below zero with a forty-five-mile-an-hour wind. The difference between birth and a breech delivery. Steel snaps. Engine oil becomes thick as sap. When forced outdoors you pray for pain. When the pain leaves hands, face, feet they start to redden, finally turning black. You cannot grow them back as a salamander regenerates a tail. Once the wind has licked the flesh away it remains gone. The wounds become merely openings into which the cold can more easily pour, working toward the body's core, relentlessly wicking the heat of your life outward. Exposure is a thermodynamic lullaby. Torpor spreads like ivy, its leaves veined white with ice. You sit finally, become too tired to smile, too cold to remember mother, lovers, children. A neighbor finds you sitting, stiff, heatless, and wraps his arms around himself, his hands clamped under his arms, looking away from you, shifting from one foot to the other, reciting some childhood prayer. You are evidence of how he may not, one day, save himself. It is embarrassing to be killed by the wind, less acceptable than drowning, thought careless, possibly indicative of insanity.

Death by oxygen: to be bludgeoned numb by the very thing we cannot do without.

Last winter on January 17, two feet of snow fell, and then the winds came up and the temperature dropped. The steady crawl of snow broke apart in the gusts and produced a drifting chop of two-to four-foot swells. The landscape would not rest. I stood in the kitchen, my weight shifting from side to side for balance and looked out over the high plain that surrounds my home. I leaned into the storm as though my small house had transformed into some blockish barge, floundering upon a white and roiling sea. The stovepipe howled. The dog hid. He knew the wind to be a magician. He knew it meant to lure us outside, entice us to have a better look at its magic. I hid like the dog. I closed my eyes, my body still rocking, covered my ears. I'd looked up the magician's sleeves, found them empty, saw the darkness.

Winter travelers pack their car trunks with canned goods, goose-down bags, dry clothes, candles, books. In some places there are hundreds of miles between towns, and a car off the road becomes only a humped mound of white in a white and windswept snowscape. Some of the elderly and most of the disillusioned carry a gun in winter, so close to death that all that remains for them is the choice by which door they might enter. They imagine they would prefer stopping their hearts while the blood still runs hot. They imagine themselves dying shouting challenges into the gale.

There are stories, particularly of frontier women abandoned by their husbands, who reeled from their crude prairie dugouts and killed themselves on some bare piece of ground. I wonder whether they were silent and resolute, or if they screamed and flailed their arms at the wind, their keening swirled round their heads. The notes they left often simply read: "The wind. I could no longer stand the wind." No words of love or regret, just explanation. A personal epitaph of emotion blown skeletal, scrawled with a burned end of stovewood on brown paper or board.

Per capita, Wyoming competes each year for the lead in national suicides. It is the wind that swells our competitive sails. Its loneliness drills into our very fabric, is worn as an insignia. Our decks stand emptied, scoured clean of everything but despair. We emerge each spring, weathered, windburned, fragile, some of us gone overboard by our own hand. I wonder if the downwind states suffer? I wonder if Nebraska and South Dakota are savaged, as acid rain savages, by the hopelessness swept from Wyoming's high plains, carried eastward. Do the winds describe patterns of suicide? Will our descendants examine their pasts and find themselves responsible for demographic patterns of psychic desolation? In the future will Wyoming be sued? Will the litigants portray themselves as hapless, wronged downwinders?

On the two-lane between Belfry and Red Lodge, Montana, there is the little town of Bear Creek: bar, post office, a handful of scattered homes and trailer houses. The hills that rise away from the creek are largely emptied of their coal, the mines gone derelict, their entrances boarded. There is a routed, wooden sign along this road, just outside the town, commemorating the Smith Mine Disaster. It tells of a note that two men made in their final minutes trapped in a section of the collapsed tunneling. The plaque reads: "Walter and Jŏhnny. Good-bye wives and daughters. We died an easy death. Love from us both. Be good."

The day I stop and read the sign I'm tired, I've been traveling, my emotions wrung, risen closely to the surface. Their deaths hit me as though deaths of my own relatives. I weep a little. I'm alone and don't try to stop. The image of the two men, friends, huddled and desperate in the darkness becomes so vivid that my car seems to darken, as effectively black as a lantern blown flameless. I feel I am suddenly plunged into a shaft of darkness, there is the unease of vertigo, the air grows thick with lack of oxygen. I think of the many ways men die. I think of courage and resolution. I think that if Walter and Johnny had survived the mine that wind, any wind, would have tickled them to happiness, sugared every moment of every day. I see them standing in the wind, chewing on it as though it is their meal. My eyes clear. I feel torpid, puny, nearly suffocated and all too human. My joints ache. My head pounds.

I drive toward home thankful for the pain. Wyoming has taught me to be thankful for pain. There is pain that saves the body; there is pain that saves the soul. I am grieving for strangers. I am stretched clean of bias and consideration. I am alert. There is no boredom in pain. Those who writhe in pain, physical or psychic, do not wonder why they are not famous, worry that they're losing their hair, care that their car is rusted through. Vanity and ambition crawl for cover.

I think of choices, and sweep the many into two: to fight or to surrender. I wonder about Walter and Johnny's struggle—their surrender. Their plaque would suggest that they'd come to a relative peace. I wonder if they blessed their last miseries as an end to a lifetime of miseries. They were thinking of their wives and children. They tried to reassure. They rose to the occasion of their deaths. They meant to salve the pain of loved ones.

I imagine them perhaps holding hands, smiling if the strength remained, and lifting themselves on individual winds up and away from concern, swept on some final updraft of grace. It is a notion that helps their dying sit with me. It is the first time I am able to imagine wind with kindness. I wish Walter and Johnny had been granted another year. I wish they could have slept with their bedroom windows open.

"There's more than one way to go crazy," a friend advises. He's a man now in his late sixties, a well-known painter. He taught himself to paint during a long convalescence, after a horse fell on him and shattered his pelvis. His name is George. Years ago George and I used to drive together to the Red Desert in the central part of the state to hunt for jade: wandering for miles, heads down in the winds, picking up likely looking stones, chipping at their rinds with our hammers. Prospecting. I remember that we sprinkled sulfur on our jeans to keep the ticks off, and still each night had to burn out a dozen that had buried their heads in us. There were rattlesnakes, but mostly I remember the soft-apple and emerald shades of the jade. I don't remember the wind. Like men squatting for hours in icy mountain streams to pan for gold, my avarice transcended comfort.

"The wind's what loosens me," I admit. "Makes me feel like I'm coming apart." I'm proud of myself for being so candid.

"My ass," he says. He pauses to spit. "If the wind would have unraveled anybody it would have unraveled Monty. Monty seem frayed to you?" We're leaning against his truck, our butts hooked on the rounded edge of his dropped tailgate. He lights a cigarette, cupping his hands around the match. The wind spreads and sweeps the smoke to the east. He snaps the wooden match and drops it at his feet.

When George and I looked for jade we would stay with an old bachelor named Monty. He was in his late seventies. He lived alone in a trailer perched on a shelf he'd bulldozed into the side of a mountain outside Jeffrey City. He worked his claim each day on the side of the mountain, scraping away a track with the dozer, climbing down to find what stone had been uncovered. His bathroom mirror was a slice of black jade so clear of imperfection and reflective that I shaved in front of it for two mornings before I realized it was precious. Monty was as happy for company as an abandoned pet, his face perpetually twisted into a grin.

He had been run over by his bulldozer decades before and healed crooked, the way a juniper bough grows on an exposed ridge. He shuffled forward with a cane gripped in each hand, his hairless head up and grinning, his eyes sparkling, watering. His ears flared, cupping in the slightest breeze. He was as dark as an old coyote turd. Besides an occasional trip to town for staples, or a meal at the diner, his sole recreation consisted of a monthly visit by an Arapaho woman from Riverton. She cleaned his trailer and did the laundry. Monty suggested that she was an utterly expansive soul, anxious to fulfill *all* of his needs, but George and I have trouble imagining that kind of altruism.

He worked seven days a week, out bobbing against a brutal wind. He slept each night rocked by that same wind. The trailer was lashed to the mountainside with half-inch steel cables to keep it from being turned into litter. All of that without complaint. George figured that Monty could be forgiven for the insinuation of the affair. He lived far enough away from the rest of humanity to perhaps consider himself even handsome.

"Maybe it's a good deal," says George. "Maybe if you couldn't blame the wind you'd start in on your wife? Go after your work?"

"It doesn't bother you?" I'm feeling sheepish. I'm thinking of Monty.

"Wind, water, and worms." He looks directly at me, widening

his eyes for obvious effect. "Learned that in grade school. Three major causes of erosion. I suppose you've got a hard-on for water and worms too?"

"I like water. I don't think about worms."

"Folks that bitch about the wind is what bothers me." He's looking away again. "Why don't you whine about something you can change?"

He pushes himself farther back, sits on the tailgate, his feet dangling. We're quiet while he smokes. "I tried to commit suicide once." He says this quietly. He studies the cloud shadows that dip in and out of the canyons to the north. "Didn't have anything to do with the wind."

He squints as he draws on the cigarette. His face is cracked, lined deeply. He seems too much a part of the earth to want to leave it. He drops the cigarette butt, stands, and grinds it out with the toe of his boot. He stretches. "Missed the first shot," he says. He turns to me, smiling. "Spooked me so bad that the next three shots I had were running shots, in the timber." He turns away chuckling, and walks to the truck's cab.

That afternoon I walk out away from my home. I'm trying to enjoy the wind. It's out of the north, to my back. The sparse feathering of prairie grass bends to the south, sweeping fanned patterns in the sandy soil. I'm thinking of Monty and George. Black beetles bury their heads as I pass. An unusually pale-green rattlesnake is draped through the gnarl of a low-growing sage. He looks like some primitive Christmas decoration. He does not bother to coil and buzz a warning. Just turns his blunt face and watches me. Two buck antelope spook to the west. The wind flexes the tan hair on their sides. I've picked three plastic grocery bags from the tops of sage and stuffed them in my pocket. The municipal landfill is five miles upwind. I walk in its drop zone.

I enter a dry gully and follow it, ascending a ridge broken by wind-stunted pine and juniper, studded with outcroppings of wind-sculpted sandstone monoliths. As the wind varies even slightly so does the pitch its whistling makes through the soft, standing stones. I look out over the high plain. It is clear the fifteen miles to Carter Mountain. The mountain rises starkly in black stone and white fields of winter snow. A three-dimensional Rorschach. The snow is forced into plumes, like mimic clouds thrown from the mountain's sheer faces by the high-altitude currents of air. Wind, I think again.

I sit against a shoulder of sandstone. I face the wind and breathe deeply. It chills me to my belt-line, from the inside out. Spring struggles here. The only green lies shyly in the depressions that held the drifted snow. The rock is stained with smears of lichen: black, orange, rust, and white. It flakes like paint.

The sandstone against my back rises up twenty feet and is cupped; the dents and pits variously shallow and deep, of different circumferences: patches of weaker rock that have ground out more easily under centuries of windy workmanship. It plays a handicapped tune, the wind against the rock: a stone-age organ when the wind comes out of the north. I close my eyes and listen for melody. I think of the suggestion that the wind itself is the accumulated choir of the dead. I wonder if the dead yearn to voice their grieving? I wonder if they must convince themselves that they no longer need to struggle for their share of air? Perhaps, after all, the wind *is* their lament? Perhaps it is also their gladness?

I try harder to listen. With my eyes still closed I concentrate on my forced exhalations, the inhalations of cool air hammered to the bottom of my lungs. I do not hear the dead. I do not hear the living rock. I hear my own breath and become for a moment wholly satisfied, in just those simple moments of concentration.

That night I dream myself outside my flesh looking in, standing away from my body, unaffected by winds, studying my sleeping form as though I have returned to some old neighborhood, standing in front of a home with no light at its windows. The awareness that I am as ephemeral as wind startles me. I am frightened and excited by this ability for movement, frightened that I inhabit my body as though it were some broken spar of rock, alive as a reef lives, perhaps, but just a home in which I've come to make some sort of song. Separate. Yet I feel an unaccustomed comfort, and curiosity. Not because I am housed, but because I know in that moment that I am surely free to leave my home.

I come fully awake with a start. I sit upright in bed, in the darkness, breathing hard. My panic is the only evidence I own that my dream is accurate. I turn on the light. It shrinks me completely into my skin. I stare at my hands, flexing them. Just that quickly, from feeling myself sweep across the upturned face of landscape, to return as a naked man, my back cramped, sitting in a bed in the middle of a Wyoming night. My wife sleeps beside me. She stirs but does not wake. I touch her hair. Feel the heat of her skin against my hand. Feel how separated I am from her dreams. A wind works against the house. I hear the rafters moan.

I think of waking her, of making love, but realize that I would mean it as some sort of religious act, and she might not be praying in her sleep. I feel my explanations would be inadequate. Certainly making love to bait God is not altogether bad. I smile and wonder how many people there are who consciously couple to transcend their form. Five hundred? A thousand? Surely ascetics, not libertines, and I started drinking young.

I slip on my robe and turn off the light. I sit at the kitchen table in the dark and stare at the moon-fried plain that stretches away from the house. It is spring. The moon is so bright that only the closest stars remain visible. The sage casts shadows against the wind. The shadows move like cats curling into sleep. Our single cottonwood rattles, still not in leaf, its shadows a game of dark lines—swordplay with swords only. I stand at the window and think that the point is to step into wakefulness with the dream intact; to come honestly alive within my skin. There is a window open. The night is warm. Papers rustle. My hair lifts and falls, and I smile and backslide fully awake, fully *self*-aware, away from reverie. I am a man again, filled with common fears and desires. But I do not hear the wind, and it is there, all about the house, and slightly in the room. I have some interest in how it brings the shadows alive, dancing, flexing. I do not think they mind.

RECOIL

The sage is blanched olive, aqua, and gray. The soil pale and rutted: an abraded layer of bentonite and alkalis, swirled like some volcanic patisserie with comma-shaped hyperbolas of silica, lime, and ash. Last year's prairie grasses are scattered sparsely, brittle as dried quills, broken over by the winds, surviving perennially on the few smears of inconsiderable nutrient. This is top land, not bottom. Moisture is rare, and there is nothing to hold it. Kick down with your bootheel and within six inches you have struck the shelf of sandstone on which you actually stand. The prickly pear is weathered the color of army-surplus underwear, scarred, healed into darkish scab. Forty feet in front of us the sandstone rises up in a series of crumbling escarpments, dun colored, stained in streaks of terra cotta. A single living juniper stands against a monolith of south-facing stone as if supported by an espalier, as though a solitary sentinel awaiting better days.

The wind is out of the north, constant but not threatening. The sky, the color of undyed linen. The sun vague, as a dandelion blossom is vague when viewed through a dozen curtains of gauze. There is no heat. Flakes of snow strike the face as insects do. They are small, nearly moistureless chips of storm: a pail of them would yield little more than a teaspoon of liquid.

To the east the Bighorn Mountains blur at the horizon, struck numb on this January day. In this weather and light they seem insubstantial evidence of some lost land, as unreachable as the coastline of Atlantis. They waver in the cold, finally declining, spreading at their northern terminus into the lesser mountains of the Pryor Wild Horse Range. I think of the wild horses there, huddled into family groups, out of the wind; shaggy puzzles of color assembling themselves for the meager combination of their heat: pied, sorrel, pinto, bay, black, grullo, and smoke. Their breaths mingled into cloud, the hairs of their muzzles frosted white, and their eyelashes. Hammer headed, ram nosed, ewe necked, goat withered, cat hammed, broom tailed, they hold their yearlings at the center of the bunch, fenced by their imperfect bodies, perfect, all of them, in their unhampered freedom.

To the north and west the Beartooths and the Absarokas present themselves only in my memory. The edge of this Canadian front has rolled in and swallowed them. We will be next. The arctic mass bears down on us as would the paroled ghost of an ice age.

I look down at the boy. He wears no hat or gloves. He was reminded to bring warmer clothes but became too excited to listen to advice. He wears only a cheaply lined jacket that advertises a Cleveland baseball team. The jacket is snapped to his chin. It was sheer luck that he's pulled on good boots. His face and hands are red, going white. He shivers, but smiles as though he remembers the face of God, vividly. I call him The Viking; have since his birth. It is his energy, his stoicism—he withstands pain as uncomplainingly as animals do—the unbridled enthusiasm with which he launches into every episode of his life.

"Try it again," I tell him.

He brings the rifle's stock up into his armpit, tilts his head and lays his temple atop his thumb where he grips the gun, just above the trigger guard; he holds his breath, the barrel wavers. He's only seven, not large for his age, and doing the best he can. He fires. He misses the tomato sauce can, high, the coarse soil lifts in a spray. He pumps another shell into the chamber and fires again. The can

falls over, rolls to a stop against a sage. He's been at it for forty minutes. He hits just enough cans to want to continue.

My wife and I had driven to the boy's house in the late afternoon to meet him as he arrived home from school. There was an
hour and a half of daylight left. He and his father were ready. We
threw the sack of empty cans in the back of the truck and a plastic bag of garbage. We're practical people. There's no sense in finding a place to shoot cans without making a trip to the dump. We'll
stop by the landfill on the way.

I'd brought a pump-action .22. I showed the boy how to check to
make sure it was unloaded before I let him handle it. It interested
me to watch him put his hands on the actual stuff of his dreams. I
wondered what it might be that I could hold that would prompt
me to feel his excitement. Perhaps a child? But my wife and I have
decided not to have children. I made a mental note to have a second look at hobbies, but couldn't imagine getting that kind of
thrill out of holding a golf club. I settled for just watching the boy.
His gladness made me as happy as I'd been in months.

"What is it?" he'd asked.

"A .22."

"A Winchester?"

His father shrugged. He hasn't any more idea than I how the
boy has learned about different gun manufacturers.

"It's a Remington," I told him. He looked disappointed. "My father gave it to me," I added.

This seemed to register. "How old were you?"

"About ten."

He'd nodded and run his hand over the rifle's stock. That was
when he forgot his hat and gloves. We were all watching him, his
father, my wife, myself. None of us remembered to remind him a
second time, and now he is caught out in the open, and this icy late
afternoon is working into his bones.

"Aren't you cold?" his father asks.

"I'm fine." He doesn't bother to turn. His father and my wife
stand behind him. They wear gloves, stocking caps, heavy coats,

and they are cold. There is only so much of his excitement that any of us can absorb. I turn up the collar of my coat.

When we'd left the house the wind wasn't blowing. The sun was out weakly. There were slanting pools of midwinter light. There were spots on the macadam where the ice was beginning to melt. There was a glare. We'd lowered the visors in the truck. With four of us in the cab we'd only needed the heater on low. Everything has changed except the boy's ebullience.

I look to the boy's father. He's stamping his feet, his nose runs and freezes on his upper lip. My wife has snaked her hands between the buttons of her coat in an effort to warm them.

"One more load," I tell the boy.

He hands me the gun and sprints to the dozen cans we've lined along the hillside to check for bullet holes. I begin stacking the fifteen shells into the tubular magazine. With a glove off, my fingers begin to thicken in the cold. I pump a round into the chamber and click the safety on. The boy has returned. His teeth are chattering; his smile still unhinges his face.

"I've hit most of them," he says. "At least once."

"I'm beginning not to care," I tell him. I hold my hand against his cheek. I pull it back. His skin seems colder than the rifle's barrel.

"I'm not tired," he says.

"I am."

We all turn to the sound of the truck's engine starting. My wife sits in the cab. She waves. We can hear the heater running.

"I'm not cold either," he says. "Really."

"You aren't the only one out here."

He nods and looks toward my wife as he takes the rifle from me. "When I've shot all these it's over?" He's not complaining, just checking the information twice. It is his preference. He grants adults the prerogative to change their minds if it is in his best interests.

"I'm thinking about supper," I tell him. "This weather burns up the BTUs."

He nods again. He doesn't ask what BTU means. He clamps the rifle up high between his arm and ribs, lays his head down to sight, and walks methodically toward the cans firing as rapidly as he can. The spent casings arc to his right, glinting dully in the frozen air. Fifteen shots. Three cans down. The ashen hillside pocked in a dozen more places. I'm too cold to try to interfere with his charge. He puts the safety on and turns. He holds the rifle in both bare hands, smiling heroically: a poster child for why young men can be convinced to go to war. He has attacked and remains unharmed. The enemy is in disarray.

"That should show them," he says. His martial fantasies have brought his eyes alive. In this boy, The Viking, there is the hint of a berserker. It is lucky that he has been born to patient and reasonable parents.

"What it shows me is that you need another lesson in how to handle that gun."

"I didn't really hurt anything."

"Tell that to the cans."

"They're cans," he says, honestly perplexed.

"What were they a minute ago?"

He looks down at the rifle, and then back to me. He trusts me, and he's not a duplicitous boy. "The enemy," he whispers. He knows the difference between the brutality of real life and the brutality of entertainment. He knows that he's just stepped in and out of a cartoon. He sees no reason to conceal the pleasure it's given him.

He hands me the gun and helps his father gather the scattered cans into the brown grocery bag.

He's the last one to the truck, coming slowly, examining the cans in the bag, pulling them out singly, holding each one at arm's length, squinting at their bullet holes. When I turn to let him squeeze behind the seat he drops the bag and hugs me. The side of his face against my belt, his arms encircling my thighs. He says, "Thanks." His ears and nose have gone red as a clown's.

On the drive home he sits on the bench that pulls down behind the seat in the pickup's cab. My wife sits with him. She has taken off her coat and wrapped him in it. The warmth in the truck is driving the cold in his numbed muscles inward, cooling his core. He shivers. It is not a hardship for him. It was only hard for him to quit his sport. When he looks up and sees me watching him in the rearview mirror he smiles again. His nose is running, and his father hands him a handkerchief. My wife cups her warmed hands over his ears. He blows his nose.

Nothing seems alive on the landscape except the gathering wind, the snow. And then we pass under a ferruginous hawk perched on the top of a telephone pole. He is a large bird, approaching two feet in height. His head swivels, his yellow eyes watching as we pass. His breast feathers flush and relax in the wind. He's hoping to get lucky, watching for anxious rodents on last-minute errands before the approaching storm falls upon us. I have the heater turned to its highest setting and still the windows fog. I clear them with my jacket sleeve.

My father was a hunter. There were guns everywhere in the house and people who knew how to use them. I have an old album filled with faded black-and-white photographs of me posing beside the bodies of bear, deer, and elk. In most of the pictures I hold my father's rifle for him, like some midget gunbearer: an apprentice. He rests a hand on my head; my brother rides on his shoulders.

In the side mirror I watch the hawk spread his wings, release his grip on the pole, and let the wind vector him southward. I remember helping my father clean the game birds he brought home in the falls. I remember the attentive eyes of our hunting dogs, large brown eyes watching us as though we were re-creating the magic of flight instead of disassembling it, our hands shiny with blood, feathers stuck to our wrists and forearms, the air smelling of blood, the good, rich odor of the opened birds. I remember spitting shot out on my plate during fall dinners. Even now I prefer pheasant to chicken, the sharp flavor of venison over the blandness of beef.

I had badgered my father constantly—as this boy has his—to let me try out a gun. I had been instructed in the handling of guns, their care, but had never fired one; I wanted to truly earn my image in the photographs. My father had finally had his fill. "Which gun?" he'd asked. I was unsure. I wanted as much as I could handle. I didn't want to be mollified.

"You pick," I'd said.

It was after dinner, summer, and he was tired from his day's work. I'd forgotten that he'd taught me to swim by tossing me into a lake, taught me to drink by pouring me a water glass of bourbon. He simply nodded, slid a .12-gauge shotgun from its case, filled his jacket pocket with shells, and started down a dirt road to a pond at the edge of his farm. I trotted beside him. It was a year or so before we were to move to Wyoming. The farm was in western Pennsylvania and its pond smallish, the outlet silt choked, marshy, grown to cattail, the side fed by the stream nearly level and trampled into a pocked and spongy surface by the stock that came in to drink. I loved the place. I'd hidden along its shores to watch muskrat, the splashdowns of waterbirds.

It was dusk. The fireflies just beginning to sprinkle the air with their ignitions. A mist rose off the water's surface, the air above the mist alive with bats ducking and rising, gorging themselves on summer insects. The earth seemed to hum with the shrill of cicadas. Occasionally a fish broke the surface of the pond, the surface rippling, catching the last of the day's light. I imagine our faces must have caught and held that light, our skin gone rose colored, softly luminous, appealing.

I look again into the rearview mirror. The Viking's head nods with the rhythm of the truck. He is starting to warm, to surrender to fatigue. He holds the rifle upright between his knees, gripping the barrel with both hands. His head snaps up, and he tightens his grip. He is so intent on seeing this task of shooting the gun to its end rightly that he holds the thing as he might well hold a truncheon, or a crucifix—with that kind of vigilance. He has forgotten that we are on our way home, that we will eat, that he will be put to bed. He is absorbed in this very moment of his life. I look at him again and see the image of my younger brother clearly, when he was a boy. It is not a hallucination. He shared this boy's daring, his ungovernable joy, the reverence for any activity that transported him into fantasy. We called my brother The Mongoose because he regularly caught rattlesnakes using only his bare hands. He was that fearless, that reckless, that sure that life could not ruin him. And like The Viking he was captivated by the spontaneous violence of firearms.

I look back up to the highway. The snow swirls on its ice-glazed surface. The light has almost left the sky. I turn on the headlights and remember my father walking out into the mud at the skirt of the pond, thumbing shells into the shotgun. A Browning. I had asked. Without any hesitation he swung the gun to his shoulder, fired twice, and I watched as two bats spiraled into the water, one flopping a bit before it drowned, gone lifeless and splayed on the water. The report of the shots swelled and echoed in the humid air.

My father pumped the remaining shell into the chamber and motioned for me to come up beside him. He handed me the gun, stepped behind me, and said, "Kill a bat."

I was a small boy—the size of the boy in the backseat with my wife—and the gun was too heavy for me to steady, but I tried. My wish had come true. I was excited about the prospect of firing the thing, but also anxious that I might disappoint my father. There were so many bats in the air it seemed impossible I might miss. It gave me courage. I seated the stock into my shoulder, my right arm barely long enough to reach the trigger, leaned back to elevate the barrel and fired. The recoil spun me in one complete circle in the mud and left me sprawled on my back. As the drowned bat was sprawled.

My father walked to where I lay and lifted the gun away. "We might have been a year too early for this," he said.

"Did I kill a bat?"

"No."

"Did I hit anything?"

"You shot a hole in the sky."

It was a long walk home. By the next morning my shoulder had swollen purple and yellow. For a week it was painful to raise my arm. I trophied the damage for the other boys at school. "A shot-gun," I told them. It was worth it.

I park the truck and The Viking's father and I watch as the boy enters the house. He is unsteady on his feet, and that is unusual. He's exhausted to the point of clumsiness. His father grips my shoulder as men do when they love one another. He is a gentle man, decisive, a painter, a cherished friend. There is a part of him that has been surprised by his son's fascination with shooting the gun. He is an attentive father. His son has been with him in his stu-dio since an infant. The first toy he built the boy was an easel. He has instructed him in the appreciation of color and composition, beauty, and still, for years, the boy has wanted to shoot a gun.

We know the boy has no accurate concept of death; just as cer-tain that he has no idea of his ability to cause suffering. We no longer hunt, but this man and I were raised with guns, hunted when we were younger, and agree that his son should know the re-alities of handling firearms, witness the damage they may render. That is what we say aloud to one another. Secretly we simply mean to please him. We adore him. The boy calls me his uncle, and I love him. He has adopted me the way a wolf pup adopts a childless adult male. He trusts I would die for him.

Today we took him out in the cold so that we could witness the expression of pleasure on his face. I brought the gun. We hoped he would hit a can. We were that greedy for his joy. We wonder if it could have been done in a better way.

"He loves you," The Viking's father tells me. He squeezes my shoulder harder.

"I'm proud of it," I say. I mean it. The boy's love is one of the few things I know I've proved worthy of. His father nods. Through the window we see the boy telling his mother about the shooting. He gestures wildly. When it dawns on me I add, "I'm even prouder of how much I love him. I didn't expect it. It's not something I've earned." A huff of wind lifts and purls the snow between us. "Grace," I say. "A gift." Our faces soften.

The meal revives the boy. His energy lifts, but evenly. When the others have cleared their dishes he asks, "Do you go hunting?" He is trying to throw an occasion into his future so that he may relish the anticipation of the thing. He thinks that someday he might like to hunt. He and I are the only two left at the table.

"Not anymore," I tell him.

"But you used to?"

"I did."

"Would you hunt a bird?" He is checking to see if I am hierarchical in my prejudices. He doesn't ask whether I fish. He takes it for granted that my convictions are so flimsy that pulling a fish into the air to die would hardly seem like a crime at all.

"I might go bird hunting." I mean to placate him. I'm caving in to the pressure. He won't be old enough to hunt for another seven years. Twice his present lifetime. Neither of us know what he might be like in another seven years.

"Bird hunting's hunting."

"I guess it is."

"Why don't you hunt bigger things?"

"Because I don't enjoy watching animals die." I speak weakly. He's already established that my claims are situational. I've slumped in my chair. I wonder how he'll proceed. I have as much as said that I get a charge from killing small birds.

"You eat meat," he says. Children do not suffer hypocrisy gladly.

"I was a vegetarian for five years." I realize the statement is lame before I am finished with it.

He smiles and picks the steak bone from my plate. "Not anymore," he says. He is a rare boy who owns the rough and muscular hands of a man. The hands look made to hold a bone.

"When you're old enough I'll take you bird hunting."

"You're sure?"

"I'm sure."

"You won't forget?"

"Not if there's someone who will remind me."

He smiles. "Do you want to see Sarge?" he asks.

The Viking owns a leopard-spotted gecko he's named Sarge. The lizard is new, just four inches long, thick bodied, and rattles its tail like some witless snake. It eats crickets by the dozen and lives in a converted aquarium by the head of The Viking's bed. I follow him down the hallway to his room. He sits on the edge of his bed, and I sit on a low three-legged stool in front of the tank. Sarge rests on a heated ceramic stone. He is plump with crickets.

"Do you want to hold him?"

"I don't."

"Are you afraid?"

"I don't like snakes."

"He's a lizard."

"He's a snake with feet."

The Viking smiles and lifts Sarge out of the tank. He grips him in one hand and pets the top of his head with the pad of a single finger. I'm not worried that he'll throw the lizard at me. He's satisfied that I'm fear riddled and that he is not. It's enough. I watch him comfort the thing.

He's an obstinate boy, loyal, easily frustrated if he's misunderstood, inquisitive, a good problem-solver, naturally kind, temperamental, judgmental, fierce, generally fair. At times when I am alone with him he reminds me so much of my brother that I often forget that I'm old enough to drive. We become just two separate boys sitting together in a room, comfortable with one another, innocent. Linked more strangely than either of us can explain.

"It doesn't bother your brother to hold Sarge," he says. The statement's not meant as a challenge.

"My brother likes snakes."

"Is that why you call him The Mongoose?" He knows that it is. My brother has fashioned him a fetish from antelope bone and hide, given him an arrowhead, and a prehistoric shark's tooth. He is allowed to call my brother The Mongoose.

"Tell me about the rattlesnake skins." The Viking asks for stories the way some children ask to have particular books read to them over and over again. He returns Sarge to the heated rock and lies back on his bed. "Sarge doesn't have suckers on his feet," he says. "He can't climb out." He doesn't want me to worry so much about the lizard getting on me that I can't tell him stories.

I tell him how my brother nailed snakeskins to boards, inside out to dry. That he took emery cloth and sanded away the dried muscle, the hardened membrane. I explain to him the patience it took to massage glycerin into the skin until it was as soft as flannel.

"What did he do with them then?"

"He made hat bands and belts. Once he glued snakeskin to a pair of our mother's shoes."

"And the rattles?"

"He kept them in a small box."

The Viking smiles. My brother has given him a rattle. The Viking's father has told me how the boy brings the thing to dinner, shaking it with all his might under the table, hoping to panic his family, finally disappointed that he can't shake it fast enough to produce a believable buzz.

"I don't think there's enough of Sarge to make a belt," he says. "Tell me about how The Mongoose never had eyebrows or hair on the front of his head."

"He wasn't born that way."

"I know. Tell me about the black powder."

I tell him how my brother kept two battalions of green plastic soldiers secreted in his closet. The closet was small, lined with shelves, built under the eave of the house. I tell him how The Mongoose would line the soldiers into opposing sides and then strike a wooden match into the spray of a can of deodorant. The Viking has heard this story a dozen times.

"Like a flame thrower?" he asks.

"Like a very small one."

"Where did he get the deodorant?"

"It was our father's."

"Do they still make it?"

"I don't know," I lie.

I tell him how the soldiers melted, retreated into shapes that resembled disfigured candles. How my brother saved his allowance to buy reinforcements.

"What about the black powder?"

"Sometimes he came too close to a saucer of it that he had poured out in the closet. It went in a flash."

"With the flame thrower?"

"Yes, but the powder flash is what took off his hair."

"How did it happen more than once?"

"My parents wondered that, too." I don't tell him that the pools of black powder were used to disable enemy tanks.

"What about the secret-agent gun?"

"This is the last story."

"Okay."

"The Mongoose had a .22."

"Like the one I shot today?"

"A different one. A bolt action. He wrapped the end of the barrel with black electrician tape. He took the muffler off the lawn mower and screwed it onto the barrel. The threads bit into the tape."

"And it didn't make a sound when he shot a bullet?"

"He stuffed the muffler full of steel wool."

"But there wasn't a sound?"

"Just a small sound."

"Like what?"

"Like cracking a knuckle."

"Wow."

I think that I might never tell him that when my family moved into town for winters out of the Wapiti valley that The Mongoose bought a handheld box periscope at the Army Surplus Store and hid in fifty-five-gallon garbage cans in our neighbors' alleys. That he listened for songbirds, located them with his periscope, eased up out of the cans with his silenced gun, and killed dozens of them before the police captured him. The neighbors noticed. I don't want The Viking to hear about the look on my brother's face, sitting alone in the back of the squad car. The thrashing he received from our father.

I'll wait for another time to tell him how I once carelessly shot an anvil and that part of the shattered bullet was dug out of my brother's side. I'll teach him how to spell ricochet, but I don't want him to catalog my irresponsibilities.

I'll also wait to tell him about the evening that my brother and I fought and how The Mongoose shot the heel off my boot, from the hip, as I was running away from him. How to explain that we had the best of instruction, practiced that instruction, and still consider it a miracle that we did not maim or kill one another. We were maybe too comfortable with guns. We were trusted with guns, but we were boys.

And there is the story about the antelope I killed the fall I was fourteen. It was my first year hunting. The first year I could have a picture taken with meat I killed for dinner. Will The Viking forgive me for making a poor shot with my last shell and crippling an animal, a fast, sleek animal that became unwisely curious about me and stopped for just an instant to have a better look? It would seem ruthless to explain how my brother and I, and a friend from a ranch on the South Fork, herded the wounded thing into a ravine steep as a loading chute. How to describe our panic and our shame? How to describe our urgency to stop its suffering, our suffering? I am afraid of the pictures that will construct in his mind, in a ghastly narrative, if I tell him that we stood above that quivering tan-and-white beast, hefting the largest rocks we could lift, raising them above our heads, dropping them like prehistoric caveboys until we knocked the last terrified fight from its mind. Thinking of that afternoon still numbs me to torpor. I do not know how to mimic the sounds that rocks make fallen against bone and flesh. And the throaty bleating is above my range of voice. I have never had to scream through that kind of fear and pain, plead for mercy in a foreign language. How to explain that mercy was not ours to give? If I tell the story The Viking will ask how it ends. I will be obliged to tell him that we three boys dropped ourselves onto the pronghorn's back, that my brother gripped its curved horns, pulled the head back to expose the throat. I will have to tell him that the animal made no more noise. That its eyes had surrendered. That it was praying to its god. And I will be required to stand and demonstrate how I stabbed the helpless thing again and again until it stopped its struggle and I had finished the task I had begun with a borrowed gun. I would, perhaps, not have to tell him that it was not fun.

If I tell him the story it will be when he is older. When I am taking him bird hunting. I will stop the truck along the highway. I will tell the story long. I will make it terrible. I will not have to try very hard.

"You know what I'd do if I was a dog?" he asks.

His question startles me. I look down at him. He lies with his hands laced behind his head. He blinks slowly, just on the edge of sleep. "What?"

He smiles. "I'd wag my tail."

I pull the blanket up to cover his chest. I kiss him. I turn out the light when I leave his room.

That night in my own bed I cannot sleep. I worry that I have wronged this boy. I worry that I have started something in him that will, years from now, collide badly with the world. I console myself by thinking of who he is, his sweetness, who my brother is, a man more compassionate than I have been able to be.

I know that it is my own fears that keep me awake. My own crimes. I think of how much I do not trust in the world. I remember that years ago, as a young adult, even after I'd stopped hunting, that I still slept with a pistol under my bed. The last evidence of a lifetime of guns? Or something more? Perhaps evidence of a belief in jeopardy, even evil. A pistol to help a man sleep?

I tangle in my bedcovers. I think of a friend, a psychologist, who struggles to glimpse the peace she feels lies at her core. She is active in Amnesty International. Because she is a kind woman, and fluent in Spanish, she spends her summers in Central America counseling survivors of torture. She is a bold and candid woman. She does not own a gun. She meditates. Last year she traveled to a foreign ashram to receive darshan from a living saint. She tells me that she believes that wrong action, in any form, is simply a kind of ignorance: behavior shrouded from the single light of God. I agree with her. I want to.

This past fall she called me. Her voice rose and fell as jagged as a dying thing. She had just returned from an Amnesty International conference in Washington, D.C. The subject had been torture; the examples global, specific, and terrible. The accumulated weight of the testimony had suddenly seemed to her evil, and actively so. It seemed more than ignorance. It frightened her gravely. Dislocated her beliefs.

She is resolute enough that she does not fear for her own life. She fears for the life of her beliefs. Meditation did not seem enough. Atrocity squatted in her visions. She became heartsickened to find evidence that so many delighted in the suffering of their victims. She was cornered. She wept. She prayed. It still did not occur to her to want a gun.

We met for coffee, and I reminded her that Gandhi did not follow the example of his nation's colonizers. I reminded her that there exist imprisoned Tibetan monks who plead with the Divine that their Chinese torturers gain enlightenment before they do. She smiled and hugged me, but it was not enough.

I turn from one side to the other in my bed. I'm sweating. The sheets stick to me. My chest pounds. In the moonlight I see this woman's life, the lives of a boy and brother I love, braid into one, and I grasp that braid and pull myself upright in my bed. I wonder if the presence of a gun attracts violence? Does the ownership of a firearm pronounce one a victim? I wonder if I am a careless man. If I am capable of change.

Not long ago I brought a blowgun back from the Amazon basin. I had traded a tribesman for the thing because I thought it lovely. I showed it to The Viking. He handled it. He puffed a dart into the back of his parents' couch. His eyes shone. I told him of the men who used them to make a living. I tried to pantomime their hunt. I described the animals that granted their lives for the people's survival.

His father told me that in bed that night the boy began to cry and could not be consoled. "They kill monkeys!" he'd shouted. A connection had been made and shrunk him into fear. He never asked to see the blowgun again. Perhaps his soul is too straight for me to bend with my indulgences of his whims?

This past winter I picked him up at his elementary school. His father had called from a meeting that was running late. The Viking and I were happy to see one another. He told me about the routine of his day, and I told him of mine. We are used to each other. He is a boy who largely speaks his emotions through expression, through gesture. I was surprised when he interrupted our small talk and told me he loved me—an unprompted gift.

"Dad says we're a lot alike. That when you were a boy you were like me."

"I think you're a better boy than I was," I tell him.

"Why?"

"Because you have more explained to you. And you understand more than I did."

"I think I am like The Mongoose, too," he says.

"I think you're right." I look at him. The sun is on his face. His face is unlined, his hair thick and rich in the light, his eyes clear, his skin smooth and darkened by his play. It is a face my brother has owned. He only knows The Mongoose as a man with arrowheads, a shark's tooth. He has his favorite stories of my brother's boyhood. He has no way of knowing my brother as a boy.

He does not know that my brother went to law school, graduated with a disinterested ease, passed the bar, preferred to run a bar. He does not know that my brother has lived with my mother for three years now. That he shops for her, cooks, brushes her hair, and to soothe her nightsweats squeezes lemons and crushes mint into warm water so that he may bathe her face and back.

He has visited my mother with his father and seen her always in pajamas, her face divided, encircled by the clear tube that brings her oxygen. He has heard the hum of the machine that distills the oxygen from the air. Heard her cough. The Viking has sat with her at her kitchen table. He does not know that it is my brother who steadies her from her bed to the kitchen; to the end of her tubing, her tether. And back again when the visitors have gone.

He does not know how the yard gets raked, the walk shoveled, the bills paid. He is too young to think it odd that a middle-aged man lives with his mother. He has not read the poems my brother writes in the evenings, and at night, and in the early morning while the coffee brews. He does not know that the poems deal in hope and redemption, that they reconstruct the women my brother has loved. Someday he will. Someday he will understand the sweetness and the shame of the men whose characters he shares.

I put my hand in his hair. He does not move his head. He looks up at me expectantly. "You both have good hearts. You and The Mongoose," I tell him. "And you are both nearly fearless." He smiles. He straightens on the seat. I return my hand to the steering wheel. I add: "Just don't put too much faith in justice."

He furrows his brow. The statement is not beyond his understanding, but it has confused him. He opens his mouth to speak, and then does not. Mercifully this is a boy who has seen only what a bullet can do to the tin of a can. The sun plays through the windshield in a sweeping glare. We can hear the voices of children playing, the grind of traffic. "The world is not always fair," I tell him. "You'll notice it more than most of us do. My brother has."

He nods. He looks down to his lap. He turns his hands and opens them so that the palms face up.

A DITCH BURNING

I am related to water. I am a descendant of its sound and movement. Part of a roiling lineage. If I bend an ear to either shoulder
I hear the suck and swell and hiss of a mountain stream. My soul
has nursed at liquid teats. As colostrum is passed from mother to
child, so the vital history of water has entered me. Water brings
me joy. I fear that water will someday murder me. My life is balanced between its threat and grace.

Everything that means home to me is a by-product of the North
Fork of the Shoshone. The floor of the Wapiti valley is a descending fall of water-smoothed rock. Its random and volcanic ridges
crumble down to the river, down with the flow of water, brought
every year imperceptibly lower and more jagged by the runoff of
thunderstorms and snowmelt. The river and its tributaries support
the grasses and wildflowers that by midsummer grow belly-deep
to a grazing horse. There is Douglas fir. Spruce. Varieties of pine,
some juniper, aspen, and at the river's banks the water-drunk cottonwood. The trees shed their needles, cones, leaves, layering the
forest floor, each season adding to the mulch of acidic duff. Bear,
deer, elk, mountain sheep, lynx, coyote, and mountain lion drink
from the Shoshone. They feed, and graze, and die, and couple in
the wild forest that the river drains. If the North Fork were some-

how withdrawn, excised, as a vein is stripped from muscle, the land would desiccate, the wildlife perish, and that small part of me that exists without fear would wither. I cling to the sound of water to be brave in the world. I go to the sound of water to remember that God is not mute.

❧ THERE IS a photograph of my mother and brother and me. It is a black-and-white photograph. The three of us stand along the North Fork, balancing on the tops of the rounded rocks at the water's hem, the water low, behind us, appearing as a badly dented and corrugated sheen. The photograph is dated September 1963. I am eleven. My brother has just turned ten. My mother is thirty-nine. My brother's jeans are cuffed. They are new and have been bought long so that he will not outgrow them before he wears them to rags. We are all dressed in jeans, and riding boots, and plaid shirts open at our throats.

The far bank is timbered in only pine and fir, and a mountain ridge shoulders up softly, exposing itself in patterns of meadow, and rimrock. There are islands of pine that appear darker, fallen under the shadows of clouds.

My brother stands to my mother's right side, I to her left. The top of his head is level with her throat, mine with her brow. It does not show in the photograph, but we all have gray-blue eyes. My hair is white-blond. My mother's and brother's hair is nearly black. We're smiling. My mother's hands are thrust into her pockets. Her legs are splayed in a wide stance. My brother's and my inside arms—the ones nearest my mother—are bent at the elbows, our hands held up, gripping the ends of a stringer. The stringer bows from our shoulders, in a curve of fish-weight between us, across my mother's waist. There are fifteen trout on the stringer. They are mostly brook trout. There are a few natives. The black, split-wing shadows of their caudal fins fall low against my mother's thighs. Lower than the fish. The sun is high, in front of us. With our free hands, my brother and I hold fly rods, the rods like brackets enclosing the equation of variables we three represent. My mother has brought us to the river to further our instruction. It has never occurred to us to wonder why she knows how to fish. She is our mother. She teaches us how to manage in the world. We watch her smooth hands grip the rod's cork above the reel. We watch the rhythm of her arms paying out the line in arcs over the river, working into the length of her cast. We follow the last presentation of the line and breathe out as the fly settles on the river's surface. If she were not our mother we would be struck by her beauty. We would argue to stand close to her. We would become nervous at the scent of her clean, sun-warmed skin. We would not have learned to fish.

☼ THE ABSAROKAS rise away from the river sharply, the rock crumbling into its separate gravels, into course sands, the walls of mountain rock turning back the sounds of the river into overlapping harmonies. It is in this chorus that my memories live. I am a man held to the mountains by this choir of waters. I am only the memory of myself. I occasionally come vivid against the sound of water running downhill.

In the spring we traveled where the river allowed us to go. The depth of the water was gauged by where it leveled against a horse's body. Chest deep? At the point of a shoulder? One spring I forded Eagle Creek at its mouth when it boiled noisy and brown. I tied my boots and chaps behind the saddle and coaxed my horse into the stream. I expected both of us to have to swim. I was aware that either one of us could die. My horse worked in slowly. He grunted with the effort to hold himself against the current. The water soaked me to my thighs. My father had told me that if we were swept away that I was to slide back, grab my horse's tail and trust that he could swim us both out. But when we were midstream I knew that if he went down we would likely tangle and roll in the current, as the trunks of uprooted pines tangle as they're swept downstream. We would wash into the Shoshone, and it would beat us to death on its uneven floor of rock before we drowned. I was frightened, excited, yet calmly aware of every sound and shift in the water, brought so completely alive that I imagined I might burst into flame. All the way across the ford I expected myself to ignite and tumble from my horse's back. When I looked downriver I expected to see myself there, red, orange, white-hot, caught in the current, sizzling on the rapids: a boy of fire traveling this highway of water.

✻ I REMEMBER my mother in camps we made on our packtrips. I remember her walking back to the tents from the spring balanced between two full buckets of water, unstable, the cords in her neck standing out with the effort of trying to keep the weight of the buckets away from her legs, smiling, her white teeth flashing in the sun. Each five-gallon bucket was weighted with forty pounds of fresh water. Eighty pounds in all. The meadow grass grew to her waist. She could not hold the buckets above the level of the swaying grassheads.

She had cupped springwater over her face before starting back to camp. Her hair was wet. Her rich, black-brown hair was feathered to her temples. Her dark skin brought deeply brown from the summer sun. The water was beaded across her face, each drop flashing violet, rose, indigo, and trembling in the sunlight.

She'd break free of the tall grass with the last bit of her strength, slump her shoulders, and lower the buckets to her sides. She would shake her arms and laugh. She would throw her arms above her head and step into a jig.

I would kneel with her beside the buckets. We would pick the grasshoppers out that had jumped and fallen in from the stems and seedheads of the wild grasses. The circular surfaces of the pails of water would flash our faces white as we moved in and out of their glare. I would dip a ladle in and drink and let the water spill over my chin, inside the throat of my shirt, and over my chest.

I would stand and carry the water buckets into the tent. I would stack an armload of stovewood under the stove. I would shoulder a single hobble tied to the end of forty feet of hemp rope and walk back into the grass and drive a green stob of pine into the soil and tie off my picket horse to graze for the night.

When I got back to the tent my mother would have heated a

basin of water on the collapsible steel stove. The rush of heat would tick and hum in the ventpipe. I would wash my face, the pinesap, dirt, and horse dander from my hands. She would set me to work peeling potatoes, dicing onions, mixing batter in a bowl. She and my brother were the cooks. I was their helper.

Once my brother entered the tent staggering and moaning like some wounded movie monster. He had been out in the grass, on the streambank fishing. He had put down his pole and caught water snakes instead, pinching them behind their heads, and softly snapping their toothless mouths onto the tips of his fingers. They could not release. Their jaws were spread to the point of unhinging. He waved his hands toward me and laughed. Four snakes on one hand. Three on the other. All of them slim, gray-green, flexing. None of them more than eight inches long. I was afraid of snakes. I backed over a pannier and fell, and scooted away from him on my heels and hands.

My mother knelt with him under the open tent flap. She helped unlatch the little snakes, coaxed them from his fingers. They set them loose in the grass. She was laughing too. I loved to see my mother and brother together. Their laughter worked together as easily as streams meet and swell.

🦢 I LOVE and fear water equally. There is nothing that has found the same measure of balance in my life. I own a fear of snakes, but find no solace in the thought of handling one. I love the scent of pine, but there is nothing about its odor that makes me uneasy. And I do not dream much of trees or serpents. I dream often of water, however, and often in my dreams I am drowned. I wake from my water dreams with a sense of well-being, as though mildly intoxicated and without want. Always they are active dreams, swirling at the edge of sleep, allowing me participation with both my conscious and my unconscious minds. It is water's gift. Water has chosen me for an acolyte. Water allows me to practice my inevitable fate.

One spring the owners of a lodge several miles from ours—a

man and his wife—disappeared. Their horses returned to their home corrals riderless. The valley from the east entrance of Yellowstone Park to Cody, Wyoming, is just fifty miles long and at the time did not boast enough people to fill a small diner. We paired off in twos and rode the upper drainages in hopes of finding the absent couple. On the second day we were successful. They were found dead, caught in a backwash of the Shoshone.

It was generally believed that their horses had gone down as they'd attempted to ford. Perhaps bowled under by the trunk of a tree. Perhaps the man's horse had fallen and his wife had dived from hers, had entered the river in a desperate attempt at rescue. It did not matter to me how the river had taken them, but it troubled me that their deaths had not altered its flow. I studied the stretch of river where they'd drowned. There were no new rapids, the sandbars swelled near its surface where they had the week before, the water flashed as it had always flashed: black, emerald, silver, and apple. The river measured itself out in the sun as blamelessly as any strong, sleek predator might. Satisfied. Sated. Innocent.

I wondered if they had been given the gift of dreaming their deaths. I prayed that they were in some way prepared.

❧ I REMEMBER my mother too busy to be bored. I remember her hurt, insulted, angry. I rarely remember her sad. On the few occasions where I witnessed her pensive she sat beside water.

I once came up behind her where she sat at a timbered bend in the Shoshone. It was below the lodge. Below where Libby Creek entered the river. There was a crescent of exposed sandbar forcing the water into a deep pool against the far bank. She did not see me. Her back was to me, her knees drawn against her chest. It was early fall. A warm, cloud-spackled day. I thought that if I was watching her that anything could. That anything could be watching me. I raised up out of the thigh-deep grass and looked behind me and to my sides and settled again. I was satisfied that we were not alone, but that we were safe.

Across the pool the far bank rose in a bulge of volcanic rock. The surface of the rock was dark, knobbed by the various erosion patterns of its inconsistent parts—an agglomerative cliff of separate stones fired together millions of years ago. The cliffbulge cast a shadow over the pool. The river ran emerald in the sun, black at the cliff's base. I thought of the cooler water there. Of the big trout lined against the current, their smooth, speckled bodies flexing lazily against the low, clear autumn river.

My mother stretched out her legs and took a pine cone from her lap. She broke it apart, slowly, a scale at a time, and tossed each bract onto the surface of the water. She was sitting on the edge of the sandbar, her feet nearly in the water. When she was done worrying the cone she brought her knees up again and lowered her head onto their caps. She put her arms around her knees and gripped each forearm and stayed that way. She rocked. The sun struck the curve of her spine. I had to watch her very closely to know that she moved slightly from side to side. She made no sound. She looked as though she had always been there, tottering, rounded by the river, egg shaped; a smooth monument against which the water parted when it was high. The light flecked on the surface of the pool, pricking it with bursts of silver. Trout rose, receded, remained hanging in the shadowed current.

I crept back on my belly in the tall grass. I waited without making a sound and then stood all at once searching the forest behind me, searching for the eyes that I felt watched me. I had stood too fast. I became dizzy and dropped to a knee, blinking against the sense of vertigo. The forest pulsed green, and darker shades of green. A scatter of ash-colored boulder-backs came free from shadow as a wind lifted and dropped the low sweep of pine boughs. The big stones were stained with lichen, pitted, shaggy with clumps and tufts of weather-loosened moss. They seemed to be slowly migrating to the river, all of them. Watching.

❧ RED CREEK falls out of its drainage with such violence that I could hear it roar a quarter of a mile away. My horse pricked his ears and stepped out at a faster pace. I think he was curious about the sound, but when he stood on the creek's bank he pawed at the ground and paced and tried to turn.

Red Creek presents itself as an uneven channel of white and snapping froth. I spurred him, and whipped him with my reins, and he snorted and stepped in and hesitated and stumbled down the stream and froze. The current pounded at his side, at the bottom of my knee, and my horse would not lift his feet. He braced up under the battering and refused to move. He simply stood with his legs splayed, groaning, holding his soft lips against the surface of the stream, his nostrils flared, inhaling the spray.

I knew he would weaken. I knew the water would numb his legs, and he would forget his struggle and fall. I thought of my drowned neighbors. For a moment I imagined that I might skip along the surface of the spume and be thrown clear, onto a bank. And then I knew the thought was as numbingly useless as my horse's legs were becoming, and a panic seized me as fierce as the stream that held us. I cursed the horse. I whipped him with the bridle reins. He did not move. He did not even flinch. I started to rock back and forth in the saddle. Not because I thought it might help us across. It was not an effort to save myself, but simply a sort of primal squirming, rocking because I was young and too inexperienced to know what else to do. And then the horse began to rock with me. Slightly. Timidly. At first I thought he was falling. Once, twice, and then unbelievably, as the momentum of my weight carried me forward over his withers he slid a hoof forward, just inches, but again when I rocked toward his head, he slid a hoof. And again. It took us nearly half an hour but he skated out of the water and stood trembling on the bank.

I slid to the ground and knelt, and pulled myself up by the saddle strings and untied the denim jacket rolled behind the cantle, and folded to my knees again. I was too scared and weak to stand. I squatted beside him and rubbed his legs with the jacket until he stepped away from me, and looked back at the water and snorted. I laughed. I then began to cry. It occurred to me that I would have to cross back through this place, on this day, with this horse.

I REMEMBER my mother in her garden. This is after she and my father sold Holm Lodge and moved to a home fifteen miles downriver. On deeded ground. She kept an acre of garden in front of their house, between the lawn and an irrigated pasture, south facing, exposed to the sun, sloping. Grizzly Ridge rose up abruptly to the west. In the winters the sun arced low in the sky, set in front of the ridge, and their home and garden plot fell under the last weak slants of evening light. In the summers the ridge caught the sun higher off the horizon and cast their home into shadow while the stretch of valley that fell away to the east still baked.

I remember sitting on my mother's porch in early summer evenings, watching her at work in her garden. Beyond her, in the middle distance, the land dropped to the Shoshone, and rose out of it to the base of a crumbling cliff face come sharp under the setting sun, mauve and ocher, casting black bars of one-hundred-foot shadows. In the far distance, on the horizon, Ptarmigan Mountain shouldered up from the lesser Absarokas to more than twelve thousand feet, its fields of snow remaining well into August. My mother would stand in her garden, smiling, waving. I would wave back to her.

I remember her straddling the rows, ankle deep in the furrows between the rows. Bent at the waist. Weeding. Thinning. Warming in the sun. Standing. Stretching the tightness from her back. Drawing a forearm across her brow. Her hands muddied to her wrists.

I remember the furrows filling with the methodical seep of irrigation. The rows turning dark with water. The spaced green bursts of broccoli, Brussels sprouts, tomatoes, beet and potato tops.

I remember her in the chill morning air. She would have pulled on a sweatshirt and black rubber boots, sidestepping her way through the furrows, the water risen over her ankles, the furrows caught in the early sun, appearing filled with liquid silver, as though the hot metal had been poured, line after line of it, to cool against the earth.

I remember her in her kitchen in the last month of summer before a frost. An already hot house made hotter by the cauldrons of steaming water filled with canning jars. The room become a sauna.

We would spend days blanching tomatoes, peeling them, snapping beans, shelling peas. I remember the pop of the tin lids as they cooled and sealed. Quart jars. Pint jars. When all the jars were filled and shelved in the pantry, she'd pull whole tomato plants, knock the soil from their roots, and hang them upside down from the exposed floor joists that made the basement's ceiling. She would pick fresh, red fruit from those basement plants until January.

In October she would dig her potatoes, beets, carrots, turnips, onions. I would push the wheelbarrow for her. We would clean the root crop and pack it in boxes of crumpled newspaper or bins filled with sawdust in her basement. My mother worked long days until the snow fell. She worked against the months of cold, white frozen water that would come and stay.

❧ THERE ARE people of the wind. Clans that belong to altitude, swamp, volcano, ice, and desert. They do not have to be as mindful of water as I do. The world tutors them differently. There is a difference in their comforts and their jeopardies.

❧ I REMEMBER walking with my mother on the river in February. We walked below the lodge, on the Shoshone. There was a derelict pole ramp built into the bank. It was where the couple who ran Holm Lodge after the turn of the century used to cut blocks of ice, and work those heavy, clear cubes out of the river with pikes, and block and tackle, and skid them onto sleds. They would whip their team up through the snow—the ice roped onto a horse-drawn sledge—to the icehouse built in the shade of a stand of pine behind the lodge. The walls of the icehouse were windowless, ten inches thick, filled with sawdust. Its floor dirt. All winter they stored the ice, stacking it against the sun's return. In the summers they hung meat, shelved their vegetables, stood crocks of milk and butter against the slick, diminishing, giant cubes, and thanked God for the variousness of the seasons.

There was a foot of snow on the river. Under the snow the ice was smooth and thick and clear. My mother and I wore snowshoes, shuffling effortlessly downriver. The ruddy, leafless willowstems grew thickly along the banks, standing brittle in the cold, clicking if we swept our gloved hands against them. The air was frozen and sparkled, alive with gnat-sized chips of suspended, sparkling ice-crystal. Our nostrils froze to the posts of our noses. Our eyelashes and eyebrows fluffed with frost. Our breath condensed into puffs of thick fog and fell away from our mouths.

We stopped below the pole ramp. We scuffed at the snow with the rawhide webbing of our snowshoes until we stood flatly on the river ice. There were bubbles of oxygen frozen into the ice. We could see the water moving below our feet. We could hear the water whisper: *wintering, wintering, wintering, wintering.* There was no wind. No contrails in the air. We could hear the rhythmic slap of a raven's wing on the thick, still air approaching, still two hundred yards upriver. And then there was a crack as unexpected and sharp as a gunshot. We stared at one another. We looked down at the ice. We did not move. We looked for fractures, fissures in the snow. We became cautious as deer are cautious. We knew that this was the way life changes. Without warning. All at once.

We stepped back onto the snow and shuffled to the river's edge and moved downstream, around a bend, watching where we stepped. The sound of water was louder. We wondered if curiosity and fear improved our hearing. We moved toward the sound, and stopped to listen, and moved again. We found where a small spring entered the river and kept it open next to the bank. The snow and ice fell away to a jagged semicircle of open, fast river. The water was almost black, and steamed. There was a slide beside the spring and a beaver lodge built into the bank. The Shoshone is too large for rodents to dam, and the beaver that do not work the feeder streams build their homes high against its banks. There was a scatter of frozen brown hairs, bristling on the iced surface of their slide. My mother began to laugh. We realized at the same time that the sound we'd heard was the slap of a beavertail on the water as he'd dived. She could not stop. Her laughter steamed and froze and dropped to the river and was carried under the ice, held there more accurately, more permanently, than our memories of that morning.

❧ FIFTEEN YEARS later I am on this same river cross-country skiing across the level foot of snow its ice supports. I am a grown man. I have a cabin on Half Mile Creek. I find a seep from the bank that warms a well of water against the icesheet and think of my mother.

I sidestep up twenty feet of steep riverbank beside the spring. There is no beaver slide. At the top of the bank I step out onto a cornice for a better look, and the shelf breaks, and I fall the twenty feet down, fall through the well of open water, and under the ice. One ski pole stabs and holds into the snow that covers the ice. My wrist is wound in the leather strap of its handle. The rest of me is caught in the flow and suck of the river, face up, my nose pressed to the underside of the icesheet. The water is fast and strong. I do not panic. I pause for just an instant and listen. I think I hear my mother's laughter.

It takes only a few minutes to reach down with my free hand and unsnap my skis and work them behind me out onto the snow. Only a few moments more to pull the whole of my body out. I remain calm, and very lucky. It is thirty below zero, and my clothes freeze immediately and hold my body's heat close to my skin. I snap on my skis and shuffle back to my cabin. I don't even suffer a cold.

When I am soaking in a tub of hot water I tell my wife that she has married a reckless, and certainly stupid, man. She smiles and leaves the bathroom to make tea. I slip lower into the water and hear it again: a light, liquid, girlish sound, and feel my mother's inconsolable joy for life.

❧ WHEN I am thirty-six my mother divorces my father. It is not a surprise. She is sixty-four. My father moves to Las Vegas. My mother has hip-replacement surgery. She buys a house in Cody and asks me to help her move.

She thinks she might like the opportunity, once in her life, to call and order a pizza and have it delivered to her door. That is what she says.

Among the twelve pickup loads of garbage I drag out of her basement to haul to the dump is a refrigerator box and a dryer box filled with carpet scraps. They represent at least twenty colors and lengths of shag. The pieces range from five-by-eight-inch trapezoids, to two-inch strips some twelve feet long. My mother stands on her porch, wedged between her crutches, and pleads with me not to toss her possessions. But this is the third time I've moved her. There are hundreds of gallon milk jugs she's saved against nuclear attack. They are tied in clusters of several dozen each like bunches of transparent, plastic grapes. She plans to fill them with uncontaminated water. There is a freezer with a burned-out motor that she keeps for storage. Drawers she's gotten at yard sales that need only cabinets built around them.

"You can't want these boxes of carpet scraps," I tell her. I say it from a safe distance.

"If I didn't want them I wouldn't have them in my basement. Aliens didn't put them there."

"What are you planning to do with them?" I have my shoulder under the larger of the two boxes, trying to slide it into the bed of the truck.

"Save them."

"For what?"

She gives me a look that expresses her shame in having raised a squanderer. "If times are ever tough I can sew them together and have one large carpet."

"The new house is wall-to-wall," I tell her. I have the box in the truck. I shut the tailgate.

"Everybody's house isn't. I'll have neighbors."

"You don't know your neighbors," I say. "What about the milk jugs?"

"For spring water," she says. She smiles. "You don't expect me to drink that stuff that comes out of the tap in town, do you?" She hobbles to the porch rail. "Well, do you?" she repeats.

I heap the milk jugs on top of the carpet scraps and drive the whole lot to her new garage.

❧ THAT SAME spring my wife and I separate. We are divorced a year later. We have spent most of our adult lives together, and the divorce is a shift that leaves us both reeling. We sell our cabin along Half Mile Creek and move out of the Wapiti valley.

She moves to Idaho. I am not brave enough to try another state. I move to a town fifty miles to the east, out of the mountains and onto the prairie of the Bighorn Basin. I move to a place called Powell.

The Shoshone has been dammed west of Cody and the sweep of land east, the way the river flows has been diverted into crops. The property that borders the river, and the irrigation canals that curve away and back into the river, bring the land unnaturally green—at least for part of the year—supporting fields of beets, barley, and several varieties of beans. Powell is a farming community.

Away from the irrigated land there is only the high desert prairie. From the air the land rolls brown and gray, down from the heights of the Absaroka and Beartooth Mountain ranges into sage, scrubbrush, cactus, all of it fallen under the brutal husbandry of the wind.

My mother's new home in Cody is halfway between the house she sold on the North Fork and my apartment in Powell. I am able to visit her more often. We share a meal now and then. I take her to dinner. But we never fish. We do not walk by the river. We are never caught together in the rain.

One day I am with her to have coffee. We are at her kitchen table. She remembers a fall when all the men were in hunting camp and she was left alone at the lodge. She came out in the morning and found the air so choked with smoke that when she walked twenty feet away from her cabin she could not see the thing. Helixes of ash as long as wooden matches spiraled down out of the smoke-thick air and covered the ground, in places several inches thick. The ash billowed when she stepped. She groped her way back into her cabin, soaked a bath towel at the sink, wrapped it around her head, and worked up through the cabins, touching the walls of each one, sure that her husband and sons would return to a charred and gutted drainage. Her eyes stung and watered. Her nose and throat burned.

When she reached the lodge she cupped her hands to either side of her face and peered into its windows. She held her palms against its doors. When she entered she found the air cool and clear. She rechecked every cabin. She hurried to the barn and tack-shed. She was sure she stood in the shadow of ruin, waiting, but was confused to find no fire.

An hour later the district ranger drove in and told her there was a fire two creeks upwind. Five hundred acres of forest burned. He said the fire was contained. He said that the radio predicted a front that evening: winds, a wet snow. My mother hugged the man and stood thankfully in the diffused glow of his headlights. She grinned through a sagged overlap of wet towel. She said aloud how lucky she felt.

I ask my mother if she misses the sound of Libby Creek. She says that when it was high with runoff she worried that it would flood and carry all she cared about to the river, and that the river would be up and scatter her life downstream, for miles, out of the forest, into country she did not know.

I tell her that I am dreaming of water, almost every night. She says she misses the greenness that water brings, that she spends the quiet moments in winter thinking about new leaves. She pours us a second cup of coffee. She tells me that she also dreams of water, but occasionally, only three or four times a year. She says it is enough—that the sound of water is in her dreams.

POWELL HAS five thousand people and is busy as islands are busy, confined to its alluvial strip of agriculture, its greened coast-line bordered on all sides by the press of stunted sage, bentonite bluffs, outcroppings of blasted sandstone. I no longer own horses and have never gotten used to living in a town of any size. I feel trapped, mildly confused, out of my element. I have been married all of my thirties, most of my twenties. I miss wild water.

The town is built along an irrigation canal, and its croplands are bordered by countless grids of ditches, the water squeezed through headgates, coaxed into the fields and rechanneled and drained away. It is a landscape of domesticated water.

When I was a boy my parents would drive across this part of the basin when we made trips to Montana. The land never seemed real to me. More like some bleak prison. And the farmland like some fat and common idiot locked away against the river.

I roam the streets. I talk to friends I have made, but I don't listen to our conversations. I am not convinced that I am living my life. I feel as though I am only moving through a slice of time between what I have done and what I will someday do. I think that if I could have thought of another place to go I would have gone there, but I am unwilling to move too far from my past.

⚜ THIS IS what I do not know. This is where the water has flowed ahead of my memory and my imagination. This is where it enters the sea and quiets, and becomes briny as our living bodies.

I do not know that within five years my brother will move back to Wyoming after twenty years of living in Florida. He will tell me that he means to change his life. Means to return to the place where he was raised. He will say that he has missed the sharp, dry autumn air. The mountains. He will check his waders for punctures. He will spool new line and leaders onto his fly-fishing reels. He will talk of the big trout that have waited for him, patiently holding themselves steady against the clear, fast water of the Shoshone. He will move in temporarily with our mother until he can find a place to rent.

I do not know that she will be diagnosed with emphysema. I will have heard her wheezing. Coughing. Seen her tire easily. But I do not know that her lungs will become sodden with disease, as though they are two buckets of membrane she carries half-filled with bad water. That she will need supplemental oxygen. That a machine that makes that oxygen will be moved into her house with forty feet of clear tubing. That she will be connected to the end of that tubing, will fit the loop of a nasal cannula over her ears, and become housebound as she dies. I do not know that she will not be able to walk to her mailbox, her car, into the sun.

The doctors will tell us that emphysema is a slow drowning. They will say that a woman's body will float on the surface of her death far longer than she will want it to. They will tell us that it is a sorry way to go.

I do not know that when my mother is alone with my brother and me she will tell us that she does not want a funeral. She will say that she is opposed to the celebration of her death, that she is suspicious of ceremony.

❧ MY FIRST winter in Powell is one of dislocation. I rent an apartment on a residential street, the main drag just one block away. I try to get used to the sounds of traffic, my neighbor's barking dogs, the numbing drone of the other tenants' television sets. I feel claustrophobic and vaguely desperate. I feel submerged.

Each day I drive ten miles north to an elevated bench of land to walk for hours and look toward the mountains. Occasionally I find fossils and squeeze them in my hands until they leave imprints on my palms. I stuff my pockets with them, carrying with me the evidence of ancient water, stepping purposefully, listening for the memories of water. But the land does not wholly seem alive. It offers itself honestly as an abandoned scape. Once a thing that held an ocean. Now exposed.

❧ I WILL be surprised that it is my brother who will shoulder our mother's care, but will find it is easy to think of them together. I will find that I have always thought of them as one. He is the son who feels responsible, feels actually sprung from our pasts. I am the son who feels he should have made our lives better.

I take out photographs I have kept of my brother and mother. I line them together on my desk. Their skins shine dark off the glossy paper, their hair nearly black, their bodies thin, angular, graceful. Black Irish. I remember stories beyond their common likeness and the comfort that they share.

When my brother ran a bar in Florida he escorted two quarreling drunks to a place behind the bar one evening, outside to cool their differences. He had them by their collars. He stood between them. He kept them apart. He reasoned with them. He told me their rancor stunk of spilled beer and stale smoke and violence.

He heard a city bus release its brakes and looked away from the men for an instant. He saw our mother standing on the curb, where the bus had just been. She said, "Stand back, Rick. Step away." And he obeyed. He stepped back from between the men and looked down to see that one of them had brought a knife into the argument, thrusting it toward the other man. My brother would have received that knife. He would have been stabbed in a parking lot behind a bar in St. Petersburg, Florida, if our mother did not love him. Wholly. Beyond the simple memory of her darker second son.

When my brother looked back to the curb my mother's image was gone. He called her the next morning and told her the story. She was in Wyoming. She said she did not remember what she had been doing the day before, but did not find it unusual that her care for him had made the trip south, and spoken.

By way of explanation my mother said simply that we live on a water planet. That all streams flow into one. And then she and my brother laughed.

❧ IN MY second spring in Powell I find a newly born pronghorn. I jump to the side. I'm startled. I am walking on the bench of arid prairie north of town. It is the second time in my life I have come upon a newborn wild animal. It has not occurred to me that this barren place might hold more than rattlesnakes, prairie dogs, and the shadows of raptors. I have seen the tracks of coyote, fox, pronghorn, and badger but have not come upon the actual animals. As the weather has warmed so have the snakedens. It is not unusual to see two or three rattlesnakes in an eight-mile walk and everywhere the prehistoric calligraphy of lizard track. The bench is a fine place for lizards and snakes. It does not seem to welcome warmer blood.

The fawn wriggles in the slime of its mother's afterbirth, glistening, as though caught in a net of transparent kelp. The doe circles nervously, bleating an alarm—a sound that mimics the sharp, high hum made as nighthawks set their wings to pull their bodies out of the dives they commit when feeding. I bend lower, and squat, and smile. The newborn resembles a large, tawny cricket. Its front legs fold about its head, the back legs ratchet into the loose ground and air in an awkward dance. Its eyes bulge, are dark and guileless. But it is a furred and steaming thing, and the sight of it makes me immensely happy. I walk away quickly and sit on a slight rise at some distance until I am satisfied that the mother will return to nurse her offspring. Something in me has settled.

NOT EVERY old woman suffers to die. Not every old woman is bound to her bed, at first able to make the fifteen feet to her own bathroom, later able only to claw herself upright and scoot her hips onto a portable commode.

It will be hard to believe that it is her soul's choice. It will be harder to believe, at the time, while she's dying hard, that her soul is glad for this chance to understand its own long history of suffering.

But that is something that will skitter in my mind. I will cling to the thought that her pain is her soul's choice, that it is a gift. I will not want to see the universe as random. My belief in karma will swell, and then I will see her biting at the air, sucking on her oxygen tube, and I will be sure that no one's mother deserves to die this way. My mind will swirl and plummet. It will seem an accident that any of us can summon moments of even imprecise optimism. I will howl. And I will shout at God.

I will sit with her in the night. The lights will be off. She will be in her bed. Always in her bed. The streetlight will break the room into shadowed tones of gray and black. Her flesh will appear as slate. Her breathing will be uneven and ragged. I will think, "I am here. She is here. She is my mother." For a moment I will not be waiting for her death. For one moment I will imagine us both already dead, ascended to heaven.

I will rest my hand against her shoulder. The wet rattling in her chest will rise up my arm, into my chest. I will think, "We are here. This is heaven." I will say aloud, softly, and wonder if she hears me in her sleep, "Here, if not heaven."

❧ OVER MY second summer in Powell I became accustomed enough to the city to stop driving away from it for solitude. I make my daily walks along the roads that section the cultivated fields into mile squares. Every day I walk. I do not think where my life has gone wrong, or right. I walk. I wave to farmers in their fields. I duck and dodge the attacks of red-winged blackbirds. They line the telephone wires, chattering, and dive at the heads of those who trespass near their nests.

During the fall harvest I toss the litter of sugar beets from the macadam roads. A few rattle free from the trucks that transport them to weigh stations. I memorize the names on mailboxes. There is one farmwife that keeps dachshunds. When I pass her place a swarm of the little dogs rush at me, barking, threatening to chew me down to their height. I think of them sympathetically as retarded weasels and smile at the woman as she hurries from her house, huffing and swinging a broom at the heads of her half-dozen yapping wiener dogs.

❧ THERE WILL be days that are impossible without the inhalator. Without the inhalator she would die on those days. She calls it her peace pipe. She loads the thing with a liquid drug that dilates her bronchi, and turns it on. It hums as she inhales its mist. She smokes her peace pipe every four hours. Some days it is hard to wait that long, but if she uses it too often the drug makes her sweat and shake and curl into a ball and imagine she is suffering a series of strokes—her electrical currents flash forward into death, abandoning her body to the simple thrum of pain.

I will be with her on days when she takes in too much of the dilating mist. I will sit on the edge of her bed, against the backs of her thighs, where her legs have curled. I will guide a handheld massager over her hips, her back, her shoulders, and lie to her, coo to her that the pain will not stay. She will cry. A part of me will panic, and I will grit my teeth against the fear. I will remember that my mother is a strong woman. I will remember that I have seen her cry only once before when I was very little and she was lost in her life, driven close to divorce, frightened that she could not care for me and my brother alone in the world. Her sobs will continue longer than I will imagine they could. She will cry and plead with her God to take her. She will feel starkly alone in the world, singular in her misery. I will not be strong enough to absorb the whole demon of her pain. I will try, and it will beat me back, and return to her, and snarl as a vicious dog snarls to protect its mistress. My love of her will not seem enough.

ALL THAT winter I walk away from my new home. No matter the temperature, the wind, the snow. In January my breath frosts so thickly in my beard that my mustache freezes to the hair on my chin. When my eyes water, the tears stand frozen on my cheeks.

For miles each day I maintain my ritual of movement across the land. And it is just that, movement. I do not try to pawn it off as exercise or meditation. I am no longer particularly dissatisfied with Powell. I am just out noticing a new country. Approaching. Passing. Occasionally I check that the mountains hold steady against the horizons.

At times I speak. I elaborate on subjects that hold a momentary interest or irritation. I hold no grudges. Mostly, I simply walk, noticing where I walk, and occasionally, I speak. On some days I recite grocery lists, the lyrics of popular songs, fragments of stories, poems, an inventory of my regrets. The sound of my own voice comforts me.

I WILL not understand her when she speaks. She will spit her speech in fragments between fits of coughing. The coughing will bring up mouthfuls of fruit-colored phlegm, or gray slime. I will excuse myself. I will stand in another room and tremble with rage. I will envision myself returning to her, shaking her until she breaks. I will want to ask her why she didn't quit smoking when she was first diagnosed. Why she doesn't quit now. And I will realize that judgment kills the soul more effectively than cigarettes kill the body. I will feel my soul shrivel. I will know that judgment stains the spirit as tars and resins stain the lungs.

I will go to her. I will put my arms around her. Her eyes will say she is sorry I am her witness. Her hands will be mostly bone and skin and vein, and she will place a hand on top of mine and squeeze because I am her grown son and she loves me, and because she has thought to pray that I will die simply, quickly, when it is my turn. She will tell me that in her lifetime of prayers, my death is not a petition she has thought she might make. She will bow her head. And pray again.

⁂ ON A particular route to the west, at its apex, where it is usual for me to turn and start back for town, there is an irrigation canal, a deep one. It becomes a way station. A place to disappear for a moment and rest my legs. I skid into its bottom to escape the level surface of the land. All winter the canal has been dry and matted with last summer's brown grasses. Its sides are slick with the thatch of broken grass and weed.

On a walk in the early spring I reach this resting place and find it blackened. Stones are exposed, pieces of charred wood, beer cans, its sides free of tangle. I kick the heels of my boots back into the loosened bank to work down to its bottom. It is newly, merely spring, and not yet warm. This irrigated prairie is fallen away from the mountains, but it is still a high place and the seasons change abruptly; there is little overlap. It could snow tomorrow, and the moisture would be only welcomed. Songbirds who arrive early can spend several weeks shuffling from one frosted foot to the other, yet, in a few weeks this canal will fill with water for the fields.

The ditch has been fired in preparation for the water it will carry. The farmers burn away the bristle of old growth, walking the lengths of their water systems with propane torches, looking up constantly to the west, tasting the air for wind. The burning is a procedure that improves the flow of water, layers the soil with carbon, and lessens the likelihood of debris-clogged culverts. It is a good practice for farmers. It is not so good for muskrat, pheasant, and fox. The ditches are their home, but they raise only their young, and cannot edge the better market for barley and sugar beets.

✻ I WILL marvel at my brother's quiet patience. Day in and day out. Our mother's death will become his occupation. There will be nights of horror that he will not tell me about. I will remarry. My mother's care will be only part-time work for my wife and me. We will visit for a game of Scrabble or cards. We will prepare special dinners. We will listen for their small desires. Fulfill those desires. Clean gutters. Rake the yard. Prune shrubs. Wash dishes. Make trips to the pharmacy.

We will orchestrate the one or two days in a year when we will wheel my mother to the curb and get her into our car. They will be her strong days. An oxygen bottle will stand upright in the back-seat where the tubing will not crimp on its way to her lungs. I will drive through the new neighborhoods. Past an old home. I will watch my mother's face tighten against the glare of the day. She will comment on the changes outside the darkness of her bed-room. I will wonder if it saddens her. I will look at the town I take for granted differently.

We will once get her the ten miles out to the home we have rented in the country. We will wheel her through the rooms. She will ask questions about our computers. Ask what our heating bills are in the winter.

We will leave her to sit in the sun in her wheelchair by the south-facing windows. We will make a lunch. When one bottle of oxygen is empty we will replace it. Fetch her inhalator. "It's quiet here," she will say. "Think of the noise children would make on these tiles," she will say. We will not know whether she would find the clatter of children bothersome or comforting. We have none. I will think that if we did, they would have lost their grandmother while they were young; known her only from the stories of her sons.

🎐 OTHER THAN a place to rest, the irrigation canal is a good place to piss. The land is flat and treeless for acres, for miles, and I imagine my neighbor's eyesight to be better than my own. I look to my right and left and kick my way to the bottom of the ditch and perform my toilet as quickly as I can. I am anxious that I might be discovered by the farmers who own the land. I am aware that the picture of a man standing poorly balanced on the side of an irrigation canal with his penis in his hand is the type of thing that small-town newspapers live for. The actual truth is that I am by nature insular, that it is perfectly natural for me to enter a ditch to piss, that I feel often exposed.

I stand in the bottom of the ditch longer than I need to, to be out of the wind. I find it a quiet place to watch clouds sweep through the sky. The horizons are above and out of sight, and I am left only with the clouds, dwarfed by their immensity, anonymous, unnoticed.

🎐 WHEN WE are granted the help of the hospice nurses I will think that it won't be long now. I will learn that emphysema patients aren't put on hospice until their doctor's best guess is that they have only six months left. Twenty-five percent lung capacity will be the kicker. Down from thirty-seven percent just last summer, four months ago.

One of the gentler nurses will tell her she will likely go in her sleep. It will not be during one of the thrashings, drowning in her own fluids. In her sleep. My mother will tell me she is relieved. She will ask me not to mourn. She will worry about money. She will ask me to call around, check to see if my brother and I could take her body into the mountains and simply set fire to it. The idea of the pyre will bring her eyes bright. I will tell her I'm not sure I can carry enough diesel fuel to get the job done. She will nod, and then smile. She is the one from whom I've inherited my macabre notions of what is funny. We will laugh, and then the pain will rise and choke off her laughter.

I will sit next to her on her bed. I will cup my hand and pat her back to help up the phlegm. She will lean to spit into the little bucket she keeps by the head of her bed. I will get her a glass of cool water.

That afternoon my wife and I will buy a small refrigerator to put in her bedroom. We will come into the house with her gift. We will find her asleep on her side, one hand gripping a bedpost. It will be the way she sleeps—hanging on to the bed—as though that will keep her anchored in the world. I will think of her body in a box. I will think of the box bursting into flame. *Like that*, is what I will think.

❧ IT IS a cloudless spring day when I next enter the burned ditch. I'm careful as I make my way down. I stomp out a little shelf for a level place to stand and look to my side and see a snake. There is a foot of him sprouted from his winter place, and draped over a small, charred log, and lifeless. He is so obviously ruined that I do not jump away from him. I think of how his cool blood was brought to boil as the farmer's fire awakened him. I picture his futile writhing in his den, away from a baked death and into flame. He is coated with a fine ash, as are my boots, and I shudder from their soles at the thought of his tortured dying. I nudge him with the toe of a boot. He does not flex or coil. It excites me even though I know he is dead. I wish him the comfortable temperature of my body, my steady heat. It is only a child's wish, and cowardly. When I cannot think of something large—no argument for comfort or restoration, no soothing aphorism—I think of something small. I leave him for the food of birds, of rodents, of insects. He is my neighbor, but he is dead.

❧ IT WILL be New Year's Day. My wife and I will be having a party. My brother will be late for the party. He will call to say that our mother's cat, a twenty-year-old black cat with a clubbed tail, is having a fit. The cat's pupils are dilated, his body racked with spasms. My brother will take the cat to the vet's. The doctor will want to put the cat down, put it out of its misery. My brother will feel that loyal old cats shouldn't die by injection. He will bring the cat home.

I will sit with my mother on her bed. I will help her wrap the cat in a towel. She will hold him cradled in her arms. She will pour water into the lid of a jar and level it at the cat's mouth and when he won't drink she will dab the pad of a finger into the water and pull back the cat's lips and drip it, a drop at a time, across the cat's clenched teeth. He will tighten with seizure several times each minute. He will hold himself clenched in the intervals, waiting for the next contraction. He will forget how to purr. My mother will look at me and say, "I thought I would go before Cubby." Tears will stand in her eyes. I will wish the cat dead. I will picture myself taking him from my mother's arms and driving his stiff little body to the landfill. I will want it over with. I will think I might be capable of killing the little bastard myself. With my own hands. He will be only a thing that has swollen my mother's suffering.

A month later Cubby will have learned to walk again. He will be gaunted, but otherwise just a tattered old animal. My mother will still be alive too. She will have taught the cat how to shake hands for cat treats my wife buys her at Albertson's. She will look up at me after Cubby has performed his trick. Her haggard face will be drawn into a smile. Her oxygen tube will whistle. Her hair will be uncombed, lifted into an unnatural pompadour from having slept all day on her side, the cat held in against the curve of her body. She will lift the old cat back onto the bed beside her. I will know who I am. Down deep. I will have glimpsed the dark cloud at the base of my soul. I will know I am a man who would kill a sick animal. I will know I am a man who still believes suffering to be unnatural.

 IT IS three days before I return to the burned ditch. It has rained once in that time, clouds have come and cleared, and the sun is on the south-facing ditchbank. Since I have come this far I think that I will slide to the spot where I put my toe to the burned muscle of the little snake. I am curious to witness the process of his decay.

I find him gone, but because I am there I drop my head back and stare up into the clouds that scud across the dome of sky. I reason that the snake has been dragged or flown to some den, or nest of live animals, trophied a bit, devoured by their young. Because I am safely out of the food chain I imagine for him, the thought satisfies me, and I turn to climb to level ground, but find him in my path.

He is slightly scarred, but clean of ash. He is gray, and motionless I think, because I am there. Behind him lies his mate. She is tensed tightly for movement, perhaps because she did not share his trial; is not healing from his wounds. Her tongue tastes the air between us, her head weaves slowly from side to side.

❧ I WILL take both of my mother's hands. She will sit on the edge of her bed. I will pull up and back, and drop her hands, and grip her under her arms until she steadies. I will turn slowly, and she will keep her hands on me until I have turned my back completely to her. She will put a hand on either side of my neck, on my shoulders, pulling down, keeping herself erect. Her forehead will rest against my back, between my shoulder blades. That is the way I will support her. I will shuffle forward. She will come behind. One half step at a time. We will move like this, in clumsy tandem, around the foot of her bed to the portable commode. She will get the worn elastic waistband of her pants down over her hips. I will lower her onto the commode.

"I'm so tired," she will say. She will look tired. Her face will be gray, puffed, inanimate. The oxygen tube will have channeled her cheeks. The groove that runs from the tops of her ears to the sides of her nostrils will shadow her face. Her hair will need washing. The sweater she will pull over her pajama top will be frayed at the shoulder. "I need this to be over with," she will say. "This isn't the morphine talking. This is me."

I will nod because I haven't the courage to disagree. I will nod because it will keep me from wondering if I need it to be over with too.

She will look up at me. Her eyes will seem out of focus. Watery. Her concentration ephemeral, flighty. I will be kneeling in front of her. I will hold her hands. There will be the sound of urine dropping into the bucket of urine. "I'm trying," she will say. The lack of oxygen and the pain will dictate short sentences. Carefully chosen words. "I think I can live another two months." This will wear her out.

I will get her to her feet, lean her against my chest, pull up her pants. I will run my thumbs around the waistband to make sure it is not folded over. I will support her back to the bed, turn on the machine that delivers the mist of drug that momentarily dilates her boggy lungs. She will settle. "I don't want to die until you get your book done," she will tell me. She will try to smile. There will be only determined fact in her expression, no hint of martyrdom. I will remember telling her that the deadline to my publisher was just two months away.

"I love you," she will say. "I'm not sure you can finish and know that I am finished too." I will bend to embrace her. I will kiss her on her forehead. Her skin will be cool, damp. Her hands will reach up and feel each of my ribs, intimately, with recognition. She will be remembering that she made me. She will take a moment to enjoy her creation, satisfy herself that her life was worth something after all.

I will tell her that she made a man stronger than she imagines. I will kiss her again and excuse myself. I will walk down a hallway and into a bathroom. I will close the door and sit on the edge of the tub and weep. I will be careful that she can't hear me. I will not be crying because I am afraid. I will be crying because she willingly suffers for my ease. I will be crying because this good, old woman is my mother and she expects me to draw breath after breath in against the cage of my ribs and carry the gifts she has given me into the world.

❧ I LOOK into the sky and back to the snakes, and to the sky again. I feel stripped naked, dramatically homeless, and am aware at once that I have been since my birth—suddenly certain that we are all transient until we die.

I bend at the waist over the pair of snakes. Their eyes demand my every movement. The female slips against her injured mate, and I wish the ditch fell deep enough to hide my shame. I tell her weakly that I did not save him, did not ease his suffering, because I did not think I could. I tell her that I am different than a snake. I speak to her again, and louder, admitting my fear of snakes. And then I scuff my boot to make them move. I want no witness to my crimes—I do not feel I've earned my own death. The fear that I have lived a careless life sweeps some nights over me with liquid flame—hot as the fires that clear these ditches for their clean water.